To Phyllisee
and our sons
David and Richard

Acknowledgements

Doubleday & Company, Inc. for permission to quote from John L. McKenzie, Second Isaiah.

Fortress Press for permission to quote from John B. Cobb, Jr., Theology and Pastoral Care.

Harcourt Brace Jovanovich, Inc. for permission to quote from T.S. Eliot, "The Love Song of J. Alfred Prufrock."

Harper & Row, Publishers, Inc. for permission to quote from Judith Bardwick, Psychology of Women; Erich Fromm, The Art of Loving; A.H. Maslow, Motivation and Personality; Philip Rieff, The Triumph of the Therapeutic; Daniel Day Williams, God's Grace and Man's Hope and The Minister and the Care of Souls.

Harvest Books for permission to quote from Modern Man in Search of a Soul, by C. G. Jung.

Houghton Mifflin Company for permission to quote from Client-Centered Therapy, by Carl Rogers.

Little, Brown and Company in association with the Atlantic Monthly Press for permission to quote from The Undiscovered Self, by C. G. Jung. Copyright (c) 1957, 1958 by C. G. Jung.

Macmillan Publishing Company, Inc. for permission to quote from Alfred North Whitehead, Process and Reality and Religion in the Making.

W.W. Norton and Company, Inc. for permission to quote from The Ego and the Id and New Introductory Lectures by S. Freud; and Young Man Luther by Erik Erikson.

Oxford University Press for permission to quote from Israel: Its Life and Culture I-II, by Johannes Pedersen.

Putnam Publishing Group for permission to quote from Simone Weil, Waiting for God and Alfred North Whitehead, Modes of Thought.

The Westminster Press for permission to quote from Process Theology: An Introductory Exposition by John B. Cobb, Jr. and David Ray Griffin. Copyright (c) 1976; and from God, Power, and Evil: A Process Theodicy, by David Ray Griffin. Copyright (c) 1976.

Yale University Press for permission to quote from An Interpretation of Whitehead's Metaphysics by William A. Christian and from Long Day's Journey Into Night, by Eugene O'Neill.

Pastoral Care and Process Theology

Contents

Introduction

Pastoral care needs a home. That is the underlying motivation of this book. Whether it is pastoral care in the generic sense or pastoral counseling in the much more limited professional practice, the caring for people that uses "pastoral" as the identifying adjective seems to be unsure of its own identity. The fact that the carer is ordained or is employed by the church does not in itself mean that pastoral counseling is taking place. What may be taking place may be straight psychotherapy. Only the address has been changed.

Pastoral care, and especially that form we call pastoral counseling, has been informed most helpfully by humanistic psychologies. But a subtle seduction has enticed much pastoral caring out of its traditional home into a framework that is scarcely distinguishable from ideological settings where psychotherapists of all persuasions do their counseling. Enabling this move for many has been the insufficiency and inadequacy of theological formulations and their implications. Many have sensed, even if they have not wanted to face it head-on, a sort of bankruptcy in their theology, a bankruptcy that does not aid their practice of caring. For example, if one's theology pictures a coercive omnipotence, the reasons for pastoral counseling are vitiated unless one's aim is to help the other simply to acquiesce in whatever happens: it's the will of God. As Alfred North Whitehead has pointed out, ". . .the worst of unqualified omnipotence is that it is accompanied by responsibility for every detail of every happening."[1] While few would carry their doctrine of God that far, having no real alternatives many have simply abandoned theology in the counseling session. Even in more traditional pastoral caring situations theology has often seemed not to be a viable resource.

It is my contention that process thought furnishes an ontological basis for including and enriching much psychological insight and for a different vision of theological material. It is evident to me that psychoanalysis, the several variations of existential analysis,[2] the American and European forms of Third Force psychology, among others, are more in the train of philosophy than science, though they all employ empirical data. I hope to show that Process Thought offers an ontological psychology which can ground Freud, Jung, Erikson, Maslow, Assagioli and others philosophically and enrich them in doing so. This would be important to pastoral care, and especially counseling, since they are so profoundly informed by these psychological giants.

Process thought also grounds theology in ontology. This furnishes a secular vision of God and also the basis for a re-interpretation of the religious vision of God. I hope to show that the process vision of God enables pastoral caring to find again its deep theological roots and to employ the powerful resources of religion in its ministry of caring without embarrassment and without imposition. This book is therefore the attempt to provide both a theological and a psychological home for Pastoral Care by way of a process ontology. These formulations are only a beginning. But I hope they constitute a "lure" for others to correct, refine, and elaborate so that in the process pastoral care might find a home.

In short, the big, exciting contribution that Whitehead (and the other process thinkers) makes to pastoral care and counseling is to provide a fresh vision of reality, a profound way of seeing people in the depths of their struggling, and a new way of seeing the whole helping process, including the ways God is involved in the process. Process thought seems to provide a new set of glasses for perceiving everything that is involved in a pastoral care encounter.

The structure of the book begins with an overview chapter followed by chapters two and four which lay out Whitehead's theory of actual occasions. Sandwiched in between is the secular vision of God so necessary to the birth and rise of each actual occasion. Chapters five through seven deal with Beauty, which is the aim of life, Propositions which lure us in our aiming, and Evil which is the aim marred by discord and trivia. Chapter eight turns us toward the religious vision of God; chapter nine tries to make good on the recovery of the soul for pastoral care; and chapter ten moves beyond the pastor as carer to a Remnant-community taught how to care. These chapters are interlaced with case material as implications are drawn for the ministry of caring.

Admittedly, process thought is difficult. Whitehead's language--and he is the acknowledged father of this vision of reality though with a rich philosophical ancestry--is carefully crafted to describe reality as he saw it. While he used it very consistently, it takes some getting used to. Since reality is frightfully complex, his systematic explanations are no "simplified editions" of that reality. Therefore, I have had to struggle to be faithful to process thought as I understand it without laboring the technicalities, and to be faithful to the reader who may have never so much as opened a book of any process thinker. (Readers who have had no introduction to process thought might want to move to chapter III and, having finished the book, read chapters I and II, which are somewhat more technical.) The first time technical words are introduced they are explained with references appended for any reader who wants to explore in greater depth the richness of Whitehead's own formulations. Overly simplified charts are used to help the eye to see what the words are trying to say. The case material is intended to clarify by illustration the particular conception being dealt with. But the case material also serves to focus the book which is the ministry of caring within the framework of a process view of the world.

A problem with which I have wrestled throughout the writing of the book is that of nomenclature.
To call the pastoral agent, counselor, has seemed
to limit the area of pastoral caring to formal,
contractual relationships after the manner of
psychotherapy. Furthermore, I see pastoral
counseling as only a small part of pastoral caring
though hopefully caring uses the best counseling
theory. The word, therapist, is too foreign to
pastoral caring and again too limiting. The term,
pastor, so rich in history, has been used
occasionally, but I felt widespread use of that
term drew too much attention to an office and would
encourage ignoring of the lay role in being a
pastor to the neighbor. Finally, I decided on the
word, carer, partly because of its history in
Christian community, and partly because of the
emotional richness that seems to inhere in the term
for many people.

And what do I call the one or ones with whom
the carer is dealing? "Counselee" had the same
problem as counselor. Parishioner was too limiting.
I decided basically to use the word client which I
have used throughout the years, a word borrowed from
Carl Rogers.[3] I wanted to avoid any suggestion that
the Other (i.e., the client) is sick or an object
to be set straight. I wanted a term that I felt
had subjectivity inhering in it. My persistent
conception has been that of carer and client, facing
each other, two centers of subjectivity, each becoming an effect in the other's life.

A second semantic problem is that of sexist
language. I have tried to avoid all sexist
language with reference to God. But this was not
possible when it came to pronouns for carer or
client. To over-use the plural seemed to detract
from empathy so necessary to any caring relationship.
Consequently, I chose to move back and forth between
masculine and feminine pronouns: in one section the
carer would be feminine, the client masculine, and
in another the sexist language would be reversed.
I hope this is not annoying to the reader. At

least the effort at "equal time" is the attempt to be sensitive to those of both sexes--myself included --for whom sexist language is not merely annoying but is downright degrading.

My indebtednesses embarrass me by my inability to articulate an appropriate thanks. They start back in Chicago with Daniel Day Williams, Bernard Loomer, Henry Nelson Wieman, Bernard Meland, and Charles Hartshorne. They move in the company of these toward more recent times with John B. Cobb, Jr., and David Griffin with whom I have spent so many immensely rich hours. John Cobb and David Griffin have increased my debt for their tough-minded critiques of these chapters done with such gentleness as have Paul Mickey, Howard Clinebell, and Richard Rapp. Students at both Pittsburgh Seminary and the Claremont School of Theology have pressed the right questions and have taught me truth as well as grace. My wife, Phyllisee, a fierce critic, is an education! Whatever remains of an esoteric nature is no fault of hers. Terri Treemarcki, my secretary, would prefer a raise, I am sure, but in lieu of that she has my admiration as I stand in amazement at her ability to decipher my scribbled pages so expertly. Also, I need to thank another secretary, Priscilla Boyd. And the last who perhaps should be first are those fellow-travelers who worked so hard in the carer-client relationship that they transformed me in the process of their own self-transformation.

NOTES

[1] Alfred North Whitehead, _Adventures of Ideas_ (New York: Free Press, 1933), p. 169.

[2] See Rollo May (ed.), _Existence_ (New York: Basic Books, 1959), chs. I & II.

[3] Carl R. Rogers, _Client-Centered Therapy_ (Boston: Houghton Mifflin, 1951), pp. 7f.

All real living is meeting.
                    Martin Buber, I and Thou
The best vantage point for understanding behavior
is from the internal frame of reference of the
individual himself.
              Carl Rogers, Client-Centered Therapy

                    Chapter I

              The Person as Experiencing

     This chapter is intended as an overview to
introduce the crucial concept of concrescence,[1]
a "growing together," in process thought. In the
language of caring it is intended to introduce the
person by way of a new vision of what personhood
is.

     Picture with me a pastoral caring setting in
which the carer and client, both feeling, thinking,
willing centers of activity, are facing each other.
What is that carer seeing? Is he or she seeing a
person to whom things have happened, that is, a
person with a hard-core ego around which the stuff
of life is wound, as thread is wound around a
spool? Has that person sitting in the chair been
worked over by life; and is he pretty much what he
appears to be: already cast in his mold? Is
there a core of that person which "goes through"
life's experiences, is shaped by those experiences,
but at its center is pretty much the same from
moment to moment, month to month, year to year?

     Or is the carer seeing another kind of real-
ity? Is he or she seeing the other as a center of
activity, pulsating with life, ceaselessly forming
and reforming himself hundreds of times in the
single hour they are together? Is the carer seeing the other as an organism experiencing the
world, making the experiencing uniquely his own,
and bequeathing what he creates out of those experiences to the next instant of his own becoming
and to others? Is the carer envisaging a flow of

                       1

life in the client so that the clock hour is re-
cording a multitude of changes within him? Is the
carer seeing him as a person, a Thou, not static,
but a dynamic center of feeling, aiming, imaging,
wishing, aspiring, fighting, surrendering activity? And does the carer sense that he or she, too,
is a person constantly experiencing the multiplicity of life so that there are never two fractions
of time exactly alike?

Process thought describes the latter vision
as more appropriate to the way things are. It
begins to describe its vision by pin-pointing where
things are happening: in the present in the experiencing of each entity. The person is made up
of millions of these entities, some lower grade
subordinate entities, some higher grade, more
dominant entities. The client may be feeling
through the intricate nerve structuring of his or
her body an ever so slight sensation of discomfort
in the ankle. That area is a society of interrelated experiencing centers of lesser grade intensity. There is another society of very high-grade
intensity, the Soul, which grapples with the
slight sensation from the ankle (and all the other
givens of its total environment). The person
seated before the carer, dressed in blue slacks,
an open shirt, and perspiring, is a personal
society of pulsating moments of experience. The
carer is also such a society. So in the room they
occupy there are two experiencing centers <u>defining</u>
<u>themselves</u> fraction of a second by fraction of a
second. The place is vividly alive for him or her
who has eyes to see. Whitehead's metaphysical
vision of how things are put together can open the
eyes of both the carer and the other to the reality of their interchange and enhance the possibility of growth for both, as I shall attempt to
demonstrate. What is crucial for pastoral caring
is to understand the nature of the dynamic inner
reality constituting the person whose needs require
skilled caring.

What the carer sees makes a fundamental

difference to what happens!

It is my intention now to keep the client in focus as a complex society of experiencing occasions with the understanding that except for details we are talking about the carer as well.

In agreement with Descartes, Whitehead states that "subjective experiencing is the primary metaphysical situation. . ."[2] This is opposed to the notion that there is a primary subject, that is, an I, to which things happen. In psychological theory Whitehead would oppose Freud's construct of the Ego, a structure upon which environmental reality, superego, and id all impose a servitude. Freud is locked into substance philosophy as he pities the ego as "a poor creature owing service to three masters and consequently menaced by three dangers: from the external world, from the libido of the id, and from the severity of the superego."[3] Freud's concept of the ego is a structure emerging from the undifferentiated Id to which things happen from the outside. While the ego is pliable it is a definable given which is formed, deformed, and reformed by the three masters: id, reality, and superego. Whereas in process thought there is no underlying reality to which things happen. There is a pulsating experiencing which for a human is the "momentary embodiment" of the human's existence.[4] When any client is not viewed by the carer as an experiencing subject, the client is being viewed abstractly, that is, the real actuality is being missed. In Whitehead's own dramatic words: ". . .apart from the experiences of subjects there is nothing, nothing, nothing, bare nothingness."[5]

Whitehead's analysis of an actual occasion[6] of experience is the effort to describe how a droplet of subjectivity arises out of its predecessors, has its "moment" of self-achievement, and passes on as datum for the next processive "instant."[7] Each moment of experiencing, whether its conscious content is a paining big toe which has just been stubbed or a brilliant flash of instant, has an

identical structure. It begins in the initial
phase, grows together through intermediate or
supplemental phases, and completes itself in the
final phase or "satisfaction." As completed it
is a new datum for the next moment of becoming.
So the world grows by the addition of a new One to
the Many. The following diagram attempts to
depict the structure of each experiencing moment.

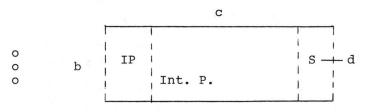

Past: "Moment" b   Present: Future:
and myriad other   "Moment" c   "Moment" d, a
feelings: o   single next
                                             occasion to
                                             represent all
                                             other future
                                             occasions

IP = Initial Phase
Int. P. = Intermediate phase (or Supplemental
          phase)
S = Satisfaction or Achievement
Solid lines (top and bottom of "Moment" c) mean
   that "moments" contemporary to each other do
   not affect each other
Dotted lines represent flow-through: the flowing
   of the past into the present, through the present
   and into the future for another "moment."

     The Initial Phase (IP) is the experience of
birth. The past, all the o's, but focused on b,
offers itself to be experienced. This is past
remote and past contiguous; it is the past of this
particular moment of experiencing. When the past
was an experiencing subject in the present, it was
experiencing unities of feeling. The present

4

moment, c, initially "grasps" these past unities
with the same feeling tone that was felt in the
preceding occasion of experience. If anger is
the feeling tone of b, then c feels (or prehends)[8]
this tone of anger angrily. Yet c feels the anger
with the twist of a new possibility, i.e., perhaps
with a touch of humor. The possibility of feeling
the anger differently may be fed to it by God. In
fact, the birth of the moment, c, is an act of God
coupled with the given of the past moment, b, which
is carried into the present as the present occasion
grasps it. To the past's gift of itself and God's
gift of a novel possibility, the moment, c, responds with its own aim, that is, what it "intends"
to do for its moment of becoming and for moments
beyond for which its own aim will have some responsibility.

The Intermediate Phase (Int. P.) is the
struggle for c to put together the givens from the
past, from God, from other lures teasing it their
ways, and its own aim for its moment in the sun.
In this phase c will make valuations, sift many
feelings, struggle for depth and harmony, as it is
guided by its aim toward what it wills to become.
Herein is the struggle between pleasure and pain,
beauty and ugliness, harmony and disharmony, strife
and peace, in the momentary adventure toward some
novel end-point, or Satisfaction.

The Final Phase, which perhaps should not be
termed a phase at all,[9] but rather the end-point,
is Satisfaction.[10] The moment, c, is over. C
has arrived. Its aim has been somewhat realized:
its struggles are finished. It is what it is. As
such it becomes a new given (part of the past) for
the next moment, d, and for other moments or
durations yet to be into which it will fit as part
of their momentary existence.

So actuality comes into being, has its "moment,"
and ceases to experience. It is no longer a subject. It is now an object and as such continues
in the experience of God and in the experience of
each occasion inheriting it. It will repeat the

structure but not precisely that particular experience of c which belongs uniquely to c.

Both carer and the other are societies of countless episodes such as I have described. As the two face each other they are not seeing what is happening if we mean literal seeing with the eye. Appearance is so deceptive. The "really real," hidden from the senses, is a pulsating Present of dynamic operations. The client, to stay with that particularity, is never the same fraction of a second by fraction of a second. Time measured on the watch fails to register the flowing of phase into phase, the birth of novelty and the perishing of the occasion, the addition of each new occasion to constitute the routing of the client. Through the hour of a counseling session the client is being born and struggles and dies innumerable times. To picture graphically what is going on in the client, we might look at it mathematically. If a carer is with a client for the fifty-minute hour,[11] that period included 3,000 seconds or 30,0000 tenths-of-seconds, a tenth of a second suggesting roughly the duration of an experiencing epoch of time for a human being. Translated into the living experience of the client this means that that person has 30,000 discrete experiences in the 50-minute period. Each person, however, is an immense society of such minute experiences. For example, we can scarcely imagine the vast experiencing going on in breathing[12] alone as the client works through the agenda of the hour. The mathematics of one period with one client is staggering. There are simply millions of droplets of experiencing, most of them unconscious, which are momentary embodiments of the client, during the session. Double that to include the carer in these mathematics and the dynamics of that hour almost defy imagination.

However, that is only one side of the story. Throughout this tremendous flux runs a powerful continuity. The client has endured a common pattern and exemplifies that pattern. Events are

not born ex nihilo and do not die without immortality. They emerge out of other occasions and
they perdure into future occasions. Thus each of
us senses a historic routing of our becoming.
For example, a characteristic defining that route
might be anger. B might be a previous instant
of anger to which c now corresponds in its own
way. No two experiences of anger within the continuity of the person are precisely the same although anger may be a dominant theme running
through b, c, d, etc. In the counseling hour
amidst the routing of continuity there is novelty
in each act of experiencing. The subject of each
experience is changing, if ever so slightly, over
against its routing. At least it is struggling
between what was and what might be. That may not
be perceptible to the naked eye, but it is the way
things are according to Whitehead's analysis of
each droplet of experience. The self, that is, the
client, is constantly creating and re-creating,
determining and re-determining, realizing and re-
realizing itself. So constant is this act of
experiencing that it must be termed process as one-
tenth of a second arises, has its brief duration,
and passes into the next tenth of a second. The
client before us, viewed within this metaphysical
description, is utterly alive and changing even if
the appearance of passivity or depression scarcely
registers a change at all. The other who is before
us is in flux, putting together the vast multiplicity of life into the unity of his being, and
contributing that new creation, his unique Oneness
at any given moment, to the ongoing flowing of
reality, his and others. The human being, as just
one type of creation, is an organism of incredible
activity.

This way of looking at the client sets the
total therapeutic experience in a perspective quite
different from most other models.[13] I shall try to
suggest four ways in which this perspective makes
a difference to pastoral caring.

For the pastoral carer to understand that the client, contrary to appearance, is a moving, pulsating, wrestling, novelty-creating person, who, during the session, has had thousands of feelings coursing through the body and most creatively in the soul, should lead that carer to see the Other in process. In appearance the Other may seem static, unchanged over the fifty minutes. The period may seem not only unfruitful but a drag. Nothing happened. Not so! Each concrescing fraction of a second the experiencing Other was responding to "old tapes," but with twists, if ever so slight, made possible by all kinds of lures, for example, the carer. (We shall analyze "lures" in Chapter VI.) It is fundamentally important to sort out reality from appearance. Reality is the struggling of the client to deal with "massive insistency" of the past, the grasping of a new possibility, enjoying the "ferment of valuation," and coming to its moment of arrival or satisfaction. This struggling and enjoying, altogether interior to the client, is the "process of activity" pretty much hidden from the eye or ear of the carer. What the carer does see or hear is the appearance of the client, the external data which are sensed by eye or ear. But these sense data, so clear-cut, are abstractions from the real world of the client. They give clues as to what may be going on or has been going on in the immediate or more remote (half-hour) past. But "appearance is an incredibly simplified edition of reality," as Whitehead has observed.[14] This is so because the client in his or her subjectivity is really missed. Appearance misses the rich putting together of the self. Appearance is always from a distance. It misses the client's inner conforming, aiming, struggling, completing. The rich interior of the client is "veiled from the observer."[15] To put the matter another way, the carer may have sensory information about the Other but he cannot conclude what the information means.

Much of the time the carer may not know with

any precision what is going on in the client. But
to know that something fundamentally active and
creative is going on is to face the client with a
profound respect and a sense of awe and in a mood
of excitement and expectation. When the carer
knows that there is a concrescing, a putting together of a past that is massively present and a
future constantly beckoning, going on inside the
client, the carer cannot view the client as an It,
an object, but will hold the client in the status
of a Thou, a subject. Such a vision of the Other
is a safeguard against giving answers, manipulating,
imposing doctrinal positions whether religious or
secular. It helps to create the conditions for
genuine interpersonal dialogue among which are
genuine respect for, and acceptance of, the Other.
It helps the carer to stay alert to the possibilities for change taking place in the client. In
short, this vision helps to keep the caring client-
centered.

II

     To be a carer who sees the client as an ex-
periencing center of birthing, struggling, and
satisfaction is to be on guard against the diagnostic trap. It seems to me that clients so often
become victims of the triumph of the diagnostic.
Diagnosis is largely a medical term. Since Freud
was a physician it was most natural for him to use
the medical model of diagnosing a mental or emotional problem. And since psychiatry has mostly
followed that model, with significant exceptions
to be sure, the felt need to diagnose according to
a chart of illnesses has continued to be fulfilled.
And since pastoral counseling has pretty well
adopted the medical model, it has adopted the
principle, if not the habit, of diagnosis. But to
diagnose is to stand outside the client. It implies
distance between counselor and client. Diagnosis
presupposes analysis which means a breaking up or
a loosening up of a whole into its constituent parts.
Analysis objectifies the client, seeking to look at
him, ask about him, listen to him, in order to find

9

out what ails him. But this activity misses the
other in his uniqueness.

Henri Bergson, a process thinker, makes a
careful distinction between two movements: the
one away from, the other into. This is the distinction between analysis and intuition, respect-
ively. For Bergson, analysis means "that we move
round the object," intuition "that we enter into
it."[16]

Analysis places the observer outside the object; by intuition the carer inserts himself into
the other by an effort of imagination.[17] By
analysis Bergson means viewing an object from the
outside, from a distance, from a viewpoint.
Analysis proceeds by translating to the object being studied resemblances from others we already
know about or think we know about.[18] By intuition
he means "coincidence with the person himself," a
"simple act" of placing oneself imaginatively in
the duration that constitutes another's life.[19]
For Bergson it is intuition alone which can give
what is essential and unique "in the person."[20]

Two illustrations, representing two types of
analysis, may help to make the point.

The first is the professional assessment. A
woman of 25 years comes to see her pastor who is
proficient in pastoral counseling. He notices
quickly some customary affects of depression e.g.,
lowered eyes, drawn face, body posture, voice
timber, rate of speech, poor self-esteem. He has
read Edith Jacobson and has embraced her assump-
tions about states of depression, especially that
basic depression is due to a reduction of self-
esteem.[21] The pastor has insights into depressive
states and observes carefully his parishioner before him. He cannot miss the diagnosis of depression. But what does he have when he makes the
diagnosis? Only a valuable abstraction, a bit of
descriptive short-hand. This woman's depression is
unique to her feeling states. We will not be far
afield in imagining that never before has this

10

occasioning of just these feeling-states happened
nor will they again. This is the uniqueness of
this experiencing woman before him. This uniqueness is one reason he does not give illustrations
of other people suffering depression, himself
included. This is also a reason he is very wary
of the facile interpretation and why he encourages
her to gain her own insights. While he knows a
major theory of depression and that she is depressed, he is not going to stumble into the
diagnostic trap, affixing to her an abstraction
and then treating the abstraction. He must get
into the stream of her becoming and try to read
from within the nightmarish concrescing that is
going on. In doing so he is already on the road
to helping her for by holding her in such esteem
her own self-formulations grasp his respect for her
and slowly form inner experiences of new self-
esteem.

    A second type of analysis is what we might
term a generic assessment. Freud made such an
assessment when he theorized that women suffer from
penis-envy which persists by displacement in the
character-trait of jealousy.[22] His very little
clinical data were derived from neurotic and
psychotic female patients and not from normal
females. But behind these data was the patriarchi-
cal society which viewed the male as the human
paradigm. Further, as Erikson notes, the early
clinicians had to "understand the female psyche
with male means of empathy. . ."[23] This was not
mythology with Freud, though its perpetuation
constitutes mythology, but it was very bad generalization which characterized the woman as being a
deficient male. It is an illustration of the
"intolerant use of abstractions," which, Whitehead
wrote, "is the major vice of the intellect."[24]
Thus analysis imposed a tragic error upon a part
of the human species; the female was read as being
motivated by a lack of the male genital. In her
trenchant criticism of the Freudian notion of
penis-envy, Judith Bardwick says, "this seems to
be the classic illustration of the danger of

11

generalizing to a normal population from an abnormal population seeking relief from its terrors."[25] Freud's cultural presupposition is guilty of missing the female per se; and, of course, missing any one female's rich complexity out of deference to a theory especially insidious because of its lack of empirical verification. Penis-envy is a sad example of one type of analysis. It is an instance of what Whitehead called the "fallacy of misplaced concreteness." Diagnosis conceptualizes a person or a group from the outside but runs the danger of missing the real subject who may be lost or at least hidden in the conceptual framework.[26]

While Whitehead differs somewhat from Bergson in his understanding of intuition,[27] both use the notion to put us in touch with material that is much deeper than sensory material: that is, with the stuff of life, the massive past, that lies back of that which is gained by the senses. What I am struggling for is the insistence both Carl Rogers and Rollo May make in terms of empathy. Rogers, for example, insists upon the counselor getting into the "perceptual world" of the client: the positioning of oneself in that "perceptual world" is what he means by empathy.[28] May's corrective on orthodox psychiatry by way of Existential Analysis or Daseinanalysis, for example, in the first two chapters of his edited book Existence, is his emphasis on the role of empathy which is similar to what I have been calling intuition.[29]

In Biblical language agape-love would seem to both guide and enable what Bergson is calling for. Agape-love is God's originally and the creature's derivately, meaning thereby that it is a grace-gift. This is its enabling capacity for it is a love transcending all human loves but including them.[30] Its capacity to guide is in its sacrificial nature, revealed ultimately in Jesus who is the "incarnation of the love which is the meaning of our existence,"[31] as Williams has shown. Thus agape-love can seek to stand within the concrescence of a fellow-traveler, taking the risks

12

involved in such a stance, assured that power and
direction will continue to come from beyond oneself. Agape-love, summing up and fulfilling both
intuition and empathy, is a positioning of oneself
within the living world of the client to feel after
him what he is feeling. The carer will traffic in
and out of that life, never fully congruent with
it, for no two individuals ever have precisely the
same traffic pattern, but congruent enough to have
the empathic sense of a fellow-traveler. The
carer will reflect on where he has been in the
journey of the client but he will be wary about
attaching labels defining where he has been and
what he has experienced. As Bergson observes, one
can move from intuition to analysis, never from
analysis to intuition. The former movement has
grasped something of the reality of the other and
then reflected upon the grasped reality. The
latter movement has never gotten to the reality.

Yet some kind of evaluation is necessary. My
preferred term is hypothesis, employed to suggest
the relativity, the tentativeness, the guarded
approximation with which we come to an evaluative
judgment of the other. I suspect a pastoral carer
is with a parishioner who has come with a problem
only a few moments until hypotheses begin to surface. They border on the hunch, to begin with, are
often vague, and probably have not yet the status
to be dignified as hypotheses. But they are the
germ of hypothesis out of which will come (inevitably) some notions as to what's going on. In ex-
tended therapy, say over weeks or months, hypotheses are modified, sometimes drastically, and are
constantly undergoing nuances of change.

If one does not employ analysis in the
diagnostic sense how does one use psychoanalytic
material, especially its hard-won theory? One uses
psychoanalytic diagnostic material as one uses any
generalization: to give a perspective to a nexus
of events, to bring to bear wisdom for which the
abstraction stands, to enrich hypothesis formation.
But one does not allow theory to crowd out or
screen the rich data which are interior to the

client as though the analysis were the real thing. The prehensive life, the subjective aims, the subjective forms: these are the world of riches which the self is putting together. Diagnosis from the outside surely misses this richness under terms of an abstraction which obscures the real stuff. The problem is that abstraction is so easily and readily taken for the real stuff. This is the dangerous temptation in psychiatry against which Menninger and Laing, among others, have been warning. Its temptation is its advantage of clarity. Unfortunately it may miss the person.

III

When the client is viewed as an experiencing center, the focus of the interview is the present. This is in keeping with Gestalt theory. However, as we shall see more fully in the next chapter, process thought is quite aware that the past informs the present while Gestalt tends to dismiss the past lest it get in the way of present awareness. As Perls has written, ". . .what happened even only a minute ago is past, not present."[32] He continues by denying past or future as realities.[33] Of course, what Perls is rightly concerned to avoid is our living in the past (retrogressively) or in the future (wishfully) and so missing the reality of the present where we are, and thus losing the possibility of gaining wholeness. Whitehead is equally intent on the present, but he sees the past as immanent in the present. The past does not remain "back there" as a lump to be related to. It resides in the duration that is now. Thus the past has such tremendous reality that Whitehead called it causal efficacy, meaning thereby that the totality of the past is causally effective in the present.[34] As we shall see in the next chapter, the past is conformally prehended or felt by the present.

With this correction on Gestalt we can say with that school that the present is all there is. The

14

future is only an open range of possibilities waiting the person's free decisions.

When the pastoral carer concentrates on the present, he or she is not seeing the past as way back there twenty years ago, as though there is a mound of pastness which must be leveled. Rather, in concentrating on the present the carer invests care in helping the client in the now to deal with any subjective form, for example, that of anger toward authority figures, i.e., parents, teachers, sergeants, who reside not "back there" but in this experiencing moment. So the emphasis is on present feeling for that is where the struggle between past and future is lodged. The client is in part a conformal feeling to his or her past, in part a conceptual feeling of a new possibility, in part a cluster of comparative feelings as he or she puts it all together. Here and now is where the client is, where she is creating, where there is opportunity for changing. This would put the Gestalt emphasis on awareness in a richer field of operation than mere environmental contact. Focusing on the experiencing subject leaves nothing but the present in its exquisite preciousness but a present which houses the past and anticipates the future.

IV

Finally, the pastoral carer is also an experiencing center! This way of looking at himself begets an orientation of Presence first to himself and then to the client. Presence is constituted of aliveness, attention, and sensitivity. It is the aliveness of one who is acutely in touch with his entire organism through the multiplicity of feeling-states; the attention of one who has zeroed in on what is the present; the sensitivity of one who through empathic understanding or imagination listens to the struggles in the "perceptual world" of the other. This quality of focus means that the carer is present to the client with a concentration that is unusual in a time when most relationships

15

are so superficial. Such presence I would see to
be integral to the practice of agape-love. Of
course, such love and its practice is not limited
to a certain metaphysical vision. But some metaphysical visions make the practice of Presence
more amenable to caring situations than others.
For example, there is little evidence that Freud
thought in terms of Presence. There is every
evidence that Buber did. A central thrust of
these chapters is that the metaphysical vision
incorporated in process thought opens up the role
of Presence in a remarkable way.

The pastoral carer has, of course, an ultimate motivation: an incarnate Presence. It would
seem that he can be a more faithful servant of
that motivation when he understands himself in the
nature of things as constantly presenting himself
to the other. While this carries for the carer
the risk of rejection, it also carries to the
other the lure of Hope. It is a hope become
concrete in one presence and thereby made objective for another.

NOTES

[1]On concresence see Alfred North Whitehead, Process and Reality (New York: Macmillan, 1929), Part II, ch. X, and Part III; also, Alfred North Whitehead, Adventures of Ideas (New York: Free Press, 1933), ch. XV.

[2]PR, p. 243.

[3]Sigmund Freud, The Ego and the Id (New York: Norton, 1900), tr. James Strackey, p. 56.

[4]Cf. John B. Cobb, Jr., The Structure of Christian Existence (Philadelphia: Westminster, 1967), p. 18.

[5]PR, p. 254.

[6]By an "actual occasion" Whitehead means the irreducible stuff or whiff or entity of experience. Actual occasions or actual entities are not to be understood in terms of images suggested by vision or any of the five senses but in terms of categories suggested by our total experiencing itself. "Actual occasion" is a construct to get at a locus of experiencing in its most rudimentary form. We do not see "actual occasions." What we see are societies of "actual occasions." A big toe is a society of many actual occasions. Whitehead is intent on describing the most rudimentary structuring of life imaginable. Consequently his thought can be described as atomistic.

[7]The reason "moment" and "instant" are within quote marks is to signify that these terms are not to be taken literally as fractions of clock-time. Such time is "spatialized" time, as Bergson terms it. "Spatialized" time is a segment of time which is under analysis or looked at from the outside. Time as conceived in process thought is "flow-time," that is, real time which is a duration some subject is

17

experiencing. Technically, duration cannot be
constructed in terms of instants. However, for
purposes of analyzing an experience, we must
revert to "moments" and "instants" which is time
as though it could be stopped which is a still
picture of time.

[8]On prehensions see PR, part III; also AI, ch. XV.

[9]Cf. William A. Christian, An Interpretation of
Whitehead's Metaphysics (New Haven, Yale, 1959),
pp. 22ff, 30, 31.

[10]PR, p. 38.

[11]Taken from Robert Lindner, The Fifty-Minute Hour
(New York: Rhinehart, 1955).

[12]I use breathing exercises occasionally to help
locate where a primary feeling is, to identify
what the feeling is, and to dispense the feeling
when necessary.

[13]Rogers' client-centered therapy, Gestalt theory,
and Assagioli's Psychosynthesis have some
affinity to Whitehead's metaphysical description.
But in Gestalt there is a substantive self, with
its needs, with its actions directed to need
satisfaction thus making the environment into
foreground or background, and with contact with,
or withdrawal from, the environment the process
for ongoing life processes. The model seems to
be a polarity between an organized and organizing
self and the environment. This is a polarity of
space rather than time and explains why Gestalt
concentrates on the Now which is time spatialized.
(Cf. Fritz Perls, The Gestalt Approach and Eye
Witness to Therapy (Ben Lomond, Ca.: Science
and Behavior Books, Inc., 1973), Ch. 1. passim.)
Nevertheless, Gestalt offers rich psychological
data for Whitehead's metaphysical description.
Assagioli, whose pioneering work especially on the
Will is a breakthrough in the clinical situation,
also sees the self as a "permanent center."

This is the "true self situated beyond or
'above' it" [the conscious self or ego].
Thus, Assagioli links himself with Kant's
noumenal self over against the empirical ego
which is impermanent. But even the "I," the
self, which is the center of consciousness, is
different from the contents of consciousness.
In his famous diagram of consciousness, Assagioli
pictures the Conscious Self, or the empirical
Ego, as well as the Higher Self, which is the
permanent center, or true Self, by a dot,
symbolic of a substance at the center of the
human organism. (Roberto Assagioli,
Psychosynthesis (New York: Penguin, 1976), ch.
1, passim, esp. pp. 17-19.)
It is not clear in Rogers whether there is
essentially an unchanging ego at the center of
the client, but Rogers is clear in any case that
it is a pliable ego, capable of basic self-
changing. It would not do a disservice to
Rogers' analysis of client-centered therapy to
place that innovative theory into the larger
metaphysical description of process thought.
Indeed, it would appear to fulfill Rogers' own
creative contribution.

[14] Alred North Whitehead, Adventures of Ideas (New
York: Free Press, 1967), p. 213. The several
quoted words in this section, as well as the
basic conceptuality, are taken from Adventures
of Ideas, ch. XIV, passim; also Cf. PR, part III,
ch. III, Sec. IV).

[15] AI, p. 219.

[16] Henri Bergson, An Introduction to Metaphysics
(New York: Liberal Arts, 1949), p. 21.

[17] Ibid.

[18] Cf. Ibid., p. 24.

[19] Ibid., p. 22.

[20] Ibid., p. 28.

[21] Edith Jacobson, Depression (New York: International University Press, 1971), ch. VI. Cf. Myer Mendleson, Psychoanalytic Concepts of Depression (Flushing, NY: Spectrum, 1974), pp. 72-88.

[22] Sigmund Freud, "Some Psychological Consequences of the Anatomical Distinction Between the Sexes," Collected Papers (London: Hogarth, 1957), ed. by James Strachey, V. V, Ch. XVII; "Female Sexuality," Ibid., Ch. XXIV. While Freud was tentative in this suggestion in the "Distinction Between the Sexes" article which was written in 1925, evidence that he deeply held this view is its reiteration six years later in "Female Sexuality."

[23] Erik H. Erikson, "Inner and Outer Space: Reflections on Womanhood" Daedalus (1964, V. 93), pp. 582-606.

[24] Alfred North Whitehead, Science and the Modern World (New York: Mentor, 1948), p. 19.

[25] Judith M. Bardwick, Psychology of Women (New York: Harper, 1971), p. 10.

[26] Bergson, op. cit., pp. 31, 32.

[27] Cf. A. H. Johnson, Whitehead's Theory of Relativity (New York: Dover, 1962), pp. 134-35; PR, pp. 216, 252; A.I., pp. 209-210.

[28] Carl Rogers, Client-Centered Therapy (New York: Houghton Mifflin, 1951); pp. 28-30; Cf. pp. 483 ff

[29] Rollo May, Existence (New York: Basic Books, 1958) pp. 11-14, 34f, 81f. For a more specified reference to empathy, see a much earlier but still very valuable book, Rollo May, The Art of Counseling (New York: Abingdon, 1939), Ch. 3.

[30]Cf. Daniel Day Williams, The Spirit and the
   Forms of Love (New York: Harper, 1968), p. 204.

[31]Daniel Day Williams, God's Grace and Man's Hope
   (New York: Harper, 1949), p. 65.

[32]Fritz Perls, Ego, Hunger and Aggression (New
   York: Vintage, 1969), pp. 92, 93.

[33]Ibid., p. 95.

[34]On Causal efficacy see PR, pp. 256ff.

Enough is left unexplained to justify the hypothesis of a compulsion to repeat--something that seems more primitive, more elementary, more instinctual than the pleasure principle which it over-rides.
Sigmund Freud, Beyond The Pleasure Principle

Chapter II

How It All Begins: Initial Phase

We begin now to detail how a human being comes together.

To be concrete let us look at a human being by way of a brief case study. One of my clients was dominated by anger: he felt the world angrily. His father was a mean, two-fisted man, who vented his rage on his only son. His mother favored his older sister, creating a climate for jealousy and hostility. When he was 14, after a vicious beating by his father, he left home and school with the threat that he would never return until he was a millionaire. By his mid-thirties he had made his first million. He had married three times, was a heavy drinker and gambler, a driver of men working for him. He was dogged by intense anxiety which erupted into acute anxiety attacks whenever he felt himself cornered or squeezed, or his existence threatened by death as when a friend or colleague died. In the long, painful months of working together, these few abstractions, multiplied by many more, were illuminated by the concreteness of his suffering.

He was a man possessed by anger, or rather, hostility.[1] Part of his struggle was to curb his hostility so that he would not destroy someone. The more we got into the flow of his life the more obvious it became that that flow was a repetition of angry conformations. The past was causally and powerfully present in the form of anger. It was as though the river of his years was a subterranean flow of anger. Whence came that anger? How did it become sedimented in his being? This chapter begins

to attack that problem. But first we must set
briefly a theoretical framework that will help us
to understand my client whom we have just met.

We shall first describe the Initial Phase or
how an actual occasion is born. This will underscore the role of conformal feelings where I locate
neurosis and the general stuckness of most pastoral
caring situations. The analysis of conformal feelings will then be translated into pastoral caring
concerns by way of a brief case study. The role
of God will be briefly described although Chapter III will amplify that role.

I

The Initial Phase

Alluding to the "duration" pictured in the
preceding chapter, we are stopping time, as it
were, to look at just the beginning of that concrescence: the birthing stage.

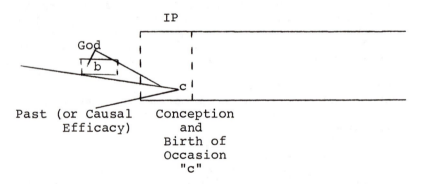

Past (or Causal   Conception
    Efficacy)   and
                       Birth of
                       Occasion
                        "c"

The Initial Phase (IP) is where actual occasion "c" is born. Actual occasion "b" is completed.
Its duration is forever determined. Now it passes
into its immortality, that is, it is ready to be
prehended or grasped by its successor, "c." Past
occasion "b" will reside in "c" which is the way
the past lives in each new present. "C's" grasp

24

or prehension of "b" is a conformal prehension, that is, "c" conforms to "b," or rather to part of "b," as we shall see. Hence, the Initial Phase is the phase of conformal feelings. As Whitehead notes, "The conformal stage merely transforms the objective content [i.e., "b"] into subjective feelings [i.e., "c"]."[2]

Before we go further in analysis I shall try to illustrate a conformal feeling. A baby has fallen out of its walker. There will be a few seconds of feeling painfully the fall. Cries, perhaps wrenching the body, will respond to the painful feelings. But in a few seconds the pain itself will abate. Yet, the sobbing continues. The baby is no longer sobbing in response to the initial fall and hurt; it is now sobbing in response to its own sobbing. The continued sobbing is a patterned response not to the original impetus but to the bodily repetition of convulsive activity. It may take several seconds or even minutes for the crying to end. Pain elicited the original responses of crying; crying itself later begets crying, perhaps minutes after the physical hurt is gone.

The newly arising actual occasion is born by responding to one of the subjective forms of the immediately preceding actual occasion. In the case of the baby the dominant subjective form of "b" was physical hurt or pain. The nascent occasion, c, somewhere within the baby feels or prehends or grasps this pain. Thus, the new occasion conforms to the old; "and so the old is the new." But the new always repeats the old in a somewhat modified way. So gradually the baby conforms to, or repeats, its immediate past experience of sobbing. In this brief experience of "fall" the baby first conformed to the pain; gradually the pain subsided; then toward the end of the experience the baby's sobbing was conforming to sobbing itself. The past has a heavy hand. It must be grasped or conformed to by the present. There is, as Freud so acutely observed, a "compulsion to repeat." But it is not a compulsion

25

under duress to a death instinct. It is a compulsion of metaphysical necessity for that is how the past comes to reside in the present.

Not all of the past is in the present, for c feels b under a perspective. That is, b is made up of many feelings which have been synthesized into a felt unity of experience. C grasps one of those feelings and so b is reproduced in c in that restricted way. C re-enacts in itself what it grasps of b. It is that of b which is immanent in c, perhaps anger, or joy, or depression. That means that a great deal of b was eliminated, or negatively prehended,[3] by c. If c's prehension of b is the feeling of anger, other subjective forms of b, such as love or momentary joy, might be lost to c, that is, not reproduced, or re-enacted, in c. Thus c might grasp a powerful subjective form of b, anger, as in the case of my client, and eliminate more frail, tender ones, such as a flickering feeling of love.[4] Through conformal feelings the past is vectorially carried into the present. How that happens, that is, how the present prehends or lays hold of its past, determines in part the initial phase of the present.[5]

C is a neonate whose very conception was possible because the past presented itself to be felt. The present is not born de novo or ex nihilo as though it were sprung forth unrelated to what has gone before. Its birth pang, for good or ill, is to conform to its predecessors, e.g., b. The immortality of b is to be part of the creation of c.

In the last sentence I said that b is part-creator of the creation of c. God is also part-creator. While we shall develop fully God's relationship to the creation in the next chapter, it is necessary that we anticipate that development now. Crucial to c's durative moment is its own subjective aim. For its brief existence it aims toward its final unity, what it will become. But its own aim toward its own completion is a response to another Aim, the Aim of God for it. As Whitehead says, God "is that entity from which each temporal concrescence receives that initial aim from which its self-creation starts."[6] God knows the total past of each becoming moment including, of course, the very datum of b to which c is conforming. God also envisages all possibility, including those possibilities most relevant to c, given its routing out of the past. God, therefore, is in the position to have that vision of what is best for c in its uniqueness. So it is that God gives to c its initial aim, the best possibility for that impasse. To God's Initial Aim, c responds with its own subjective aim. So Whitehead can write, "Every act leaves the world with a deeper or a fainter impress of God."[7] God presides over the birth of each occasion by nudging it into becoming with an aim to which it must respond. In this sense God does create each actual occasion.[8]

II

An Excursis: From Actual Occasion to Person

I have been describing the birth, by way of conformal feeling, of an actual occasion, the briefest experiencing center conceivable. Before proceeding with the role of conformal feelings within pastoral care, we need to trace the connection between actual occasion and human existence. A human being[9] is a society of ever increasingly complex systems which themselves are societies of actual occasions. For example, there is the nervous system which is composed of numerous societies of actual occasions throughout the body. The stomach, a nerve center, is a locus of innumerable actual occasions of experiencing centers, which prehend or grasp conformally past occasions making up the history of that system. That system itself is related to other environmental systems. Much of the time we are not consciously aware of this nerve center until some distress, i.e., ache, finally gets our attention and we name it hunger, or until symptoms develop which might be diagnosed, ulcerated condition, etc. Nevertheless,

experiencing at levels below consciousness is
constantly going on. Such experiencing is repeated in systems throughout the body, including
the brain. Most of this experiencing is by way of
low-grade actual occasions, devoid of consciousness. In a hierarchical structuring of experience,
lower grade occasions feed superior grade occasions
all the way up to the soul, which, as we shall see
in Chapter IX, is the dominant society within that
routing we call personal existence.

For the most part in these chapters we shall
be dealing with the macrocosm called person rather
than the microcosm called actual occasion. But
we need to remember that only actual occasions are
the experiencing centers. The person emerges as
a distinct entity from the "welter of multitudinous
microscopic actual occasions."[10] Real life is in
actual occasions. When we talk of persons conforming, or experiencing, or prehending, or aiming,
we are speaking of a generality, that is, a massive
clustering of actual occasions. Being a person is
an endless process of unifying into ever more complex societies millions of experiencing centers.
Soul makes the process of person-building possible.
I can call myself a person because there is a continuous defining characteristic from past to present in my experiencing. There is an underlying
similarity in the ways I have experienced, and continue to experience, the world. Because of conformation there is a basic underlying character,
an enduring personality, amid the flux. Each successor moment has summed up its predecessor moments
with some peculiar completeness.[11] So when we
speak of a person we are referring to a synthesis
of summing up. It is important to make the distinction between actual occasion and person, as we
have just done, to insist on the atomicity of experience. In turn atomic existence when clustered
together into personhood shows how intricate a
personal unity is.

III

Conformal Feelings and Pastoral Care

We now return from our excursus, explaining the move from actual occasion to person, to argue that conformal feelings are at the root of most pastoral caring situations; and, I would also argue, at the root of neuroses and psychoses generically.

Many, if not all, situations requiring pastoral caring or counseling would appear to be stuck on the phase of conformity. The person feels conformally the immediately preceding tenth-of-a-second which has felt conformally its preceding tenth-of-a-second, and so on, until a route of conformity is established. A pattern of conformal response is embedded. We respond by hooking into the immediately preceding experience which hooked into its immediate predecessor. As the baby's sobbing, long after the physical pain has gone, continues to feed on itself, so we, seconds after the anger-producing event, continue to conform to the anger. Thus, we perpetuate it by continuing to hook into it. It appears that there is a "compulsion to repeat" on the part of all of us as we respond conformally to immediately past data. So patterns of continuity between past and present are formed. This is not mere repetition for we repeat but with a difference. Almost imperceptibly the baby's sobbing flattens out and may even turn to gurgling laughter. Novelty is introduced. But with some this repetition becomes a powerful pattern, a fixation, which binds us neurotically to the past. Probably all people respond temporarily in this way when they are under great stress, i.e., important loss. This may be a form of regression in the service of the ego, a concept developed by Kris.[12] But for a large group of people who really are stuck in the routing of their lives, conformal feelings would appear to be at the nucleus of their problem.

29

At the beginning of this chapter we met a client crowded with anger and asked how that anger came to be such a defining characteristic of his being. I want to return to that case study to translate the theory of conformal fixation into caring theory. I remind the reader that this is not a typical pastoral caring case, but it is certainly not a-typical for pastoral counseling. Furthermore, while this case dealt with a neurosis, I would argue that the metaphysical description above applies with equal validity to those situations where neurosis is not a factor, such as the typical work of grief. Even in these "normal" situations the sense of loss encourages conformal feeling after conformal feeling which we recognize as states of regression, periods of fixation, compulsive needs to repeat, in short, a sense of being immobilized with new possibilities not even so much as a wish. That is why hopelessness is the hallmark of loss as it is of any other experience of being stuck.

Very early the dominant motif had been set. My counselee's father and mother were both angry people--at least that was his perception, and that perception helped to constitute his reality of anger. His odyssey of anger began by prehending angrily the subjective form of his parents, which was anger.[13] They were angry; to them as angry he conformed. Unfortunately, he perceived them under an abstraction; that is, anger so dominated that it crowded out other possible and perhaps fragile perceptions such as love even meagerly shown. Throughout his childhood he rehearsed the conforming feeling of anger, continuing that rehearsal into adulthood so that anger became the perduring feeling-tone of his life. As he conformed so he became. To be sure, there were novel expressions of anger, many positive in the sense that they were socially acceptable, as when he turned his hostile aggression[14] into a fortune. But anger was where he was stuck. He repetitively conformed to his own conformities so that he became a self-fulfilling prophecy.

30

Duration of anger upon duration of anger built up in the flow of his life so that there was an enduring characteristic of anger defining the flow of his being. So powerful was this defining characteristic that it dominated all his other conformal feelings, toward others, i.e., toward a sister, wives, workers, a psychiatrist, blacks, the blue-bloods of the community, God. The anger that built up toward God emerged as a basic problem. His parents were "very religious, at church whenever the doors were opened." There were two strikes on God before my client ever left early childhood. Evangelist after evangelist, as part of sawdust trail revivals, dangled him over the fires of hell, tormenting his soul into responses of nightmarish fear and anger toward God that only accentuated the chronic anxiety into acute attacks.

My client illustrates a particularly important point in process thought. It is the impact of non-sensuous perception. This perception is deeper than mere sense experience. Non-sensuous perception is the past being grasped, or felt, or hooked into by the new moment. It is the past being carried into the present. This is not conscious perception except in relatively rare moments of conscious memory. It is the subterranean flow of feeling out of the vast multiplicity that was a fraction of a moment ago and now will become part of this new moment. Non-sensuous perception is how the past is causally in the present. In illustrating non-sensuous perception Whitehead used the conformal feeling of anger in the following excerpt:

> The first phase in the immediacy of the new occasion is that of the conformation of feelings. The feeling as enjoyed by the past occasion is present in the new occasion as datum felt, with a subjective form conformal to that of the datum. Thus, if A be the past occasion, D the datum felt by A with subjective form describable as A angry, then this

31

feeling--namely, A feeling D with the subjective form of anger--is initially felt
by the new occasion B with the same subjective form of anger. The anger is continuous throughout the successive occasions of experience. This continuity of
subjective form is the initial sympathy
of B for A.[15]

Perhaps we can diagram this crucial point in
this sequential way:

 = A feeling D angrily; B feeling
A angrily, etc. (Since D is in
A, D also becomes a part of
B through A.)

My client was A (angry) feeling D angrily; then B
angrily feeling A's angry feeling of D, and so on
to build up an enduring pattern of anger along the
route of years. To paraphrase Whitehead, Anger
was the expression of cumulation; it was physical
memory.[16] Part of the tragedy of such cumulation
is that much of life is excluded. Not all of the
data which life gives to us can be included. This
is due in part to the fact that we are finite
creatures and cannot grasp or embrace all of the
data of life.[17] It is also due to any overwhelming preoccupation in the initial phase with an
enduring conformal feeling. My client was so defined by his conformal feelings of anger toward
his parents that he missed the fuller richness
that those parents surely were. They were not just
angry nor did they act just angrily. This became
clear as he straightened out his vision of his
parents and found much to his surprise that he did
have slight memories, and pleasant ones, of them
other than angry. I am suggesting that his pre-
occupying feeling of anger excluded what they might
otherwise have been to him. There were mini-grade
perceptions of his parents which prompted in him
an ambivalence: some love even if dominated by
anger. It was the love, as well as the sense of
guilt it produced, which prompted him to care for

them in some expensive ways out of his fortune. The point is, however, that when a dominant conformal feeling such as anger grips a person by totally (or almost totally) defining him, that feeling crowds out a lot of other data, such as softer feelings, eliminating them from participating positively in the ongoing experiencing of life. When his parents' meager displays of love did not become formative in his childhood, there was nothing to modify the dominance of anger. This is why Erikson writes about the basic need for a continuity of love from parenting figures.[18] The tragedy was that my client missed the 'more' that his parents were other than simply being angry.

What helped anger to become dominant in my client was the value he came to place upon it.[19] Although valuation plays its part later in the concrescence, that is, after the conformal phase we are now discussing, it needs to be introduced here because it encourages the reproduction of feelings. A person puts such weight or attaches such significance to a certain feeling as to guarantee the persistence of that which is valued. My client valued anger so highly, that is, became so enmeshed in it, was so preoccupied with it, that his concentration on anger helped to guarantee its immortality in him. Had he been able to shrug it off, which children can rarely do, or value it downward, he might have tended to attenuate it into triviality if not elimination. But he so fixated upon it that it became second-nature to him to conform, conform, conform; angrily. Anger became a habit of his soul, to borrow from Plato. He guaranteed its survival "down a route of occasions forming an enduring object,"[20] and so his personhood was defined as angry.

What we are seeing in the staying power of conformal feelings is what Freud termed fixation but with this difference. Freud located fixation in static, spatialized time around the oedipal complex. The fixation would continue to dominate the patient as though he or she were still circling that fixating event. Whitehead enables us to view fixation in temporal duration <u>within</u> the experiencing subject. There is no single over-arching moment or event that locks the future in the grip of the past. There are traumatic events, oedipal being one, to which the conformal pattern might well belong. But the fixation comes through the process of the subject's tenth-of-a-second by tenth-of-a-second responses which form into a routing of life with a definite pattern. There is no stopping time, pinpointing the locus of fixation in the third-to-the-fifth year, and circling that oedipal event until the fixation is surrendered. The criticism of Gestalt psychology is that this is not where reality is. Whitehead would make the same criticism. The problem lies not "back there" but "in here," in the person who <u>is</u> prehending conformally. His <u>pattern</u> of pre-hending becomes foreground and the long (or short) history of that conformation becomes background, to use Gestalt terminology.

It was my client who conformed to the anger of the preceding moment, which moment conformed to its predecessor, and so forth, literally <u>ad nauseam</u> for him. While outwardly he gave the appearance of being free, inwardly he was bound. The basic fault lay along the whole route of his life. <u>How</u> he took his world determined <u>what</u> he would be. While we are anticipating Chapter IV, we need to note Whitehead's Ninth category of Explanation: "That <u>how</u> an actual entity becomes constitutes <u>what</u> the actual entity is . . . ."[21] If the process is marked by undiluted anger, anger will be the dominant subjective form of the experiencing subject.

It is to the credit of both Freud and Jung that they saw the past as somehow massively involved in the present. Jung spoke of the power of memory-traces: ". . . everything that will be happens on the basis of what has been, and of what--consciously or unconsciously--still exists as a memory trace."[22] The collective unconscious and

the archetypes which crowd it are part of the inheritance of each actual occasion. Freud, too,
accepted racial memory though he did not do as much
with it as Jung. Rather, Freud's contribution was
to analyze childhood experience, especially certain experiences, where he located the notion of
fixation. For example, Freud underscored the
power of the past in his description of superego
development. It was in this connection that he
developed the notions of introjection and identification. Introjection is a lifelong process but
peculiarly powerful in childhood whereby important
figures, i.e., parents, "out there," are internalized within the self. The self is constituted
in part of introjects, inner presences of persons
or things, or parts of persons or things. Then
the self identifies with these introjects. So the
superego is formed by internalizing the powerful
parents and identifying with them inside the self.
They thus live in the self and so their ideals and
their judgments continue to operate as Ego Ideals
and Conscience. These are spatial terms rather
than process terms, but at least Freud, as Jung
after him, tried to deal with the massive impact
of the past. Freud came very close to process
terms at one point in his last statement regarding
superego development:

> . . . a child's superego is in fact, con-
> structed on the model not of its parents
> but of its parents' superego; the con-
> tents which fill it are the same and it
> becomes the vehicle of tradition and of
> all the time-resisting judgements [sic]
> of value which have propagated themselves
> in this manner from generation to genera-
> tion. 23 (Underlining added)

Freud is speaking of subjective form, that is,
parents' superego, being conformed to by a successor subjective form. This is the vehicle of
tradition by which the past continues into the
present. That Freud did nothing with this creative

possibility means that he was locked into a way
of thinking that was spatial and abstractive, not
processive and concrete.

Whitehead's metaphysical analysis sees the
past as far more massive than even Freud or Jung
ever conceptualized. But massive as that past is
for Whitehead, it is not locked in iron. Since it
is dynamically grasped by the present, each new
present can and must determine what it will do with
the past. One value in stressing conformal feelings as a base of neurotic and non-neurotic conditions is that we remove the biologically determined
instinctual element. In the case of anger, for
example, Freud located its genesis in the death
instinct as a derivative of hostility. This leads
to pessimism about human nature when it is grounded
biologically in the dual instincts of life and
death, love and hate. Process thought re-inter-
prets instinct in terms of causal efficacy, the
route of inheritance from the past, which carries
something of the power of instinct without some of
its cast-in-iron implications.[24]

In discussing conformal feelings we have accentuated the negative. Our case study has dealt
with the conformal feeling of anger. This was intentional in order to provide a different theory
of fixation. It helped us to see how neurotic and
despoiling patterns develop, e.g., patterns of
hostility, depression, rejection. But conformal
feelings can be as positive as they are negative.
A continuity of love, a pattern of openness, a
basic sense of well-being are also in debt to, and
are propagated by, conformal feelings. Erikson's
well-known eight stages of human development from
basic trust in infancy to ego integrity in the end
stage, or from basic mistrust to despair,[25] are
abstractions standing for what goes on in the inner
concrescence of each becoming, of which always in
the initial phase there is a conformal feeling.
Trust, autonomy, initiative, industry, etc., are
words labeling a certain type of conformal patterning. Whitehead's brilliant ontological

description of how conformal feelings take place is framework for a growth psychology as well as a therapeutic psychology. If we concentrate on the latter, it is because our concern is to underscore the therapeutic. As the theory of conformal feelings helps us to understand how neurotic (and all stuck) patterns develop, so does it help us to understand therapy. The dominant therapeutic insight in psychology is that therapy comes through inter-personal relations. Experiences of new reality, such as acceptance and respect, are introduced into the stream of the client by way of the carer (and vice-versa eventually). Conformal feelings are one way these new experiences are grasped by the client. By hooking into the carer's accepting of him, new patterns of self-acceptance and self-respect have their beginnings and their validation.

In each conforming "moment" God is also experienced by way of the divine aim given to the new occasion, as we pointed out earlier in the chapter. Up to this point we have not re-introduced God's role. Yet, that role is crucial in the begetting of each actual occasion and macrocosmically of the person. The following chapter will deal with this in detail. However, we need to look briefly at what God does in the birthing of the actual occasion to offset somewhat the conformal prehension.

God has a subjective aim, an unchanging urge, to bring to every momentary becoming an "ideal strength of beauty." This is the eternal vision of the Divine. In biblical language it would be the agape-love of God for the total creation; or as the Hebrew ḥesed is translated in the Revised Standard Version, a steadfast love, with the emphasis on steadfastness, for each particular becoming. It is God who offers the Divine Ideal with pinpointed relevance to each new becoming. God's targeted aim helps to bring to birth a new moment. God holds in the divine living experience the totality of the past so that God knows each of

us in absolute intimacy. God also envisages the
totality of possibility. Out of this divine omni-
science God brings to bear on the occasion-to-be
just that aim which is ideally best for its momentary experiencing. We must say "occasion-to-be"
because God in concert with the immediate predecessor occasion gives birth to the occasion through
the divine aim. I am not using the language of
God's will for that connotation is too often coercive. Rather, God is engaged in persuasively
luring the creation forward by giving to each
throughout the flow of its life just that aim which
is best for it at that moment.

The occasion responds with its own subjective
aim which will be its own goal for that duration
and will help to guide the future of its own life
and that of others. The occasion's response to
God's aim probably rarely corresponds perfectly
with the divine Vision. But there is always a
fainter or stronger impress of God lingering in
its own subjective aim. It is out of the commingling of aims--God's and the occasion's--that each
occasion is born. Out of God's aim novelty is
possible. Along with the conformal feeling, each
feels God's urge toward a new aspiration. So life
has continuity with the old and refreshment of
purpose toward the new.

When we remember that God is actively seeking
to persuade every occasion in the total creation
toward its own highest good, and when we know that
we cannot comprehend the innumerable actual occasions in even one human organism, we are staggered
by the size of God's omnipresence. God was massively present throughout the total routing of my
client. Now if God's subjective aim is eternally
toward strength of beauty, and if God's struggle
was to persuade my friend to alternatives to
anger, which is so corrosive of the human spirit
and of human relationships, what happened along
the routing of the years? Why did God's vision
not prevail?

My client (and every tragic human situation) is a first-rate argument against a traditional theism in which God's power is absolute. David Hume's well-known words in the mouth of Philo are to the point:

> Is he [God] willing to prevent evil, but not able? then is he impotent. Is he able, but not willing? then is he malevolent. Is he both able and willing? whence then is evil?[26]

Peter H. Hare has termed traditional theism "bankrupt theism."[27] Whitehead would agree. His theism rejects the twin notions of God as absolute power and coercive power.[28]

What happened along the years of my client was not the will of God. God was in the struggle to help my friend to pry loose from the all-encompassing subjective form of anger. There were victories along the way: anger turned to the profit-motive, a socially acceptable goal. There were significant others, viz., a golf pro, a business colleague, his third wife, his wife's pastor to whom he related for a few months, all feeding alternative slants into his conforming pattern to make possible limited break-throughs. God undoubtedly used these as part of the divine aim toward re-construction.

But we are forced to acknowledge that evil was very real.[29] One could not be two minutes with this friend and fail to see in this fellow-traveler the suffering and pain of a person whose experiencing was disharmony and trivality, the struggling of a soul treading in the chaos just to stay afloat. In the midst of that raging evil God, too, was embattled. I believe but for the divine aim, so steadfastly presented, my friend would have totally succumbed to the massive past. There was the Agent of grace persuasively at work. To that Working we turn in the next chapter.

NOTES

[1] Hostility is an urge to do injury or destruction whereas anger is more transient and more compatible with love. Cf. Leon J. Saul, The Hostile Mind (New York: Random House, 1956), pp. 3, 4. However, I am using anger and hostility interchangeably since my client had subjective forms of both. Of course, anger is a complex affect. My client suffered, for example, emotional deprivation to which anger was a response. But for the sake of illustration, I shall focus on anger alone.

[2] Whitehead, PR, p. 250.

[3] Negative prehensions are those feelings which exclude items from positively contributing to an occasion, as when C excludes the datum of love from b, while grasping b's anger. This might be called an excluding prehension. See PR, pp. 35, 66 especially, and 346.

[4] For the reader who wants to explore further the conformal feeling reenacted under abstraction, see PR, pp. 361-365.

[5] PR, pp. 34, 249.

[6] Ibid., p. 374; cf. p. 373.

[7] Alfred North Whitehead, Religion in the Making (New York: Macmillan, 1930), p. 159.

[8] To round out the birthing process of each occasion I should point to an important addition John Cobb, Jr., makes to Whitehead's analysis. He argues that an occasion's subjective aim might also arise out of a hybrid prehension of preceding actual occasions. A hybrid prehension is the feeling of, or the grasping of, a conceptual feeling of a preceding occasion and objectifying that occasion as it is represented by

that particular conceptual feeling. For example, b's aim for itself and for its successors might be a more just social order. C might represent all of b by this complex aim and make that aim its own. This addition by Cobb does not violate Whitehead's analysis; rather, it enriches these words: ". . . God and the actual world jointly constitute . . . the initial phase of the novel concrescence." (Whitehead, PR, p. 374.)

[9] It will help the reader if I state as clearly as I can how I intend to use certain terms which may overlap in everyday use. Human being will refer to the whole structured society, the total psycho-physical organism. Person will be equivalent to soul, which is the "organ of central control of very high-grade character in the brain." (PR, p. 166.) Because of soul there is "central direction" and a route of endurance from past to future. Self will be used to signify individuality, one's own person, in contradiction to another person or thing. This will usually be a hyphenated use, e.g., self-creation. (In the index of the corrected ed. of PR references are almost exclusively to this hyphenated use.) This is the way Heinz Hartmann uses the term. See his Essays on Ego Psychology (New York: International University, 1964), ch. 7, esp. p. 127. Cf. Whitehead's similar usage, PR, p. 233. Ego will be limited to Freud's structural psychology of Id, Ego, and Superego. Freud defines each of these terms functionally, e.g., what it does.

[10] Donald W. Sherburne, A Whiteheadian Aesthetic (Hamden: Archon, 1970), p. 59.

[11] Cf. PR, p. 531.

[12] Ernst Kris, Psychoanalytic Explorations in Art, (New York: International View, 1952), p. 177 (and passim).

[13] Freud understood the build-up of Superego in precisely this way, viz., the child's superego is constructed out of the parents' superegos. See below, p. 35.

[14] Not all aggression, of course, is hostile. Freud failed to make this necessary distinction.

[15] Alfred North Whitehead, Adventures of Ideas (New York: Free Press, 1933), p. 183.

[16] Whitehead, PR, p. 305.

[17] Cf. Whitehead, PR, pp. 35, 338-360, esp. 346.

[18] Erik H. Erikson, Childhood and Society (New York: Norton, 1950), pp. 75, 220ff.

[19] Whitehead discusses valuation in the technical terms of Adversion (valuation upward) and Aversion (valuation downward). See PR, pp. 35, 280, 388, 406, 422.

[20] Whitehead, PR, p. 422.

[21] Ibid., p. 34.

[22] Carl Jung, The Archetypes and the Collective Unconscious in Collected Works (London: Routledge and Kegan Paul, 1959), Vol. IX, Part 1, p. 279.

[23] Sigmund Freud, New Introductory Lectures on Psychoanalysis tr. by James Stachey (New York: Norton, 1965), p. 67.

[24] John B. Cobb, Jr., A Christian Natural Theology (Phil: Westminster, 1965), p. 81.

[25] Childhood and Society, ch. 7.

[26] Dave Hume, Dialogue Concerning Natural Religion (New York: Hafner, 1951), p. 66.

[27] In _Process Studies_ (Vol. 7, No. 1, 1977), p. 51.

[28] _PR_, pp. 11, 19, Part V; _AI_, ch. X.

[29] For the role of Evil in Pastoral Care see ch. VII.

From a still wider and more comprehensive point of
view, universal life itself appears to us as a
struggle between multiplicity and unity--a labor
and an aspiration towards union. We seem to sense
that--whether we conceive it as a divine Being or as
cosmic energy--the Spirit working upon and within
all creation is shaping it into order, harmony, and
beauty, uniting all beings (some willing but the
majority as yet blind and rebellious) with each
other through links of love, achieving--slowly and
silently, but powerfully and irresistibly--the
Supreme Synthesis.

Roberto Assagioli, <u>Psychosynthesis</u>

Chapter III

The Role of God: A Secular Vision

It is not my purpose to develop, or re-present,
a process understanding of God. Rather, it is my
intention to pinpoint certain aspects of that conceptuality which seem to have peculiar bearing on
pastoral care.

Let us begin with what I consider to be the
most critical problem in contemporary pastoral care
and counseling, namely, the missing element of God.
That element is missing for three basic reasons.
First, the informing models of pastoral care have
been and continue to be secular ones which are often
embarrassed by references to Deity. More specifically, they are derived from the psychologies of
Freud, Jung, Adler, Perls, Rogers, Erikson, among
others; and from Ego-psychology, Behavior Modifica-
tion, Reality Therapy, Rational Emotive Therapy,
Transactional Analysis, Growth Models, Systems
Analysis, Encounter Groups, Marriage Enrichment, and
Parent Effectiveness Training. With exceptions in
this list there is scarcely a place for even a secular version of God. Yet some pastoral care, and
most pastoral counseling, have swallowed whole the
secularity of humanistic psychology. Second, especially in pastoral counseling, but even in the more
traditional areas of pastoral caring, there has been

45

a sensitive reluctance on the part of many pastoral carers to insinuate either the notion of God or the presence of God into the counseling conversation. Learning well from the various psychotherapies not to impose an agenda, and especially the religious datum, God, the typical pastoral counselor has at this point eschewed all God-talk. This eschewal has been supported by the rather well-founded notion that in dealing with neurotic clients, for example, God-talk might well miss the neurosis proper, i.e., sex phobia, or shield it by way of spiritualization. Third, traditional formulations of the doctrine of God have seemed to be ill-prepared to be an asset in most pastoral counseling cases. God appears to be irrelevant because the divine Being is "totally other" and immutable, or God is heavy-handed because the power associated with the Divine is coercive, or God is part of the problem because of models of God which are terrifying. Often the pastoral carer has the uneasy sense that his or her own faith is not where the traditional formulation is and so compartmentalizes ministry, operating out of one compartment when preaching, for example, and another when counseling.

The pastoral carer is assumed to be, and is, a religious person. He or she may be religious within one of Whitehead's definitions: "Religion is what the individual does with his own solitariness;"[1] or in Wieman's sense of the search for the Ultimate Good; or in Tillich's sense of the reach for Ultimate Commitment; or in a more institutional sense (i.e., churches, rituals); or in the several patterns of human behaviors known as pieties; or in the mystic sense of becoming Oned with the Eternal;[2] or of being claimed in the 'Moment' by the Eternal (Kierkegaard). For our purposes it does not much matter. The pastoral carer is a religious person one of whose most formidable data is that God is and is important. Yet this person for reasons cited does not usually 'objectify' his or her own God-content in the interview. This often leaves a residue of guilt, or at least a sense of incompleteness, on the part of the carer. He or she feels caught

between personal and professional identities which
are impossible to reconcile. Subjective aims become blurred; subjective unities constituting the
person suffer. Pastors leave churches in favor of
counseling centers; limit their practice to traditional situations performed traditionally; or com-
promise by settling on penultimate goals, that is,
relief of the presenting problem or the real psychological problem and ignoring the ultimate goal,
viz., a relationship with God.

I have lifted up these problems to indicate
the context in which pastoral caring has the obligation to assess carefully the role of God in the
caring situation and to develop a theory of practice
commensurate with that role. Within process terms
we shall examine the metaphysical requirement for
God and suggest how this way of looking at God can
make fundamental differences to pastoral caring.
In subsequent chapters we shall examine the religious vision of God and the concept of God as Savior.

I

God as a Metaphysical Requirement

In his Science and the Modern World (1925)
Whitehead pointed to Aristotle as the last first-
rate European metaphysician who was "entirely dis-
passionate" in introducing God into his system; he
did it to complete his metaphysics.[3] Whitehead then
goes on to say that the "general character of things"
must require "that there be such an entity" [God]
before any "evidence on a narrower experiential
basis can be of much avail in shaping the conception."[4] In this paper I am following Whitehead's
logic: a metaphysical requirement preceding a more
narrowly based conception. Furthermore, Whitehead
followed this logic himself. We cannot make the
claim for Whitehead which he made for Aristotle,
for, as Emerson said, Christ is ploughed into our
history, and Whitehead prehended that history both
generally and in a canalized way in an English vic-
arage. Nevertheless, Whitehead comes very close to

47

his own metaphysical intention: the "general character of things" must require God before the conception can make very much sense.

We can now ask the question in what way or ways is God required by Whitehead's metaphysical vision?

The first is that it is God, along with the past, who gives birth to the nascent occasion. An occasion does not exist as an underlying substance. It is atomic, a droplet of experience which has its phases from conformal beginnings to final completion. The question is, How does it begin? While it is causa sui once it begins through to its satisfaction, it must be born. There was a time--a fraction of a second earlier--when it was not. In that "former" time there were other occasions arising but not it. Now, it is its turn to come into being. Whence that origination?

For Whitehead it begins with a gift, actually a double gift as we saw in the previous chapter. Preceding occasions are given to it in concert with an Initial Aim from God. What the new percipient receives from the actual world immediately past is its physical beginning; what it receives from God is its mental beginning. "Physical" refers to our grasping or prehending the past, the actual world from which we spring. "Mental" refers to our grasping or prehending the ideal world with potential for new attainment. If we were only physical, we would repeat the past ad infinitum like the rocks and the sand which are only slightly open to novelty. If we were only mental, we would be nothing but lonely abstractions unrelated to actuality. So the world and God give us our di-polar nature.[5]

God's gift to the nascent occasion is in some important respects more fundamental than the initial data from the preceding world. The preceding world is infinite in variety. Which "world" will the new occasion inherit? It is God who makes that determination by giving a divine aim that begins the career of the new occasion. God's initial aim

locates the occasion <u>here</u> in this particular flow
of time. That aim <u>gives</u> the occasion its "stand-
point" from which it will inherit a certain routing
of the past. It specifies where that occasion is
located and therefore which past it will feel.
That location is its birth-place so that out of all
the massive past it will be in line to inherit this
routing of occasions and not others except very
indirectly.[6] Every occasion at birth is a Janus
figure: facing backward and forward. It faces its
routing: conformally. It faces its future and the
best possibility for it given that routing:
conceptually.

God's aim is to give each nascent occasion its
best "shot" for its richest possible attainment.
God envisages all possibility; the infinity of
possibility forms part of the nature of God. God,
immediately experiencing all the infinity of pastness and all the infinity of possibility, brings to
bear upon the nascent creature that particular aim
or goal uniquely suited to that creature. The goal
may be minimal, poignant, tragic. God's aim has to
be relevant to what has been. What is to be cannot
be to dream as though there had been no yesterday.
As Whitehead realistically writes, "This function
of God is analogous to the remorseless working of
things in Greek and in Buddhist thought. The
initial aim is the best for that impasse."[7] This
is not the 'best of possible worlds.' Whitehead
calls Leibniz's judgment an "audacious fudge" to
redeem bad theology.[8] The concept of the working
of God in process thought is not constructed on the
basis of a wish formation, as Freud postulated in
The Future of an Illusion. God is eternally bent
on giving to each occasion that goal really possible
to it "given its situation."[9] Whitehead's simple
general statement is: "God confronts what is
actual in the world with what is possible for it."[10]

Whitehead's God is biased! God's untiring,
ceaseless purpose is for each to achieve novelty,
whatever novelty is really possible. God loves novelty, but novelty that is value-laden, that is, the

attainment of the richest, most exquisite value possible for each creature in the world.[11] Repetition is not the attainment of value although as a conformal feeling it is a necessary step toward value. Beyond that step, however, repetition is the stereotyping of value, the flow of life in rutted existence, so that value becomes coated over. It actually becomes encrusted value, warmed over from a previous time. The urge of God, endemic to the divine nature, is to give to each potential occasion its fresh start by aiming it toward a final unity as deep and wide and rich as its becoming can take hold of. "God moves us beyond mere facts of existence to values of existence."[12]

While God's gift of initial aim co-constitutes (along with the past) each new occasion, the divine initial aim does not complete the occasion. Each occasion develops its own aim, vis-à-vis God's aim. Thus, the inner aim of each is in response to God, although for the most part this is an unconscious response. Relatively rarely are we aware of our aims being responsive to God until perhaps when we look back and see what we did not see in the moment.

The subjective aiming of each person is so crucial, since it guides the entire inner activity, that we must introduce it here, over against God's aiming, though we shall return to it more fully in the next chapter.

Every subject is purposive. It directs itself toward its immediate achievement and beyond to include the relevant future of itself and others, as we shall see in the next chapter. It is this aim by which the ordering of our lives takes place. Order is teleological: it aims toward an end point. Out of the multiplicity of the world each new moment aims to create a new thing in the world: itself. Then it adds to the world what it has created. From its inception, and continuing through the internal struggle to make something of itself, an experiencing unity is taking place, a unity that is "congruent with the subjective aim."[13] It is this aiming which is the final causation of the actual occasion,

the teleogical lure guiding the growing together
of the subject's experience.[14] It is the nature of
the human being to reach, which is its aiming, and
it follows its aiming throughout its brief subjective experience, gathering unity into its final
realization. The subject gathers itself together
around the goals it sets. In this sense we are all
future-oriented, including the immediate future and
the more distant future. We have aims directing us
forward. Around these aims the core of who we are
and whom or what we serve is constantly being
formed and re-formed.[15] To borrow a pregnant suggestion from Sartre, our "projects" define us. Our
projects are our aims. Our aims are made possible
by God's endowment. It is God in Whiteheadian
thought who initially influences our subjective
aims by giving us the gift of the divine envisagement. God, who envisages all possibilities, pre-
sents to us just that vision appropriate to us at
any one moment, a vision that takes seriously the
routing of our individual histories. We must respond to the vision of God, but we respond with an
aim of our own, an aim that all too often resembles
but faintly that vision. The world begins each
epoch of experiencing with God's aim for its greatest good. Thus, God presides over the birth of
every entity. "Apart from the intervention of God,
[by way of God's initial aim] there could be nothing
new in the world, and no order in the world."[16]

We have been struggling with metaphysical generality not religious feeling (which we shall look
at in Chapter VIII), with what Whitehead has called
the "secularization of the concept of God's functions in the world. . . ."[17] Religious feeling "is
not an essential element in the concept of God's
function in the universe."[18] God functions whether
or not we are conscious of that functioning and
whether or not we connect with it religiously. William Christian following Whitehead distinguishes between "metaphysical" and "religious" functions[19] and
in a tightly packed summary concludes that God is
required by the system[20] and "is not a merely decor-
ative addition to that theory."[21] John Cobb, Jr.,

after a carefully argued chapter on God's relation
to the creation, concludes: "My suggestion is that
if we adhere to the definitions and principles for-
mulated with maximum care, we will be left with the
question as to what causes new occasions to come
into being when old ones have perished, and that
when that question is fully understood, the only
adequate answer is God."[22]

II

The Secular Vision of God and Pastoral Care

In process thought God is necessary to all
activity, including human. This conclusion is
based on categoreal requirements rather than religious data.[23] God is in the process whether acknowledged by us or not. This can be meaningful to
all forms of therapy but especially to pastoral care
because the carer in that tradition at least acknowl-
edges a divine Working in the midst of things. The
pastoral carer does not have to assume religious
background or interest on the part of any client.
The secular vision of God's working provides a perspective in which pastoral caring can begin to be
true to its roots without being coercive or offensive. In what follows I shall try to detail what
this means for pastoral care.

1. God does not need to be bootlegged into a
counseling or caring conversation. God is in the situation! If there is a constant Working in our midst,
contributing to our conception and birth every 1/10
of a second, so to speak, contributing just that
vision of what is best for each occasioning moment
in the flowing of our lives, then that Working is
massively present in every caring situation. God's
providing the initial aim for every becoming is a
metaphysical functioning and so is part of the weaving and the wovenness on the loom of our existence.
It is part of our Givenness.

If God is so massively present, how can we possibly avoid paying attention to the Working of God without fatally abstracting from Reality? If pastoral caring has as an ultimate goal making visible the interconnections of life, so that the linkage between a life-crisis, viz., loss of a spouse, and ultimate issues is clarified, as Daniel Day Williams has argued it should be,[24] are we not doomed to failure if we tiptoe around the notion of God? Why then should it be difficult, or awkward, or embarrassing to introduce the notion of that Working into our caring situations?

I am not suggesting, of course, that we be cows or bulls in china shops. There must be a delicacy of timing, a sensitivity of tone, and an objectivity that refuses to coerce the other. But does not Whitehead give us permission, and even require us, to deal with the metaphysical secularity of God in every aspect of life, as he has done in his metaphysical description? Cannot we do this without the need to propagandize or without the compulsion to develop certain subjective forms that we call religious, viz., commitment or behavioral forms? This may not be as far as we want to go, or should go, but must we not go this far? Otherwise, so it seems to me, we are depriving our clients of a salutary vision of how things are together. The deprivation consists in their not getting a metaphysical sense of what reality includes: an Ally whose constant aim is for their good no matter where they are in their burdened existence.

What I have specifically in mind is illustrated by the following vignette. I call it a Teaching Parenthesis and I use it regularly at the outset of a formal caring relationship as I did with Helen who had been referred to me by a Jewish psychiatrist. She came from a very conservative Protestant background. Her problem was conformal feelings of rejection repetitively renewed out of her childhood home with attendant feelings of hostility and guilt. She had transferred these feelings to God whom she identified with parental images. A small part of this I learned from the referring psychiatrist.

53

After two data-gathering sessions with Helen, I carefully developed my Teaching Parenthesis with her, as I do with most clients whatever their background, convictions, and presenting or real problem. It went like this:

Co. "Helen, as we begin to work together, I think you ought to know what I see at the center of things; not that you need to see it that way at all. I see a Ceaseless Working at the center of your life and mine who is gently trying to persuade us at each moment to reach forward to fulfill our potential. This Working does not demand perfection but struggles with us second by second where we are to direct us forward." (Pause.)

Cl. "Would you call that God"?

Co. "You can. Right now I am content to share with you my vision that there is an Ally who will be working with us at every step, a gentle Ally who wants for you the very best."

Cl. "Where did you get that idea? It's so different from my understanding. It seems freer. My intuition told me there was such a God."

Co. "Well, Helen, let's leave it there. We can come back to it anytime. I just wanted to let you know where I am."

I find no reason why Helen cannot return to this agenda any time and handle it within a formal counseling session, or why I cannot re-introduce the vision if I intuit that it might be appropriate and salutary to what is going on. My experience with clients is that this is not impositional when sensitively done. Furthermore, it affords a fresh perspective on a primordial source of strength and hope. My freedom to do this is the gift of the

54

metaphysical vision that this is the way things are and the sooner we lift into consciousness the secular working of God the richer are the possibilities for alignment with that Working even if religious feelings and commitment lag behind.

How necessary this is should be obvious from our analysis of conformal feelings. Whitehead does not minimize the massive effect of the past in the present by way of conformal feelings. But Whitehead also sees an equally massive operation of God--The Initial Aim--providing the creative antidote to mere repetition. God's ceaseless activity in urging the experiencing subject to aim at a novel response to the stuff of life is, for me, the fundamental basis of therapy. The client can embrace a new future and not merely repeat the past into the future. God's gift of the divine vision in the birthing stage of each actual occasion is built-in SIZE.[25] At the center of things is massive Presence to lure those who are locked-in toward ingressing new possibilities.

Focusing on God's urging the client toward a new possibility helps to focus the pastoral interview on the present. God is not "back there" for there is no "back there." The past resides everlastingly in God's present experience as we shall see in Chapter VIII. At least some of it also resides in the present experiencing subject. Yet, there is a constant temptation on the part of the carer as well as the client to linger "back there," as though that is where reality is. The past cannot be changed, of course; it is a fait accompli. Even God cannot alter it. But God labors with each new becoming to receive the givenness of the past and to put the potential creativity of the new subject upon it. God loves a new thing and wants the fresh new droplet of experience to stamp the gift with its own character. This is a present transaction and bears the thrill of a momentary burst of novelty. Seen from this perspective the carer can use the truth of Gestalt that the Now is all we have and is where therapy takes place.

2.   The second way I think this secular description of God's functioning is important is what
it does to the outlook of the pastoral carer.   So
many caring situations look hopelessly stuck.   That
is an abstract judgment from the outside, but it is
supported so often by the self-perception of the
client.   Yet, great good comes out of caring situations: people get unstuck; conforming or fixated patterns are broken; saving insight occurs;
growth takes place.

Since all reasons have to be in actual entities, the reasons for change must lie in the percipient occasion or in God, the divine entity.
God's initial aim creating the first phase of the
subject's own aim and the subject's own continuing
creative concrescence account for whatever novelty
takes place.

The counselor and the client have an Ally in
the room.   The client may not be conscious of this
Other, but the counselor, informed by process insight, knows that there is a cosmic Working for
good.   That Source of good, perhaps not yet available to the client's religious feeling, is metaphysically stimulating the counseling process by
giving to every entity a new vision for its momentary duration.   God's total concern is the production of value: a new unity of the most intense
beauty possible for this momentary experience.
This is what God is about: to create something of
value out of the multiplicities which feed the
person.   God is not neutral.   God loves novelty.
The intent of God is to lay gently upon the client
the lure to become a new being.   The words of the
Seer on Patmos, put into the mouth of God, are
appropriate: "Behold, I am making all things new."

A vision of this Working should let counselors
relax within their role.   A very small fraction of
what goes on is their responsibility.   There is
the human other, the client, in her power of self-
creation.   There is the enormous Presence of Deity
envisaging new possibilities for her and creating
the initial phase for each momentary duration of

her new life. Locating creativity between the
Divine Working and the human response we have a
metaphysical grounding for the hypothesis developed by Carl Rogers: that individuals have the
capacity to deal with their psychological situations: that is, ". . . for self-initiated, constructive handling of the issues involved in life
situations."[26] The capacity is partly in each
individual, for she is causa sui; but the massive
Presence of God is impressively there to "lure"
each moment toward "higher reaches of being." If
Whitehead's vision of God's secular functioning
corresponds significantly to the way things are,
then by virtue of God's omnipresent creative activity in every actual occasion of a human self,
culminating in the human soul, the therapeutic
situation is bursting with potential. This would
be the secular version of the doctrine of grace.

God's ceaseless Activity should mean that the
carer can trust the silences. In fact, we now
have a metaphysical ground for the intuition that
silence is creative. One of the more difficult
aspects of caring on the part of the pastor is to
allow the silences within a pastoral conversation
to do their work. That work, within process understanding, is to encourage the client to enter
into his solitude in the presence of a counselor,
to get in touch with his past, which is resident
within him, including his collective and personal
unconscious, to open up to lures, including God's
that beckon him forward, and to shape himself in
the inwardness of his becoming. Solitude is the
"space" in which the concrescing or pulling together can take place. Silence between two people
is not the same as the silence of being alone.
Silence between two people, if it is the silence
of love, allows for each, within the creative presence of the other, the solitude in which to be
under the most gentle persuasion to put things together. Whitehead, as we have already noted, goes
so far as to say that that is what religion is
about: what one does in his or her solitude.
Every counseling or caring situation is profoundly
religious. It is ironic that so often the

religious pastor cannot tolerate silence so essential for the other to be religious. It is as though he compulsively must be "doing something" to effect the desired change as though the silence he can offer is not in itself the creative milieu for change. But if God is operative as process thought envisages, then God is operative in the silences and within the creative solitude of the person's inner world. Perhaps the pastoral carer's main contribution is to guarantee the silences for God and the other to do their work.

In the same vein, the pastor can trust between sessions with more integrity. He or she has metaphysical grounds for such trusting. It is easy to be seduced into the notion that everything of importance that happens in the caring situation happens in the session itself. Probably more of what importantly happens occurs between sessions. This is partly in response to the previous session and partly in anticipation of the next one. In any case the client works over feelings, struggles for insight, and makes gradual shifts in attitudes in behavior outside the session in commerce with concrete lived experience. God is the primary Ally in these struggles. This should give encouragement to the pastor not to hold on to the client in the in-between times, or to carry the other's burdens, but to let her go, trusting her to the love of God which concretely means a "particular providence for [each] particular occasion."[27] The doctrine of providence is taken with absolute seriousness in process thought!

Since God has initial aims for the carer as well as the client, the carer may learn to trust his or her "hunches" as leadings from beyond the self. There is danger in following out one's intuitive judgments. We are easily deluded and often confuse our aims with God's. Nevertheless, with sensitivity and caution we need to listen to our intuitions. I think it was Robert Lindner who said that all the therapist has to work with finally is the datum that is himself. Process thought maintains that that datum includes God who adds directionality in the process. When intuition is empathically derived, meaning that one is within the living world of the client, intuition needs to be trusted. This is all the better grounded when God is viewed as luring the carer in the helping situation. The more often God's aims can rise to consciousness in the pastor, the more the pastor in the role of carer should be willing to trust the possibility that his own intuitions may be part of the divine directivity for the client-centered relationship.[28] Consciousness of the divine aim is probably a relatively rare experience when measured by the vast unconscious prehension of God. Nevertheless, concentrated openness to the divine aim does make conscious response possible. While every moment carries the experience of God, in some moments that experience rises to consciousness, as we shall see in Chapter VIII. For our purpose now, it is enough to suggest that the carer should be responding with raised consciousness to the divine aim; in so responding the carer should be free to trust this Leading. This can relieve the pastoral carer of some anxiety by letting him be more natural which in itself is efficacious for growth for both carer and client.

3. There is yet one other way in which God as the provider of direction is helpful to the pastoral carer. Every caring situation is complex. Group counseling, whether a dyad, a family, or a cluster of diverse individuals, exacerbates the complexity. It is this complexity which is like an avalanche of data overwhelming the carer. Imagine the vastness of the data in a familial situation of four people: millions of operations throughout each psycho-physical organism brought together in the group; all of this unseen activity multiplied by four (multiply it by five to include the carer who is an integral part of the nexus of the group); and all of this constantly changing in the restless flow of new experiencing.

Every family structure is a system marked by centrifugal and centripetal forces. The centrifugal forces are idiosyncratic, expanding outward as though fleeing from the center to assure the personhood of each. These forces are metaphysically necessary to assure the subjective aims and final realizations of each person. God lends a hand to the centrifugal aims in the group so that the richness of diversity can be included in each self. Because of God each is something definite. The something that each one becomes is his or her unique achievement. In a family of four those "unique achievements" can be at loggerheads with each other. Each is a stream of individuation which often operates centrifugally as over against the others. In fact, a basic reason for family counseling is that the family exaggerates the centrifugal tendency and so becomes disintegrated. Each flees from the center going his or her own way. Then a new system based upon sickness may take over. All may be "sick"; or they may "choose" to concentrate on one to be designated "sick" just to keep the family intact if possible. Centrifugality is a tendency of individuality. God plays a role in individuality even at risk to a larger whole.

But God also works within the family system since every part is related to every other part. God is the centripetal force not only to bring order and value to each individual but also to the entire family. We can believe that God is trying to weave a pattern of symmetry and harmony throughout the system of a family network similar to the divine intention throughout the network of the individual. Because all of reality is social, God's aim is a unifying vision to lure the family into a systemic unity, but a unity that guarantees the uniqueness of each. Thus, God is always involved in a delicate balancing act between individuality and community. If individuals in organizing their own lives regard themselves without windows opening upon the familial others, they can fancy themselves as having no responsibility to

the family network. If the community in organizing its macrocosmic life together coerces or reduces or blights a member of the family, it can be
equally irresponsible. God's task would seem to
be to provide the unifying vision by which both
the individual members and the family are not
merely protected but can balance claims and counter-
claims into dynamic harmony.

The pastor in the midst of family dynamics,
trying to help the family effect a more healthy
or satisfying network, can count on God to be at
work to bring to the family a unifying vision that
will include the rich diversity of each self and
at the same time the systemic wholeness of that
particular family life. That is to say, the pastor can count on God to correlate the several
initial aims being offered in the course of a
family counseling session, including those to which
the pastor is responding, so that there is always
present the divine urge toward a harmony out of
rich diversity. This makes it unnecessary for the
pastor to understand or comprehend all the complexity. He or she will need some sense of what
is going on. But what is "going on" is in some
profound measure the working of God. Perhaps with
something of this understanding pastors would be
less inclined to eschew family counseling.[29] Because of limited pastoral time, because of the
vast needs of families, because no situation is
unrelated to family dynamics, because of the potential for effecting change through family counseling, pastoral carers need to make the family
system the base of their caring practice. Highly
conscious of the divine Ally trying to persuade
the family into a new, richer wholeness, the pastor can with some confidence essay to do with
families what few others in the helping professions are privileged to do; for no other in our
society has such ready access to the family as does
the professional leadership of the church.

61

In this chapter we have focused on a Presence which gently, tenderly, patiently seeks to persuade every emerging event to reach beyond mere conformity toward the greatest possible value open to it. Because of this Activity novelty is ingredient in each fresh moment. Since novelty is essential to life Whitehead can write, "The world lives by its incarnation of God itself."[30] The word, incarnation, suffused with religious meaning for the Christian, might mislead us. The thrust of this chapter and even of Whitehead's use of the word, incarnation, is a secular thrust. We have tried to lift up a vision of the way things are, a vision of a Working that presides over the birth of every puff of existence. The religious person can make of this what he or she will, as we shall do in Chapter VIII. But there is great value in the secular vision itself for pastoral caring: there is a Caring at the center of things whose labor is to help the person to transcend himself by realizing possibilities of which he has not even dreamed. Authentic pastoral caring is in league with that Caring.

[1] Whitehead, RM, p. 16.

[2] Cf. Anon, The Cloud of Unknowing (Baltimore: Penguin, 1975).

[3] Alfred North Whitehead, S.M.W., p. 173.

[4] Ibid., p. 174.

[5] Cf. PR, p. 374.

[6] Cf. PR, pp. 104, 434-36; cf. Cobb, NT, 152-53, 204-205.

[7] PR, p. 373.

[8] Ibid., p. 74. Perhaps this is the place to note that Whitehead cannot uncritically be used to undergird the Growth Potential Movement so at ease in the United States. Whitehead takes causal efficacy too seriously and tragedy too realistically to be sanguine about human growth. Whitehead's notion of evil is grossly underestimated. See Chapter VII.

[9] Cobb, NT, p. 205.

[10] Whitehead, RM, p. 159.

[11] See Chapter 5 for the development of the Aesthetic dimension.

[12] RM, p. 158.

[13] PR, pp. 31, 32, 41.

[14] We shall detail this phase in Chapter IV. But see: PR, pp. 227-28; 342-43; 373; 375; 390; 416. Also Christian op. cit., pp. 302ff, 314ff; and Cobb, NT, pp. 151ff.

[15]PR, p. 343.

[16]PR, p. 377.

[17]PR, p. 315.

[18]Ibid., pp. 315, 316.

[19]Christian, op. cit., p. 324.

[20]Ibid., pp. 334-336.

[21]Ibid., p. 311 cf. p. 301.

[22]Cobb, op. cit., p. 214.

[23]As David Griffin has pointed out to me, Whitehead saw more clearly the contribution of religion to metaphysics after writing Science and the Modern World. However, through the first four parts of Process and Reality, it is the secular vision which is dominant. That is the vision seen from within the categoreal system.

[24]Daniel Day Williams, The Minister and the Care of Souls, (New York: Harper, 1961), ch. 1.

[25]Cf. Bernard M. Loomer, "S-I-Z-E Is the Measure," in Religious Experience and Process Theology, ed. by Harry James Cargas and Bernard Lee (New York: Paulist, 1976), pp. 69-76.

[26]Carl Rogers, op. cit. pp. 22, 56.

[27]PR, p. 532.

[28]"Directivity" is a choice word of John B. Cobb, Jr. See his Theology and Pastoral Care (Philadelphia: Fortress, 1977), p. 47.

[29]In reviewing over 800 pastoral caring cases in Th.M., D.Min., Ph.D. and continuing education seminars, I have discovered that less than ten percent have dealt with family counseling.

[30]<u>RM</u>, p. 150.

I am neither spurred on by excessive optimism nor
in love with high ideals, but, am merely concerned
with the fate of the individual human being--that
infinitesimal unit on whom the world depends, and
in whom, if we read the meaning of the Christian
message aright, even God seeks his goal.
                    Carl Jung, The Undiscovered Self

                    Chapter IV

        How It Comes Together: Self-Creation

     To introduce this chapter let us look in on
a fellow-traveler whose medical diagnosis was
cancer. The prognosis was not good. He was 50 at
the time of the diagnosis.

     For almost a month after the diagnosis he
continued to deny the importance of his disease.
It was as though nothing that threatening could
happen to him. A nightly bedroom scene helped to
destroy that illusion. He would retire earlier
than his wife. Alone in the darkened room, with
the covers drawn up around him, he gradually
grasped the possibilities through imaginative
feelings that he might die. The room, the bed,
the covers became a symbolic tomb. He slowly
allowed himself to feel the thick darkness; he
sensed that he was utterly alone in his skin; he
felt the fragility of himself. For the first time
in his life he had the visceral sense he was not
in control. He now recognized what he had never
consciously allowed himself to know: that he had
always had a sense of being omnipotent. That that
sense was infantile in origin is to say, among
other things, that it had always been a part of
him. For most of his adult years position and
status had supported the illusion of omnipotence.
With his head he knew he was finite, of course,
but this was not his visceral feeling. His
nightly experience, in the context of cancer,
cobalt, and surgery, revealed himself to himself.
Through some rigorous self-analysis he came to
see that his character had been formed around the

                        67

desperate need to protect a frail ego. A rich
insight slowly emerged that a compulsive need to
control was a defense against narcissistic wounds.

Despite insight, however, darkness, aloneness,
and powerlessness continued to terrorize him.
These were the enemies he had to cope with, and
his accustomed ways of coping were important. He
remembered feeling he might be annihilated and
trying to wonder how that would feel. So caught
up in the existential moment he failed to see the
irony. It was incredible to him that he would
cease; yet it was he wondering about his ceasing.
His fear of death was precisely there: that he
would be no more. Immortality seemed so wan. God
was "out there"; he was here, a solitary one (he
recalled often Kierkegaard's "solitary individual")
who was powerless to control any longer his own
future.

Through months of confronting this cessation
to his life he gradually came to absorb the possibility of his death. As gradually two other
related experiences began to interlace his being:
the new relieving perspective that he was not
omnipotent but thoroughly finite and fragile; and
a home-coming to a process vision of God as
visceral now as it had been conceptual before.

These large brush-strokes do not do justice,
of course, to the flowing of subjective experiencing interior to our friend. They can only point
to the plethora of feelings--from agony to
ecstasy--through which he constituted both his old
life and his new. Integration, dis-integration,
re-integration are words which may suggest the
multiplicity of occasioning which made up the
river of his years. What is needed is a way of
looking at any person--in this case, our fellow-
traveler--to see, at least in part, what is going
on inside. There comes to mind Carl Jung's
profound concept of Individuation, which suggests
the processive formulation of the Self. By
individuation he means a process by which uncon-

sciousness in all its richness, and consciousness which is more than ego, are integrated into a "separate, indivisible unity or 'whole.'"[1] The person is this integrated whole. When either unconsciousness or consciousness is suppressed, some form of symptomology eventuates, as was the case with our fellow-traveler. The routing of personhood is the life-long struggle to achieve autonomy between unconscious material and new situations, e.g., cancer, one encounters. Jung's announced psychotherapeutic aim centered around this individuating struggle: "to bring about a psychic state in which my patient begins to experiment with his own nature--a state of fluidity, change and growth, in which there is no longer anything eternally fixed and hopelessly petrified."[2] Jung's vision of the person struggling to become whole is a profound vision. Yet it lacks the analysis by which the individuating struggle toward wholeness can be conceptualized. Jung's great achievement was to illumine some of the contents of individuation, e.g., the powerful archetypal realities, and to correct what he called the "overvaluation of consciousness."[3] But precisely what happens within the duration of the individuating experience is not clear.

Whitehead in his metaphysical analysis of an actual occasion has clarified the concrescence, or the growing together into unity, of each moment of becoming. As we translated and hopefully enriched Freud's significant notions of fixation and the compulsion to repeat by way of conformal feelings, we see Jung's important notion of individuation also enriched and made more usable by locating it within the metaphysical description of how every person puts it all together, for better or for worse. It is the thesis of this chapter that Whitehead can help us view our friend struggling with cancer from the inside.

We need to detail briefly, at the risk of oversimplification, what Whitehead calls the Intermediate or Supplemental Phase of an actual occasion's subjective experience. Once again we are stopping time, as if we could, to look into the interior operations by which each of us becomes a "whole" out of the parts, a new unity, "I," out of the rich multiplicity of the environment.

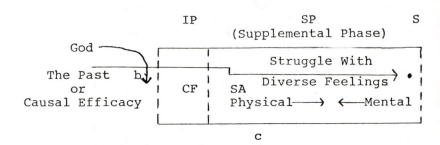

We may recall that in the Initial Phase (IP) c has grasped the whole actual world of the past as it is located in b, which is the immediately preceding moment, by way of a conformal feeling (CF), e.g., anger. C is also the recipient of a lure from God to aim its career in a slightly different direction so that the past will not be merely repeated and that the present might enjoy a novel experience. Thus, c is born. From now on c will be putting together itself, starting with its own incipient subjective aim (SA) refining that aim throughout the concrescence, and concluding with its Satisfaction (S), that is, its final arrival at its own unity or wholeness. In this minute duration c will individuate out of a massive past toward possibilities relevant to it into some kind of unity that will add one more novel entity to the world. "The many become one, and are increased by one."[4]

I

Subjective Aim

The existence of c, in distinction to b and all that has gone before it, begins to aim for what it will become. That aiming will be under power-ful duress to the conformal feeling that helped to

70

give it birth, and it will be in response to God's
Aim for it. But finally as c grows together it
will determine its own aim! Everything else in the
concrescing moment clusters around that aiming, the
king-pin or central element systemic to the concrescence. Each occasion reaches forward for what
it will become and it shapes all the data to fit its
aim. Each duration is not powered by instinct as
in Freud though the past is pervasive; nor is there
a "ground plan lying dormant in an individual from
the beginning," which if known completely, would
allow his fate to be in "large measure predictable,"
as Jung proposed.[5] Rather, each human organism is
teleological, drawn powerfully by its own aiming
toward its own final achievement of selfhood. The
aim may be positively correlated with God's aim for
it, in which case the organism will be in some sense
imaging God; or it may be turned away from God so
that there is but the faintest resemblance. But
the aim will carry some impress of the vision of
God for that concrescence; it will be the guiding
light for that duration.

Every aim of each concrescence is a response
to a conceptual feeling, that is, a feeling that
reaches for a new possibility. We have already
seen that every aim is a response to a lure from
God, that is, to a vision God has in mind for this
particular instance. But it is also a response to
a possibility suggested to it by the preceding
moment. By something akin to the law of association, which Whitehead builds into his metaphysical
scheme in the category of Reversion, a possibility
which becomes incarnate in the preceding event
suggests another possibility, perhaps dramatically
different, perhaps almost identical, for the new
concrescence. For example, the client might feel
conformally the sadness of the previous moment but
with a pull to feel it in the present with a twist
of pleasure. Then the sadness would not be identical with the previous moment. It would be felt
slightly differently: with just a touch of pleasure
which could be a masochistic feeling. In other
words, every subject's aim for its concrescence is
tied to a possibility.

Possibilities have metaphysical status in
process thought. They are called Eternal Objects
and "exist" as potentials for the world to ingress
in each concrescence. They are part of the nature
of God for God eternally envisages all the possibilities as a realm of interrelated potentiality.
They constitute the future as they wait to be
realized or actualized in each new present. The
pen that is on my desk is defined by a number of
related possibilities one of which is blackness.
Our cancer victim whom we met at the beginning of
this chapter had his life turned around when he
could really entertain the possibility of his own
finitude. His defense of omnipotence was less
needed when he discovered it was ok to have limitations. He no longer suffered compulsively the need
to control. Cancer was the context for the break-
through of salutary possibilities.

Every Aim is targeted toward the realm of
possibility which constitutes the only future we
have. Each Aim is a response to a conceptual
feeling, that is, to a feeling of possibility.
God gives to each moment that possibility which is
best for it. Cancer may be the kairotic moment in
the fulness of which time God can provide a
radically new possibility, e.g., the acceptance of
finitude with release from the pretensions of
omnipotence, for the richer aiming of a person.
But possibilities come from other sources as well,
viz., from reversions or associations as when one
possibility suggests another.[6] Furthermore, the
problem of aiming is made terribly complex because
possibilities are "bundled" together in a relevant
ordering so that any number of them might be more
or less relevant. Much of the time we feel very
ambiguous about choosing among several possibilities.
No one possibility stands out. We know the pain
of the decision as when we weigh the pros and cons
of heart surgery. On the other hand, part of the
stuckness of many clients is that they feel their
possibilities are shut down; they are prisoners
to an aim that seems to allow only for the past to

72

"repeat" itself, as was the case with my angry
client in chapter two. The feeling of these
clients is that they have no way to turn; to change
the figure, all their energies are concentrated on
barely treading water.

Aiming is fundamental to health. Life does
not lie with the past which has already perished
and now is immortally set as datum for future
moments. Life is connected with the future, with
possibilities waiting to be taken hold of and made
part of a new present. So while every occurring
moment is a Janus-figure, facing backward and forward, its forward facing is toward its own novel
unity as it embraces the richest possibility for
its brief duration.

At the very inception of the Supplementary
Phase there is struggle. If we could but listen
to the struggle speak we would be listening into
decision-making at levels lower than consciousness,
at the birthing of Aim which will guide the entire
concrescence. There is God's initial Aim, envisaging for us the richest possibility relevant to us.
There are the aims of others, from our immediate
past and in our remote past which affect us:
parents for children, a lay person for his pastor.
All these aims, by association (or reversion),
suggest still other possibilities. These many aims
lure the birthing moment itself to aim for a final
realization of unity or wholeness. And beyond the
birthing experience, throughout the entire concrescence, up to the final realization the struggle
of aiming goes on. Indeed, aim is precisely what
is determined by the concrescence. We are not
describing a static aim that is set, determined once
and for all, and then guides the flowing of life.
That is not true of our basic experience. We are
describing a process aiming (hence my repeated use
of the gerund) which both guides the process and is
determined by the process. Aiming becomes aim
through the process; and aim immediately gives way

to aiming. We achieve our aims only to be forced
on to new aiming in the next bit of experiencing.
All of us sense the struggle: sometimes the agony
of perplexity, sometimes the ecstasy of laudable
alternatives, sometimes the hopelessness of closed-
in or fogged-in goals. The flow or sweep of a
person's life is the flow or sweep of his or her
aiming. When the flow has seemingly stopped, he
or she is likely to become a client. The aim is
there because it is a metaphysical necessity of
life. But it is often trivialized by overwhelming
conformity; it is seemingly blocked and one feels
untracked; there are too many competing lures and
one feels she has to escape; or the possibilities
are hidden by a cloud of loss, i.e., death of a
spouse, and the future seems pitifully bleak.

The importance of Subjective Aim for pastoral
caring is that it gives metaphysical grounding to
teleology. We are oriented purposively. Realistic
but transcendent goals are essential to human
existence. This is why Jungian therapy is right
when it focuses on the future whether in dream
analysis or getting the client to talk about his or
her goals. And it is why Psychosynthesis is right
in its therapeutic use of guided imagery. Images
beckon. In pastoral caring, whatever the selected
therapeutic technique, a critical jointure with the
client is around aims. While most discrete aims
are unconsciously determined, there is a continuity
of aiming that can and must be dealt with. As the
carer helps the client to wrestle with his or her
aims, assured that God is at the center of that
wrestle, the client can begin consciously as well
as unconsciously to orient life teleologically
(where it is meant to go); and along with that
ordering to individuate toward the novel unity
possible for him or her. This is the primary move
in helping the client to get unstuck by breaking
with mere conformity.

Translating this theory into case material,
we can view our cancer victim as teleologically
confused. For psychological reasons, he really

needed to deny his human limitations, denial
serving as a defense mechanism to cover over
feelings of inferiority. Infantile omnipotence--
the lot of us all due to our early illusions based
on wish-fulfilment as though wishing made it so--
became a deep-seated part of his adult identity to
support the denial. Positions carrying large
responsibilities, which placed him in centers of
power and control, also supported the denial. His
aiming, therefore, was badly confused. When things
went out of control, when the omnipotence was
threatened by friends or enemies, the denial would
give-way. Anxiety attacks would ring the old bell
that he was being rejected. Panicky, he would
attack. His aiming was thus always curving
around himself: in Freud's language, neurotically;
in Luther's language, sinfully.

The diagnosis of cancer and the subsequent
months of treatment exposed his vulnerability.
Denial could no longer cope. He later acknowledged
that he felt this to have been God's opportunity
to get through to him on a different plane of
aiming. Little by little he felt his own life's
directions changing. Almost daily he felt a new
pointing in his life, as though the flow of time
was bearing him in a 180° reversal. Teleologically
he seemed to be somewhat righted. He felt his
life being re-routed. For example, he began really
to see the roses he spent so much time gardening;
he listened to birds with a new intensity; time
with friends and family developed a quality of
relationship instead of an agenda to be accomplished. He did not sense less struggle; only a
different struggle. He felt he was more on track
with the realities that were environing him,
especially the reality of God. This seemed to
give him more of a sense of well-being, that is,
he was defining his being with more appropriate
aiming.

II

Comparative Feelings

Up to this point we have been relatively
simplistic in what goes on in any concrescence.
We have talked of a datum out of the past, e.g.,
b, an aim from God, a reverted or associated
eternal object or possibility, a subjective aim.
But these are abstractions from the immensely rich
feeling-states that are composing the concrescence.

Whitehead grounds his metaphysical vision on
the principle of relativity. The social nature
of reality is the doctrine that everything is
relative to everything else. "In fact if we allow
for degrees of relevance, and for negligible
relevance, we must say that every actual entity is
present in every other actual entity."[7] Each
actual occasion sums up the world within itself.
This gives even more size than Jung imagined to the
residency within each of the Collective as well as
the Personal Unconscious. The memory traces that
both Jung and Freud intuited as existing in the
present are given a vehicle for their inclusion,
the vehicle of prehensions or feelings. Every
person is a series of experiencing centers grasping the vastness of the past into themselves and
not merely the simple contiguous occasion, b. Of
course, b is never simple. For b inherits x, y,
and z before it. So the experiencing center c not
only grasps b by prehending it; it also has hold
of b's grasping x, y, and z. For example, I not
only read Whitehead, but I read Christian grasping Whitehead and I read Cobb grasping Christian
and Hartshorne both grasping Whitehead. And so the
world grows in amazing richness.

But that growth is made possible by each
experiencing subject's feeling conceptually the
range of possibility. Not the whole range, to be
sure, but a limited slice of that range relevant
to where the new occasion is. The term "range"
implies a network of possibilities that can help
define the new occasion, or for our purposes a

76

society of occasions called a person. If it be a person, the graded possibilities for a particular moment might be anger, hostility with intent to do harm, anal aggression, oral aggression, passive aggression, a bemused frustration, etc., all a cluster of associated possibilities.

Between the past which rushes in through the back-door and the future standing at the front-door as luring possibilities, the present is in struggle to fulfill its aim toward its own unity. The struggle is among feelings to produce the richest possible subjective form or content. Some feelings will be emphasized into high-grade importance, what Whitehead calls adversion, and some into triviality, what he calls aversion. It is a struggle dominated by the subjective aim of the concrescing occasion, a struggle described as enjoyment by Whitehead. The experiencing subject enjoys its own actualizing of itself. We should be warned that enjoyment is an ontologically-oriented term which means that each occasion is involved in the process of putting itself together whether that be pleasurable or painful, constructive or destructive. The cluster of occasions called the self is deciding itself for this instant of creativity. This is its enjoyment, even if that be torment, of creating itself out of the rich multiplicity that comes in through the back-door and beckons from the front.

Between the back-door and the front-door some powerful living goes on. There are tensions between loyalties to the past and attractions from the future; between what is more important and less important; between the insistent demands of now and the enriching joys of later; between the duress of duty and the call of pleasure. We all know the struggle; we often feel it ambiguously. It is the struggle between instinctual material and superego restraint, to borrow from Freud; between collective and personal unconscious and consciousness in Jung's scheme; between need-deprivation and need-satiation, according to Maslow.

It is the way we feel the lure toward Beauty, the yearning for something better, the appetite to incorporate more of life. Victor Frankl puts it well: "During no moment of his life does man escape the mandate to choose among possibilities."[8] The choosing is the locus of the struggle.

In the choosing we constitute ourselves. Whitehead would approve of Jung's statement: "[One's] environment cannot give him as a gift that which he can win for himself only with effort and suffering."[9] Whitehead sees enjoyment as the occasion's self-creative moment. He is fond of the phrase, causa sui, to describe this continuous synthesizing of the data. The self forms itself, determines itself, realizes itself and so is constitutive of its own final unity. Here is the self's freedom, here its responsibility. The self deepens itself or canalizes itself, at the same time that it widens itself; or it creates itself superficial and narrow. It struggles toward intensity of realization at the same time as it strives to maintain balance. The self is always in a more or less situation as it is eliminating here, upgrading there, in its relentless pursuit to cause its own being.

Perhaps the word best describing this very complex individuating experience is integration. That is what the total organism is trying to achieve. The multiplicity of feelings, both physical and mental, is the stuff which the experiencing organism is trying to put together, unseen, and yet before the very eyes of the carer. It feels its world adverbially: joyfully, sadly, bleakly, fulsomely, angrily, humorously, ambivalently, depressedly, disjunctively, conjunctively, narrowly, widely, deeply, superficially, openly, fixedly, etc. Each of these feelings is a subjective form, or a bit of content of the experiencing center, for "how an actual entity becomes constitutes what that actual entity is,. . ."[10] The carer is seeing, if he or she has eyes to see, creativity in concrete operation: the many are

becoming one: the Person for better or worse.
Out of his own experiencing the carer can intuitively place himself within the interior struggle
taking place inside the client even if the
contents themselves are uniquely hidden within
the recesses of the client. The ontological
structure of every individuating experience is
this: each, guided by his own aim, feels his
way toward his own wholeness. To that wholeness
of "satisfaction," the aesthetic goal of every
concrescence, we shall turn in the next chapter.

III

An Illustration: The Nursing Home

I want to try to illustrate how it is all put
together by way of one of the most difficult and
often depressing pastoral caring situations, the
Nursing Home. If the contents of this chapter can
illumine that experience, they should find ready
translation into almost any other. Conversely, if
these contents cannot illumine what goes on in
nursing homes, then their metaphysical status is
in jeopardy. A further reason for choosing the
Nursing Home is that, as difficult as it is, it
is more typical of pastoral work than a formal
counseling structure from which I tend to draw
illustrative material.

A sign on a wall of a nursing home in the
West reads: "Old age is not for Sissys." One
obvious inference to draw from that sign is that
some very hard tasks are handled by the aging
and especially by those occupying nursing homes.
A related inference is that nursing home popula-
tions are "in charge" of their situations, at
least minimally.

A nursing home is viewed by many as a
laboratory approaching surd evil; that is, there
is no way to rationalize much of the existence
there as containing any elements of good. They
see the former quality of life to be gone. The

79

residents for the most part appear to have nothing
more to wait for than death, many not even aware
of the wait; and the visitor takes the persistent
sense data of odor, moaning, crying out, and human
disarray as realities too offensive to cope with.

Yet even among the most distressed cases we
must see the distress as partly the resident's
but largely ours. There is enjoyment going on in
the myriad actual occasions making up each life.
Enjoyment as we have noted is a metaphysical term
indicating subjective experiencing at whatever
level of concrescence. Enjoyment is the term
covering the process by which the total prehensive
experience, guided by the subjective aim,
culminates in the final unity or satisfaction when
that duration is ended and the subject becomes a
piece of the datum to be felt by the new occasion.
It is the unyielding insistence of process thought
that subjective experiencing is the nature of
reality which offers a new perspective on nursing
home life. We dare not let our abstractions as to
what ought to be, or our memories of former times,
dominate our evaluation of what is going on with
the residents now. Abstractions are important as
nursing home staffs try to do some regulating and
as visitors try to impose some ordering of life.
But to conclude that the resident is only an object whose life we regulate is falsely to posit
vacuous existence. We miss the concreteness of
the resident. Regulation is necessary. But it is
just as necessary to perceive the resident as
essentially a totally prehending, concrescing subject within whose limitations the structure of
reality is no different from any other reality
including the hale and hearty visitor to the
nursing home. The nursing home resident is a
self-determining person, within limits, to be sure.
He or she does aiming, makes adjustments, reaches
some level of Self-realization, and so becomes a
new addition to the world, both for himself or
herself and others, and for God. Each resident
is causa sui for each puts things together in the
wonder of his or her existence. Proof of our

objectifying the other as "not with it" and so not a percipient being is the frequency with which we talk about the resident's "condition" as though that person were not a person. Medical doctors as well as lay people, pastors as well as nurses, talk over the client in the presence of the client as though he or she were an object rather than an experiencing subject.

Take the seemingly simple matter of a resident's eating. For some it is a ritual of conformal response. A 95 year old resident, not very rational, asks when dinner will be. When told that it will be at 6 o'clock, she responds, "That's too late for dinner." The logic is hers, perhaps a conformal logic to past times and places, one of the few things she seems to be remembering with some clarity. It is impossible to honor that remembering with any lengthy conversation, but it is genuinely satisfying to know that in that duration some remembering is going on. There is often regression in eating habits including the return to primitive patterns where it's all right to eat with one's hands, to dirty one's face, to soil one's blouse. Members of the family may be aghast and embarrassed. But that defines their subjective forms rather than the aged mother's. Here may be the sheer physical delight of chewing, even without teeth, "gumming" it to tell it as it is, of tasting, of swallowing, of feeling full. It probably will be aesthetically distasteful for "outsiders," but for a resident to put her mouth, or even her face, into her hands full of chocolate pudding may be an aesthetic delight as fully satisfying to her in her present concrescence as a gourmet dinner once was.

For the resident to be put into bed with the feel of mattressed security underneath, with the covers felt as a cacooning environment, and for that resident to go far back in her memory traces and compose herself into a fetus-like posture, feeling all the while the caring hand of the aide on her shoulder, is for that resident in very elemental ways to enjoy the flow of prehensive feeling and maybe at the edges of consciousness to sense almost a primordial peace.

Process thought finds a modicum of freedom, or spontaneity, in the most mundane of events, viz. the actual occasions that make up a blade of grass. How much real, that is, actual, freedom there is in the myriad events that make up a single resident of a nursing home! A mother might have the shortest conceivable duration of recognition of a daughter, but her will might continue to play a strong role in ways conformable to its own history with an accompanying sense of some control. The mother, wheeled about the halls, might put her foot down as a brace against going out doors, or might catch hold of the railing to declare a new direction to traverse, even though signs of recognition might be most fleeting. Or a long-term resident might repeat her daily beseeching to any passer-by: Where am I? Am I dead? Are you my mother? As she tries to rise from the chair to which she is tied, she implores, "Man, will you help me?" The response, prompted by an external logic, "Annie, be careful or you'll fall," elicits an inner logic all its own: "If I'm going to fall, why don't you help me?" Her enjoyment of a logical moment, perhaps only flickering to consciousness, advises us to be careful lest we predetermine that her level of enjoyment must be so little human it is no longer really human. Process thought insists that we treat with utmost respect and appreciation the subjective experiencing of the other, no matter the appearance. For Reality may belie appearance, and does. The latter is the more superficial.[11]

God's initial aim draws from the resident his or her responding aim, and extremely limited novelty is often all that is possible. Hope is in a God who has not forgotten these, and whose aim is for them to enjoy whatever is possible for their organism to delight in. God's caring is seen here, not in a theological tour de force in which God can do everything but for some mysterious reason, known only to God, won't. In the view of process theology God cannot do everything. Yet there is a Caring that struggles with a body that has outlasted its mind, perhaps, to provide as much lure as that enfeebled organism can respond to. There is a certain beauty in the struggle that God and each organism are engaged in to give even a limited sense of life to each experiencing moment within the nursing home. There are moments of pathos, tragedy, humor, depression, rationality, incontinence. The moments mark the flow of concrescences in which life is struggled for, owned in some passing flux, and left as influence for the next encountering occasion. The encounters are not on the floor of the New York Stock Exchange, nor a struggle over Union policy, nor a decision to buy a new home. But when the flow of subjective encounterings is going on in a nursing home, life at some level of beginning, struggling, and concluding is taking place. Heroic goings on, which include God, the resident, nurses, aides, are taking place. Only when we close our eyes to these inner dramas and see the macrocosmic whole spread out before us--itself a denial of process-- do we make the fatal judgment that it were better that they were dead. Fatal because we become oriented that way, as though all we are doing is a holding operation. Nursing home dramas are life-dramas--full of subjectivity--and we ought to help the dramas to become as satisfying as possible!

Process thought takes our minds off the sensory data, which are so related to Appearance, and forces us to look intuitively into the prehensive, actualizing centers of nursing home residency. Process thought teaches us not only where to look but that what we are "seeing" is the "really real." This metaphysical way of seeing into reality could revolutionize pastoral care in nursing homes, and, if adopted by dedicated staffs, would enhance the quality of their caring and the enjoyment of the residents so busily engaged in

their ongoing self-creations. The Appearance
would not be taken for Reality but would be seen
for what it is: ". . .an incredibly simplified
edition of reality."[12]

IV

The Caring Work of the Pastor

Now I want to relate the description of the
supplemental phase in the becoming of an actual
occasion to the caring work of the pastor. I am
borrowing as the framework for this section a
summary of the therapeutic approach outlined by
Jung.[13] It is my judgment that this framework is
as essential to pastoral caring as to psychotherapy itself, although because of a different
training modality some of the specific techniques
may be different for clergy, e.g., dream analysis
may be shunned. Jung has argued that Freud contributed to psychotherapy Confession and Explanation; Adler added Education; Jung himself,
Transformation. It is helpful for me to see this
in a hierarchical structure beginning at the
bottom, with equal value attaching to each level:

> Transformation
> Education
> Explanation
> Confession

Feeling must be correlated with confession and
insight with explanation; re-education might be
preferred to education; transformation stands
uncorrected. This structure can be correlated with
the contents of our present chapter. However, not
all pastoral caring situations need, nor can they
use, all four aspects of the psychotherapeutic
model now being considered. For instance, much
pastoral caring in a nursing home would employ
Feelings and Transformation, but not Insight and
Education, whereas formal counseling relationships
would or should include all four. Those
situations that are only primarily supportive might
be less likely to include the four, but in all

probability where there is a genuine problem and the intellectual ability to reflect upon it, the full therapeutic approach would be requisite.

A. Confession or Feeling. Freud developed as part of his treatment theory the practice of catharsis, the sharing or the confessing in the presence of the analyst the inner secrets or concealments of the patient. Since for the most part such "secrets" were unknown to the patient, that is, were part of the unconscious, whether repressed (Freud) or archetypal (Jung) or both, Freud developed such techniques as dream analysis and association to unlock the hidden part. Jung has summarized the aim of catharsis: "The goal of treatment by catharsis is full confession; not merely intellectual acknowledgement of the facts, but their confirmation by the heart and the actual release of the suppressed emotions."[14]

As Jung observed,[15] the prototype for catharsis is the religious institution of the confessional. In the history of pastoral care, however, the confessional was related to the unburdening of sin, or more precisely, sins. In pastoral caring, aided by Freud's expanding and deepening of the notion of catharsis, we now have an enriched perspective on the ancient practice of the confessional. I believe that both the religious practice and the Freudian enrichment are profoundly deepened and made more effective by way of process insight into concrescence.

The value of confession is to lift up into self-awareness in the presence of a trusted friend the prehensions or feelings which are constitutive of the client. Feelings are the basic stuff. They are our grasping of the past and of the possibilities beckoning us. They inform our willed intention or aim for this moment and the relevant future. They are competitive with each other and a "decision," probably always with a touch of pain, must be made to negate some and embrace others. The

client is profoundly what he or she is feeling.[16]
For the most part our feelings do not emerge into
consciousness. Nevertheless, they leave their
tone and that tone is pervasive of the total
organism, for example, chronic depression.
Feeling-tones have continuity, that is, they
linger on effectively in a person's accumulative
experiencing, viz., chronic depression.

The task of the pastoral carer centers
around feelings. His job is not the why question-
-not yet. The how and what questions are now
asked. How are you feeling? What are you feeling?
The client is feeling! Prehension is the term
describing her reality of feeling, that is, how
she grasps her world.

What the carer should be helping the client
to do is to try to become more aware of the reality of feeling, the basic stuff of life. Feelings
are the foundational structure of our reality. Our
experiencing is our feelings of past and future,
our own aims, the struggles among competing
feelings. Feelings, in process thought, are where
it is at! Therefore, Freud's insistence that
Confession, that is, the raising of feelings to
the surface there to be felt anew, is all the more
necessary in process thought since feelings are the
primary ontological structure of each of us. So
the major job of the carer is to help the client
focus on feelings.

In the past 15 years I have probably read or
listened to 2000 case verbatims prepared by
students at all levels of preparation for ministry
from the basic divinity degree through doctorate
of ministry programs. A consistent weakness is
the failure of almost all to deal with feelings.
Students will elicit a response to the simple
question, what are you feeling? They almost
invariably make their own response by way of a nod
of acceptance or a word of acknowledgement,
perhaps with a note of sympathy or support, and
then move on to another topic as though that one

is done with. Whereas only the verbal response
has been made. The client is rarely helped to
stay with her feelings-tones; to re-feel them; to
re-invest them with importance; to struggle with
what they are and what they are trying to say; to
uncover the aim which is guiding them; to linger
on the adverbial forms they are taking to see what
chronically they are producing, e.g., anger,
depression, guilt; to locate the feelings which
form the nucleus of the sense of being stuck; to
feel the boredom and ennui of the trivial over
against the fleeting, teasing sense that there
ought to be something better. Freud uncovered the
psychological reasons for staying with the
feelings of the client. Process thought has uncovered the ontological reason for staying with
them: the structure of actuality is a feeling-
structure. Both Freud's and Whitehead's reasons
ought not to allow a serious carer to flit from
topic to topic. To do so is to skip over the
inner dynamics as a flat stone skips along the
surfaces of the water. When a client says: "I
hurt," saying it in innumerable ways, the response
is to help the client to take up his abode among
those feelings for a sufficient flow of time so
that the client really feels hurtfully his world
by being existentially enmeshed in it. Then it
is more difficult for him to escape from that
harsh reality into the removed world of abstraction, which may be for him the temptation to
intellectualize his problems. So often pastors
are seduced into the intellectualizing games with
the client. It is easier than insisting on staying with feelings; and it is more fun because it
can be a matching of wits. Furthermore, pastors,
many with the need to be problem-solvers, and
abetted by wrong-headed theology and lay people's
expectations, are tempted to skim along the
surfaces of their client's being to provide
answers. But these are answers generally to the
wrong questions. The real questions are down
among the client's feelings.

A related temptation is to equate consciousness with reality when it is essentially but a

simplified edition of reality. It is as though
the carer thinks the client has gotten a hold on
things and can move on when the client has attached
a verbal symbol to his feeling. That prematurely
removes the client from the problem spot as he
relates to the idea which he is expressing. For
example, it was not sufficient for our cancer
victim to be able to name his psychological
problem as denial. That would have only tagged
it. He needed to linger on the continuing feelings of omnipotence, infinitude, and the need to
control. Because the present is all we have, he
did not need to go back into childhood to feel.
He had to rub his own nose, as it were, in his
current feelings which included childhood feelings.
There was the past immanent within him as was
also the fouled-up future. He had to bring up
into consciousness all the old feelings and to
live with them. But the struggle was in the
vortex of feelings which he had carefully learned
to cover over. For any therapist to let him run
away from those feelings below the level of
consciousness would be to fail the vital movement
of Confession which essentially is to live with
the feelings sufficiently that when they are
articulated they are done so with the relieving
burp of undigested material.

Whitehead's appraisal of consciousness is
worth quoting here for it might equip the carer
with the necessary understanding to linger with
the client on the bottom-line of experience.

> Consciousness flickers; and even at
> its brightest, there is a small focal
> region of clear illumination, and a
> large penumbral region of experience
> which tells of intense experience in
> dim apprehension. The simplicity of
> clear consciousness is no measure
> of the complexity of complete ex-
> perience. Also this characteristic
> of our experience suggests that
> consciousness is the crown of exper-

ience, only occasionally attained,
not its necessary base.[17]

Consciousness is a part of the content of every
human life. It is extremely important to therapeutic concerns as we shall see in a moment.
But it is not the "base," not where the intense
experience, so dimly apprehended, is. To dwell
on what is merely conscious is to miss the
complexity and vastness of experience and so the
locus of where the pain is: the feelings.

B. Explanation or Insight. The purpose of
concentrating on feelings, however, is for the
sake of insight. Catharsis is not enough. One
could wallow in feelings and never get out of the
slough. Jung points out that the second stage of
therapy, as developed by Freud, was explanation.
According to Jung, what is to be explained by the
therapist is the phenomenon of transference, that
is, the transferring to the therapist of childhood
memory--images which are infused with emotionality.
For example, the therapist becomes the long-needed
or long-hated father.   The purpose of the explanation is to help the patient to "see" what is
going on so that, given insight, he will use his
new knowledge to give up old patterns and to
seize hold of life in new ways.[18]

I would prefer to call this Insight therapy
instead of Explanation therapy. Important as the
transference phenomenon is, explaining it is not
sufficient. The carer-client relationship, while
based on transference, is more than transference.
One task of the carer is with sensitive reserve
and tentativeness to help the client gain insight
into her feelings which she has been lingering on.
For example, if the client is bogged down in
feelings of hurt occasioned by the re-emergence of
childhood guilt whenever her mother tries to control her by hanging up on the phone or by giving
her the "cold, silent treatment," and if the
client has lingered with repeated feelings long
enough to sort out their composition, e.g.,

89

guilt, anger, resentment, hopelessness, an interpretation tentatively offered by the carer might
help the client to gain freeing insight. The
interpretation might run along these lines:

Ca: Does it seem to you that your mother is
still trying to control you even though
you are 35?

Cl: Yes, the same as it's always been.

Ca: If you let her, what will happen?

Cl: It isn't a matter of letting her. She
just always does it.

Ca: Why do you suppose she does it?

Cl: That's mother. She has always been that
way.

Ca: What does she try to gain from that?

Cl: Me, I guess. She must feel that she will
lose me if she doesn't run me.

Ca: Your mother's life sounds pretty small
and limited to me.

Cl: It is. She and Dad are two people who
exist side by side. There's very little
movement between them in their lives
together.

Ca: Let me suggest to you that she won't get
movement if you let her control you.
You've grown beyond her. She's trying to
bring you back. If you refuse to come
back, you give her a chance to grow.
Everytime you knuckle under to her, she
doesn't have to find new ways to live.
Her old patterns are encouraged.

Cl: You mean that if I refuse to be controlled by my mother, I help her as well as myself?

Ca: Does that seem likely to you?

This vignette from a counseling period suggests the role of consciousness-raising to insight. It presupposes arduous concentration on feelings and their catharsis. Then it seeks to lead the client to interpret what is going on. Now we are concentrating on consciousness as a subjective form. Intellectual feelings grasp possibilities which are newly offered. The client as a Janus-figure, once mired down by old patterns, with sheer physical purposes controlling out of the past, now turns toward a literally God-given set of alternatives. She could not be authentically herself without the future, without embracing the possibility of new life through her intellectual feelings. All higher life, especially human, is life lived toward novel possibility, reaching out into the rich realm of potentiality. These are imaginative feelings, the reach for an ideal possibility. In this reach is life. As Whitehead puts it, "The essence of life is the teleological introduction of novelty, with some conformation of purpose."[19] Insight, which is internal sight or perception, is consciousness raised to the level of imagination. It opens up vistas of novelty by which to actualize life at richer levels of attainment. What we are really talking about is Reason whose function, according to Whitehead, "is to promote the art of life." He goes on to say, ". . .Reason is a factor in experience which directs and criticizes the urge towards the attainment of an end realized in imagination but not in fact."[20]

Reason enables insight. Every hurting Other, staying sufficiently long with the mixture of feelings to feel their pain, needs something of an Aha! experience to wed feeling with meaning. "So that's what I have been doing all these years," our adult fellow-traveler with the infantile sense of

91

omnipotence might have exclaimed. "I have been afraid of more rejection and I have been protecting against it. Was it my size I was compensating for? the vicious family fights? a fear of failure my mother could not tolerate?" In this vein he would now be trying to attach meaning to his feeling-world. Thought in the form of imaginative feelings struggles to give insight that can be clarifying and releasing. The function of reason is to open up life that aiming can move off in another more fruitful direction.

C. Education or re-education. Jung goes on to show that Freud needed Alfred Adler who contributed the third stage, Education. Adler also employed Insight, which was to help the patient discover and understand his or her life-style which emerged in the helplessness of early childhood. But Adler sensed that merely to uncover the antecedents to a present plight did little good to resolve the plight. He insisted that life-responses could finally only be changed by new life-responses or habits and that education is the primary means to this end. The role of the therapist is to help the patient "in finding concrete ways of reorienting himself toward greater social interest,"[21] which means to develop new attitudes and more realistic ways of handling problems in all spheres of life.

At the center of Adler's proposal is the dominance of purpose. Purpose is the aim of the actual occasion or the succession of actual occasions that constitute personal experience. . . toward what? Toward the conduct of life that re-sults in a richer, more satisfying wholeness which re-issues again in higher complexity of satis-faction, and so on. Now Reason has moved beyond insight to issue in conduct. There is always a pragmatic turn to reason. To paraphrase Whitehead, it must direct and criticize the urge towards attainment of an end realized in imagination but not yet in fact.[22] So the function of reason, which is to live, to live well, to live better,[23] is only fulfilled when reason is turned toward

concrete ways of dealing with the environment.
Thus, the carer must help the client both to
imagine novel ways of handling the environmental
data and then to implement some of those ways to
develop new patterns of coping.

Suggestions gently put forth by the carer or
elicited from the client might be as concrete as
the technique of the Gestaltist's use of the empty
chair; or persuading the wife whc complains that
her husband is like a fifth child, not to call him
in the morning but to let him be late for work
after she has warned him; or supporting the 35
year-old "child" to tell her mother she will no
longer tolerate her hanging up on her. Or it might
be as general as T.A.'s charting of the Parent/
Adult/Child patterns of behavior and asking how the
client intends to change the picture. The point
is to help persuade the client toward a new
pattern of aiming, to make the pattern concrete so
that attitudes and behaviors do modify, and thus
to vivify and establish change. Final causation
is on the side of change; yet novelty is so under
duress to old patterns. There is required rein-
forcement by way of the carer and by way of some
satisfying experiences to give courage to aim
toward new habits both of the soul and of the
organism's behavior. The carer will, of course,
be full of care not to impose his or her aims since
the pastoral model is divine persuasion. At the
same time the carer will take courage that the
divine persuasion is at work aiming the client
toward conduct more commensurate with the art of
life.

D. Transformation. Jung thought a fourth
stage in the treatment process was needed. He
called it Transformation.[24] I would prefer to see
Transformation not so much as a fourth stage, but
as the nature of the context for confession,
insight, and education. As such it is the sine
qua non of caring.

By Transformation Jung meant that the carer and client must mutually influence each other for there to be any reaction in the client. ". . .if there is any reaction, both are transformed."[25] If the carer is not transformed, neither will be the client. Jung argued that the carer (doctor in his language) must pass through the very stages we have been discussing: confession, explanation, and education "so that his personality will not react unfavorably on the patient."[26] Jung's concern is to make explicit the mutuality implicit in the caring situation.

Process thought provides ontological grounding in its social theory for the notion of the Transformation. Grounded there it takes on a metaphysical character the generality of which gives to the psychological concreteness even greater significance. One of the bases of process thought is the principle of relativity. Whitehead states it succinctly in these words: ". . .every item of the universe including all the actual entities, are constitutents in the constitution of any one actual entity."[27] The universe is social through and through. Its fundamental nature is as a social process. Whitehead's whole concept of prehensive unification is social; how the universe disjunctively comes to reside conjunctively in one actual occasion. In a beautiful and penetrating analysis of internal relations Bernard E. Meland concluded:

> the notion of being 'internal' is,
> itself, a shared, even bodily,
> feeling expressing participation
> in the mystery of the nurturing
> matrix. To be conscious and
> articulate as a personal encounter,
> this internal relation must of
> necessity rise to an I-Thou
> relationship; but it rises out of
> a depth of togetherness which is
> ontological in character.[28]

94

As critical as Jung and Buber were of each other, Jung would embrace the I-Thou nature of the therapeutic relationship. Process thought locates it ontologically. The carer inherits from the client as does the client from the carer. The client is as much datum which the carer prehends as is the carer datum for the client. Not only will the client never be the same again; neither will the carer. That is the risk of inter-subjectivity. It is also the risk of agape-love, as I shall try to show in Chapter 9. Either the carer will be transformed by the client or nothing will happen. Erich Fromm puts the point in curative terms: ". . .the psychoanalyst is cured by his patient--provided they do not treat each other as objects, but are related to each other genuinely and productively."[29]

The social nature of reality, by which each prehends the other, places awesome responsibility on the carer. It is he or she who makes the intervention, establishes the compact,[30] and assumes the role of carer whether implicitly or explicitly. We shall spell out something of that responsibility in Chapter VI. What helps to make the responsibility so awesome is that the carer engages to be transformed! Entering into any caring or counseling relationship means that the carer will be changed in and through the relationship. For the carer will be open to the client, prehending the total datum that is the client, and being transformed by the different reality that is the client. It is sufficient for the present to have picked up Jung's creative suggestion of Transformation, without which redemptive changes do not take place, and to have enriched its significance by locating it ontologically within the social nature of reality.

NOTES

[1] Jung, The Archetypes, Vol. 9, Part I, p. 275. For full discussion see pp. 275-354.

[2] C. G. Jung, Modern Man in Search of a Soul, (New York: Harvest, 1933), p. 66.

[3] Cf. Ira Progoff, Jung's Psychology and Its Social Meaning (New York: Grove, 1953), pp. 143ff.

[4] PR, p. 32.

[5] Jung, Archetypes, op.cit., p. 279. (Although Jung does allow the "autonomy of the unconscious" to be viewed either as an "effect (and therefore historical) or as an aim (and therefore teleo-logical and anticipatory)," his references to "ancestral preconditions" and the "a priori factor" shaping the individual's fate, indicate clearly his preference for the historical loca-tion. Cf. ibid., p. 280.

[6] I am aware that Whitehead "abolishes" the category of reversion with the introduction of God. (See PR, p. 382). I fail to see why this is necessary. We are surely "lured" by possibilities other than those given to us by God. This is precisely part of the conflict in human existence. Yet I agree with John Cobb, Jr. and David Griffin that God is the only reason that novel possibilities, that is, those not felt in the actual world of an occasion, are felt by that occasion. As Prof. Cobb adds in a critique at this point: "Of course, such novel possibilities may be quite different from the ideal ones."

[7] PR, p. 79. Cf. pp. 76, 224.

[8] Victor E. Frankl, The Doctor and the Soul (New York: Knopf, 1978), p. 76.

[9] C. G. Jung, The Undiscovered Self (Boston: Little, Brown, 1957), p. 58.

[10]PR, p. 34, cf. p. 35.

[11]Cf. AI, ch. XIV.

[12]Whitehead, AI, p. 213. Cf. PR, pp. 245ff, 369-372, 408.

[13]See C. G. Jung, Modern Man in Search of a Soul, ch. 2. (This appears in the Collected Works, Vol. 16, ch. 5.)

[14]Modern Man, pp. 35-36.

[15]Ibid., p. 31.

[16]The reader should be reminded, perhaps, that Whitehead's doctrine of feelings or prehensions runs the gamut of feelings from purely physical feelings of the past to intellectual and imaginative feelings of higher sentient beings. An intellectual feeling is one way eternal objects or possibilities are grasped, that is, they are thought. These thoughts may be imaginative feelings, or intellectual feelings, or they may be much more primitive, viz., conceptual feelings which are the functioning of the mental pole of every actual occasion, whether in a molecule of coal or in a cell within the human body.

[17]PR, p. 408. Cf. C. G. Jung, The Archetypes and the Collective Unconscious, Collected Works, Vol. LX, Part 1, pp. 28ff where Jung states his understanding of consciousness.

[18]Jung, Modern Man, op.cit., pp. 36-43.

[19]AI, p. 207.

[20]Alfred North Whitehead, The Function of Reason, (Boston: Beacon, 1929), pp. 4, 8.

[21]Cf. Ruth L. Munroe, Schools of Psychoanalytic Thought (New York: Dryden, 1955), p. 508. Also cf. Jung, Modern Man, op.cit., pp. 44ff.

[22] Function of Reason, p. 8.

[23] Ibid.

[24] See Jung, Modern Man, pp. 47-54.

[25] Ibid., p. 49.

[26] Ibid., p. 53.

[27] PR, p. 224. Charles Hartshorne has also skillfully developed the social nature of reality. See his Reality as Social Process (Glencoe: Free Press, 1953), esp. Ch. 1.

[28] Bernard E. Meland, "The Self and Its Communal Ground," Religious Education (Sept.-Oct. 1964), p. 368.

[29] Erich Fromm, The Art of Loving (New York: Harper, 1956), pp. 25, 26.

[30] I prefer the word "compact" to "contract" for it has an affinity with theological language, more especially with the biblical notion of covenant, while "contract" is a term used extensively in psychoanalysis and other psychotherapies. I was introduced to the term by Karl A. Menninger and Philip S. Holzman in their Theory of Psychoanalytic Technique, (New York: Basic Books, 1973), 2nd ed., Ch. II, although the rationale is mine.

The most that any one of us can seem to do is to
fashion something--an object or ourselves--and
drop it into the confusion, make an offering of it,
so to speak, to the life force.
                    Ernest Becker, The Denial of Death

                       Chapter V

        In Search of Adventure: The Aesthetic Project

        In every brand of therapy the therapist is
involved in the setting of goals for his or her
client, or perhaps more accurately, for the therapeutic conversation. These may be set explicitly
or implicitly, the more explicit the better. They
will usually focus on the presenting problem or
the real problem if that is different from the one
first presented. How vividly I recall my psychiat-
ric supervisors both in New York and Pittsburgh
constantly pressing me to specify my goals with my
clients. But they were always my goals and they
seemed to be wanting my goals for my clients. They
either did not ask, or I did not perceive their
asking, what might be the client's goals. While
I am sure that they expected that my goals would
be formed in the therapeutic situation with the
client, the focus always seemed to be a bit off
center.

        In this chapter we shall be dealing with goals.
I hope to show that process thought has a way of
looking at goals which would fulfill the demands
of any good supervisor but take the focus off the
carer and put it on the client. I further hope to
build upon Chapter III to demonstrate that God who
is endemic to process plays a decisive role in the
setting of goals as part of process.

        Perhaps it should be said at the outset that
neither truth nor morality is of the highest value
in process thought. Truth, which is the conformation of appearance to reality,[1] functions to serve
beauty, apart from which truth is neither good nor

bad.[2] This is in keeping with good psychological practice which helps the client look at his fears of failing on the job, for example, in the light of his history. Hopefully, resulting insight may move the client towards a fresh set of perspectives in which fear of failure no longer dominates. This would be truth serving beauty: the re-creating of the self. Morality, likewise, serves beauty. This is not morality in the deontological sense of moral obligation. It is morality that intends to promote that which is intrinsically good. Again, this is in keeping with good psychological theory and practice which eschews morality as duty in favor of an inner morality which the client develops in re-creating himself. According to Whitehead, ". . .Beauty is left as the one aim which by its very nature is self-justifying."[3] It is the aim toward beauty which characterizes the teleology of the universe.[4] Consequently, I see the production of beauty as the goal of all pastoral caring.

Beauty: What It Is

Beauty takes many forms such as the arts which fertilize life.[5] But the most precious form is the beauty of a soul at any moment of its self-completion. The client, whether in a hospital bed, a retirement village, or on a chair opposite a counselor, is a soul seeking beauty. That is the aesthetic fact in process thought. I am not pointing to an art-object, such as a painting or a musical composition, although that has its own reality and is (or may be) beautiful. I am referring to a beauty actualized in the person as at any moment it has become itself, for better or for worse. That moment of "satisfaction" or arrival would be its achieved beauty out of its struggle in that puff of experience. (Of course, it could be ugliness, as we shall see in Chapter VII.) The process by which it has attained its full-summed or attenuated beauty is an aesthetic process replete with rich data, contrasts, intensities, discord, harmony, teleology, and integration. The goal of life is not death, as Freud wrote,[6] but beauty, both as consequence and as aesthetic process. It is this aesthetic process and its meaning for pastoral care with which we are concerned. In essence every client is a soul seeking beauty. Profoundly, the art of caring is the art of helping a soul become a thing of beauty.

Two statements from Whitehead can tutor us as we look at the aesthetic process: ". . .an actual fact is a fact of aesthetic experience." And: "All aesthetic experience is feeling arising out of the realization of contrast under identity."[7] Let us unpack these statements by way of another look at the concrescence to which they apply. Informing the concrescence from the past is the antecedent world. The subject must preserve some identity with that world. The subject is new but not wholly so. It is also the child of yesterday. There is continuity from yesterday to today. Also informing the concresence is the future. There are new relevant possibilities, some suggested to the subject by association from the antecedent world, some from God by way of God's aim for this new subject. By way of these possibilities the subject will entertain some contrast as over against the antecedent world. The subject is a Janus-figure struggling between identity with its past and contrasts with that past offered by relevant new possibilities. But it is not a one-dimensional past. So the subject has many feelings out of the past. Neither is the future visiting it with a single possibility to which it can respond with a simple Yea or Nay. Part of the struggle is what to include and what to exclude out of the past and out of potentiality. Part of the pain of every experiencing moment is the inclusions vs. exclusions required by our finitude. The concrescence is becoming exceedingly complex. It is jammed with a maze of competing feelings. If these are predominately at the surface level they will promote vagueness and shallowness. In that case while there are deeper feelings, they may be damned up by defense mechanisms. They then churn in the unconscious while life is lived superficially on the top side of the defenses. A considerable part of the ego's energy is spent keeping the defensive lid on. Consequently, life seems depleted as well as superficial. This is a common complaint in marriage counseling, made more often than not by the wife, whose complaint is that "we have no communication any more." What is often meant is that their lives are lived on the superficial level of frenetic activity where each sterotypes the other. The depth and richness of interpersonal exploration, once a part of their lives, is no longer mined. A defensive mood begins to cast its shadow across the marriage. She accuses him of taking her for granted. He accuses her of not understanding him. Neither finds the potential of novelty in the other. It's old-hat; the marriage has turned sour. Beauty in the marriage has grown thin; the marriage may be overlaid by a veneer hiding ugliness underneath.

What is vital to life is that we be in touch with the depth of our feelings, for this gives to life a necessary intensity. Intensity comes from a narrowing of feeling, what Whitehead calls a "canalizing" of feeling. Within the stretch of feelings there must be depth for there to be richness. The subject does feel some feelings more deeply and importantly than other feelings. If this were not so, life would spread out like a prairie flood in which there would be an inundation of feelings simply covering the landscape. But too focused feeling, that is, feeling canalized too narrowly, omits the richness of wider interests. Some lives seem to resemble a fissure: such narrowed intensity as to make life one-dimensional robbing it of rich variation. Other lives are like flooded marsh lands: no depth of focused feeling. Proper width and proper depth help to keep life richly varied but centered with minimal trivia and boredom. Beauty requires the stretch of breadth and the intensity of depth. This is the milieu of richness which is the essence of beauty.

102

Out of the maze of feelings, the experiencing subject is weaving a pattern. It is trying to synthesize the old and the new, the wider reaches and the deeper interests, into a Harmony for that moment of becoming. At times we are all conscious of the inner competitions clamoring to be heard. Such consciousness, however, is just the tip of the iceburg. The unconscious, collective and personal, houses the vast past as it seeks immortality in a new present beckoned to by new but relevant possibility. The unconscious is the pictorial locus indicating where powerful feelings are vying for place as the self seeks to unify them into a composity Harmony. Or Discord might be the synthesis. As Whitehead has observed, there is value in Discord, too, in that the very restlessness occasioned by the discord is motivation of aim toward some other ideal.[8] Finally, however, such discord can and does become so destructive that illness eventuates.[9] But whether it be Harmony or Discord that dominates, some unity will be formed. That is the inexorableness of process.

What is happening in each puff of experience is that the many feelings competing for attention must be harmonized by the experiencing subject. The final harmony, or unity, that is, what the subject becomes, is its intrinsic value. This value is the creation of every soul, the resulting beauty of its adventuring to synthesize its maze of feelings into an ordered whole. Such value is a "new achievement" for the universe.

Aiming: The Struggle for Beauty

Central to this adventuring toward a harmony of contrasts is the subjective aim of the one experiencing. We saw in the previous chapter how the aim of each subject toward its own final unity or satisfaction is first a response to its antecedent world and to God. Its aim is its own intention, in response to the stuff of its life, guiding it to some final form or realization for its brief moment. It is the subject's aim which steers the process so that there is the "internal conformation of the various items of experience with each other," which is Beauty.[10] The subjective aim is the "regulative factor in the aesthetic complex."[11] The aim is neither a casual gaze out over the landscape nor is it a beady eye on the target. It is an "act of aiming,"[12] that is, an act toward actualizing a new possibility. We must not understand this aim to be necessarily conscious. Much of the time it is not. Whether conscious or not it is the organism's effort to synthesize discordant feelings (Whitehead), wishes (Freud), primordial images (Jung), needs (Maslow) with lures from the future which always pose some contrast with the past. Thus, the subjective aim guides the process as it targets a goal that will, in its sense of things, contribute most to itself and to the future of the nexus of which it is a part.[13] This very process is aesthetic; that is, it is a constant weaving or patterning of itself toward the richest harmony possible. Each person is constantly involved in thus forming himself or herself into what is beautiful which is an abstract description for the tiny droplets of beauty processively being formed and then yielding to the next experience of beauty-making. The inner act of aiming works through the anxieties, hopes, fears, hostilities, guilts, shames, loves, joys, etc., to bring the richest closure possible to an atom of experience which then gives itself to a new moment of patterning.

Every client is teleological by nature. She must take aim on what she will become out of the mass of feelings that are hers. Since her aim is response to other aims for her, including God's Aim, she has some direction for her aiming. Whitehead has tried to show that God's "purpose in the world is quality of attainment."[14] Given God's massive presence through each minuscule segment of time, such massive presence being an

actual flow of purpose, the client has in her
unconscious a directivity[15] guiding her to that
"quality of attainment" appropriate to her now.
But since God's aim is among a number of other
aims, we must acknowledge that the divine aim may
not emerge with certain clarity. Yet it would
seem that the more attention is consciously and
steadfastly fixed upon God, as in meditation and
prayer, the more in harmony with the divine aim
we might expect the human aim to be. (To this
we shall return in Chapter VIII.)

The human aim is the Eros, or drive, or will,
or intention toward its own actualization. This
is the volitional thrust of the human being.
Commitment, so important to religion, has its
home right here in the subject's aiming.
Commitment is a continuity of aims, one subjective
aim after another, with more or less of a common
strand of aiming running through the momentary
aims. There is a continuity of aiming binding the
many moments together into what Jean Paul Sartre
terms a Project, which is the fundamental direction
or commitment of each life. "Project" is a helpful concept to indicate a subterranean continuity
of projects. Thus a person's life is not on a
trajectory out of the past, propelled from the
unconscious, as in Jung's psychology; rather, each
life is being pulled forward by numerous lures,
its aim upon aim forming a continuity of commitments. Along that route lies the aesthetic
project, which is the constant patterning of the
person out of a rich inventory of feelings.

Imaging God: Life's Dynamic Design

It is apparent that in process thought we
cannot speak of human aiming apart from divine
aiming. Not all that beckons us comes from God,
of course. This does not mean that other
beckonings are thereby evil. But God's aim or
vision for each occasion is the most perfect
possibility relevant to that particular growing

together of experience. For God has the totality
of all achieved actuality everlastingly in the
divine experience as well as the envisagement of
all possibility. It is Hartshorne's insistence,
as well as Whitehead's, that we must ascribe to
God the "matchless power" to hold together in the
divine experience the infinity of contrasts
offered by the actualization of the world and the
potentialities yet to be achieved.[16]

The beauty of God is this richness: the
Harmony of the infinity of contrasts formed and
forming in the ongoing divine experience. This is
the Size and Stature of God, to borrow words from
Professor Bernard Loomer. Here stature stands for
qualitative attainment: what God has attained, is
attaining, and will attain in the divine inter-
course with the world.

Out of the immensely rich feeling-tones of
the divine experience God loves us with precisely
that aim which is best for us given where we are
in our own mix of feelings. To be in the image of
God would seem to mean at least this: to will or
aim toward a unity humanly attainable, with the
richest possible contrasts, after the manner of
God. God is the model of such beauty of attainment. But it is also God's vision for each of us
that continually aims us to that degree of beauty
possible to each as we put our lives together. In
this double sense can Whitehead point to "God" [as]
the measure of the aesthetic consistency of the
world."[17] To move in the direction of beauty, that
is, to give such stature to our lives that the
width and depth of competing elements are brought
together in rich harmony, is to have an appetite
for adventure which is the vigor of the future
overcoming the staleness of the past.[18] This
adventuring is to imitate God, the cosmic Adventurer, whose own life is the richest harmony out
of an infinity of contrasts and whose desire for
us is just that harmony possible in the human
situation. Every person is potentially an
adventurer. In actuality, for many the adventures

are so tame, so safe, so stale. Monotony, which
is life without adventures, is an antecedent to
suicide because monotony is the repetition of
stale unity of pale contrasts. This is inauthentic
or meaningless existence, prompting some to
prefer to die rather than to endure the monotony
of tameness.[19]

Bernard Loomer has set the human task in
these words: "The aim of life, at the human level,
is to create people of greater stature."[20] This
means to help people to become beautiful; that is,
that their patterning of inner experience be
qualitatively rich as they bring together great
diversity of feelings into a harmonious unity.
Some lives are so narrowly integrated that they
seem aesthetically bankrupt. The older brother
of the Prodigal Son is a case in point. Other
lives are on a merry-go-round of slight pulsations
circling the same landscape. The world is flat
and tasteless, but the pain is anaesthetized by
the appearance of movement. T. S. Eliot's J.
Alfred Prufrock[21] sums up these trivialized lives.
He asks, as though yearning for a new moment:

"Do I dare disturb the universe?"

But he backs off ruefully:

"I have measured out my life
with coffee spoons;"

Then the soliloquy of self-awareness for which he
has no answer:

Should I, after tea and cakes and ices,
Have the strength to force the moment
  to its crisis?
But though I have wept and fasted,
  wept and prayed,
Though I have seen my head [grown
  slightly bald] brought in upon a
  platter,
I am no prophet--and here's no great

matter;
I have seen the moment of my greatness
  flicker,
And I have seen the eternal footman
  hold my coat, and snicker,
And in short, I was afraid.

We can believe that God's intent for human
life is to create intrinsic value, not once and
for all, but in each moment of unifying experience.
This is the beauty of the divine life, a beauty
meant by God to be imaged along the total flow of
human responses. This is high adventure in the
train of the cosmic Adventurer.

The Mid-Life Blahs: An Aesthetic Crisis

It is now appropriate to make some connections
between the aesthetic project and pastoral care.
To help people create greater stature, that is,
to help them fashion themselves into complex
unities of beauty, I take to be the ultimate goal
of pastoral care. This is in keeping with the
notion of ultimacy used throughout these chapters,
for ultimacy points to some vital connection with
God. Beauty is finally the soul's response to the
vision of God for it within the welter of relationships environing the soul. Furthermore, I think
this goal is the aim of all therapy, although it
is not customarily expressed in terms of aesthetics.
The therapeutic goal is to help people improve the
intrinsic value of their lives and so to enhance
the quality of living. The plight of clients is
that they are stuck like a phonograph record whose
groove imprisons the needle for repetitious
circling. Novelty is never absolutely missing;
but for the human being who is ontologically free
to bring about his or her own aesthetic being out
of the immensely rich offerings of life, it is as
though it were when that human being is warped by
repetitious circling. To be stuck is to fail the
venture of being human.

108

The mid-life syndrome is a tragic illustration of potential Beauty trivialized. It is the location of much stultified life. Erik Erikson characterizes the middle years of life as the stage of either generativity or stagnation.[22] Whether "generativity" is the most apt word or whether it is even the most appropriate to this stage, I still find debatable. But Erikson's choice of "stagnation" is a precise description for vast numbers of people enduring the middle years. Whether these years begin to unravel between the polarities of young/old,[23] or find it more difficult to maintain what Becker calls the basic repression, the fear of death,[24] or sag under the impact of career disappointments, the empty nest syndrome, stereotyped marital images, etc., the middle years of so many seem freighted with stagnation, boredom, ennui.[25] So many people of this age operate as though they are stuck with no vision into the future. It is often as if they have no real future, only a repetitious, monotonous roll of years ahead. As Erikson sums it up: "The principal thing is to realize that this is a stage of the growth of the healthy personality and that where such enrichment fails altogether, regression from generativity to an obsessive need for pseudo-intimacy takes place, often with a pervading sense of stagnation and interpersonal impoverishment."[26] Every pastor has an abundance of case material before his eyes every Sunday morning.

The congregation has numerous members who have leveled off, their growth practically finished, for whom change is threat enough to arouse ire. Many have already "decided" on absentee membership as an unconscious cross-reference to the stunted life they are sensing. They have reinstitutionalized many of their defenses.

What they need is to be directed toward new goals. They need to set these goals and not the pastor, although she must orient the feeling-tone of the congregation and individual members toward a spirit of new adventure. The pastor has a

unique opportunity to become a Socratic mid-wife
in the birth of novelty although she does not
determine the novelty itself. Her pastoral
function is to lift up the divine Directivity in
such compelling ways that God might regain their
attention, re-capture the old appetition of
imaginative feelings, and lure them into new
adventures toward higher reaches of aesthetic
harmony. Perhaps, then, the illness that looms
so large in middle age can be addressed. Jung
has described the illness in terms of the theological virtues: ". . .it [illness] arises from his
[patient] having no love, but only sexuality; no
faith, because he is afraid to grope in the dark;
no hope, because he is disillusioned by the world
and by life; and no understanding, because he has
failed to read the meaning of his own existence."[27]
By the very words he uses, Jung would seem to be
teasing pastors out of mere maintenance operations
into imaginative efforts in caring and programming
to help their people transcend mid-life blahs.
The theoretical material in this chapter should
help to illumine the problem and point to ways to
care about the people with the problem.

A Process Contribution To Maslow

The conceptuality of this chapter appears to
be congenial to the thought of Maslow in his rich
concept of self-actualization.[28] His need theory,
which I find so suggestive, is pyramidal.
Beginning at the base with the physiological needs,
he moves upward through the safety needs, the love
needs, the esteem needs, to the climactic and
primarily human need for self-actualization.
These needs he finds to be instinctoid by which
he means that they are "in some sense, and to
some appreciable degree, constitutional or
hereditary in their determination."[29] Maslow
separates himself from much of the gross in
instinct theory, that is, from tying the human
being so close to animal instinct that there is
no instinct unique to the human species, e.g.,
reason.[30] Nevertheless, the picture Maslow

develops is the self innately constituted with
"human urges or basic needs"[31] each need normally
requiring some satiation before the next can be
realized. This suggests the image of a trajectory of need fulfillment powered by instinct. In
other words, potentiality is innately present and
needs but to be released for health. So he aligns
himself with Rogers, Fromm, and Horney, among
others, who see the role of the therapist to be
that of releasing the client to grow and develop
according to his intrinsic nature.[32] Without
wanting to negate the value in Maslow's creative
work, I must argue that his implied metaphysics is
the old Substance metaphysics in which there is an
underlying biological structure which has certain
needs intrinsic to itself. As such it is an
essence containing its own potential which, if not
unduly repressed and enjoying some satiation
throughout the hierarchy of needs, will develop
"in its own style."[33] This is humanistic
psychology yearning to see people fulfilled but
finding the seed of fulfillment in their
instinctual nature, the natural growth of which is
blocked only by unfulfilled needs. Maslow did
write just a month before he died about commingling
the "humanistic, the transpersonal, and the trans-
human."[34] In that Preface, as in his other
writings, is found the refreshing openness of
Maslow for whom any closure on theism (or any other
topic) would be intolerable. Yet we must
acknowledge that his is an avowedly humanistic
psychology, whereas pastoral care by definition
requires a divine Agency. The difference, which
is a difference of the first order, is that in
humanistic psychology potential is innate whereas
in process thought the potential to be realized
is not in the person as such but in the total
situation including God. It seems to me the
ontological structures of Whitehead can include
the constructive insights of Maslow and, I believe,
enrich them in at least two ways.

First, the carer operating within process
categories would see the client's struggle for

111

self-actualization to be innate to the process and
not to a set of instincts. If there were needs
unsatisfied in the past, these would be part of
the discord being experienced in the present.
Harsh parental expectations coupled with only
slight gestures of approval and affection might
well leave a client's safety, love, and esteem
needs hungering for fulfillment. As the pastoral
carer watches the young client bite his lip as he
haltingly tells of his present stress, she can
empathize with the strain under which the client
struggles to bring something better out of the
mix of his life. Perhaps through the role of
transference some belated satisfactions might fill
in the needs of safety, love and esteem. Then the
carer would become a new bit of reality evoking a
new set of feelings in the client. But the focus
is on the interior of the client, for that is
where the self-actualizing struggle is going on.
The struggle is ontological in nature; that is,
it is of the nature of actuality to struggle toward aesthetic harmony. Ontologically there is
an aim toward wholeness. It requires the rapt
attention and support of the pastor as a caring
person, for actuality is social through and
through and depends therefore upon interpersonal
relations that are qualitative in nature. What is
happening cannot be controlled, managed, or
determined from outside. Nor can its precise goal
be specified. It is enough that the carer understands that the client is involved in the
aesthetic project, however pale and meager, to
actualize himself into a new unity, hopefully with
increasingly harmonious results. That understanding should be very reassuring to every pastor.
The carer should be able to see in her mind's eye
an aim, or a series of aims, literally a flow of
aims, running through competing, contrasting
feelings; rejection, depression, anger, hurt,
love/hate, longing, sadness, sparks of enjoyed
remembrance, titilating moments of affection.
These feelings are tumbling over each other,
competing to be heard, to be felt, to become
"permanent" residual forms defining the experi-

encing client. The carer can know that there is
innate to the process a compelling feeling or subjective aim which is teleologically targeting on
bringing all the contrasting feelings together.
By virtue of process and by way of this compelling
aim the client is always becoming a new unity,
always actualizing himself into unities of dis-
cords or harmonies, where evil or good might be
descriptive terms, or more likely along the
spectrum from evil to good, disorder to harmony.
But the point for the carer is that there is the
client's "act of aiming" which plays the crucial
function of harmonizing feelings. The subjective
aim is an appetition toward unity, what Christian
has called "the immanent ground of final causation."[35] Thus the client is guided by his own
ideal by which he unifies his feelings and creates
himself. But the aim does not arise out of
instinct; it arises as a response to the past and
to God. The client's aiming, so generated, the
carer can count on. There are indications that
the client can train the strength of his aim so
that he can be more resolute in forming aesthetic
moments of larger, grander Beauty. For example,
Roberto Assagioli, the father of Psycho-synthesis,
has done a penetrating piece of work on the
phenomenology of the will and has supplied helpful
exercises to strengthen the will.[36] The carer,
assuming an act of aiming going on, can support
that act by non-verbal and sometimes verbal
encouragement.

But the carer cannot presume to know what the
goal is. It is exactly here that psychological
theory can be helpful and dangerous. Helpful
because it can generalize about depression, let
us say, and out of its generalized theory suggest
goals as directions for the carer trying to help
the depressed client. Dangerous because those
goals will undoubtedly miss the concreteness of
this particular client since no other experiencing
subject has ever been in his unique flow of experience within which he is creating himself.

Secondly, in process thought, as we have seen, the goal for each concrescence is a derived goal; that is, it is not spontaneously created by the experiencing subject. Many previous occasions, aiming beyond themselves, help to set the aim for the new occasion. Thus we have a continuity or pattern of aiming derived from the past. But it is the divine Agency, so massively present in the flow of time, who gives to the new occasion a brand new possibility and so the opportunity for a novel ordering of itself. God, too, has an eternal Aim for the creation, an Aim constant, steadfast, faithful, unwavering. That Aim I identify with Agape-love. The intention of God appears to be to fulfill that Aim of steadfast love by focusing upon each occasion a possibility undreamed of by that occasion, but one that fits precisely that occasion in its moment of becoming. God's eternal caring is to focus a relevant aim upon the birthing subject to lure that subject to aspire to become something intrinsically valuable, a thing of beauty, a novelty unprecedented, unexpected, unpredictable, in Paul's words, a fresh creation.

God always introduces a possibility that will transform that person by helping him or her to take aim on creating something new over against what is. God aims at transcending mere maintenance. God will be found at the point of risk-taking and adventure over against maintenance and sanctification of what exists. The divine Aim is constantly to widen the horizon and broaden the concerns of every person. The notion of self-transcendence must be underscored. God's vision is not tamely to lift up a present desire which might well be only a re-casting of past goals. God is helping to occur new potentialities for the person and not just the potentiality in the person, as Maslow imagined. God's vision is something beyond our present wants, needs, unconscious motivations. It is to help us change those wants, needs, desires, motivations, and so radically to help us transcend ourselves.[37] God's aim is that we be "transformed by the renewal of [our] minds."

114

(Rom. 12:2). Perhaps this is what the Psalmist knew viscerally when he poeticized of God: ". . . All you do is strange and wonderful." (Ps. 139:14).

The pastoral carer must be fundamentally willing to let the divine Activity have the dominant role within the client. This tests the level of trust the pastoral carer places in both God and the client. The alternative is for the pastor to determine the goal or goals for the client and so impede or obstruct the divine Activity and corrupt the client's aiming. There is required of the carer a sensitivity both to the divine leading and to the internal activity of the client so as not to intrude on the drama of Beauty in the process of forming.

Nevertheless, the carer must be concerned with goals. I think of these goals as dimensional: the ultimate goal, penultimate goals, and operational goals. The ultimate goal of pastoral caring is salvation. Daniel Day Williams has defined this in Tillichian terms to mean: the fulfilment of human beings "in a new relationship to God and. . . [their] neighbor in which the threats of death, of meaninglessness, of unrelieved guilt, are overcome. To be saved is to know that one's life belongs with God and has a fulfillment in him for eternity."[38] The penultimate goal must be apropos the presenting problem, or if that is a screen for another deeper problem, the real problem. The goals are to help the client to deal with his perceived problem by helping him to gain, or re- gain, functional autonomy within the welter of relationships that feed the person and issue from the person. Operational goals are the means for helping penultimate goals and/or the ultimate goal to be met, e.g., choice of therapeutic means, referral, meditative and other spiritual practices. It is possible that the carer will not get beyond the penultimate goals, rejecting the temptation to coerce toward the ultimate goal. Yet the pastoral carer, unlike other professionals, has the responsibility to work toward the goal of

salvation. Daniel Day Williams developed the
suggestive principle of "linkage" by which to move
from penultimate goals to the ultimate goal.[39]
Every part of human experience is linked with
every other part. Williams, a process theologian,
argued that there is linkage between therapy and
salvation: viz., between one struggling with
neurotic guilt and the beginnings of his wrestle
with God. The psychological material, as it is
worked through, can open up rich insight into the
meaning of God for human life, can lead to a new
relationship with the Divine, can bring Peace
unimagined at the outset of therapy. As Williams
concludes:

> From a Christian point of view, then,
> human needs must be met on two levels.
> There is the obvious insistent need of
> the body and the mind for that which
> sustains and nourishes. But the
> immediate problem may be the door
> through which we walk into the arena
> where ultimate questions are asked
> and answered. The search for therapy
> is transmuted into the quest for
> salvation.[40]

The carer does not pretend to know the
client's inner aims nor God's aims for the client.
Neither does the carer set specific goals for the
client nor do his aiming for him. Positively
the carer needs to be sensitive to her client's
inner aiming which is so full of pain and yet so
pregnant with possibility; and to encourage that
aiming to develop appropriate to itself and to
God who gives the direction and the impetus. If
we accept one of Whitehead's definitions of
religion as "what the individual does with his own
solitariness,"[41] by which Whitehead had in view
"the awful ultimate fact" of the soul as it
concresces toward its own aesthetic unity, we can
say the pastor's goal is finally to help that soul
to be fully religious. The art of pastoral caring,

then, is to assist the Adventure of life in the
direction of Beauty by helping the client to focus
on the Cosmic Adventurer. To the pastoral carer
these words of Hartshorne bear the essential vision
for the practice of her art:

> Let there be as much unity in contrast
> as possible, both within the new pattern
> and between it and the old patterns--
> so that the pattern of ongoing life
> shall be unified and diversified. . .
> This is the aesthetic imperative which
> the artist feels laid upon him by the
> scheme of things, and it is the voice
> of God as truly as any other impera-
> tive.[42]

NOTES

[1]Whitehead, AI, p. 241.

[2]Ibid., p. 267.

[3]Ibid., p. 266.

[4]Ibid., p. 264.

[5]Cf. Whitehead, SMW, p. 202.

[6]Sigmund Freud, Beyond the Pleasure Principle tr.
by James Strachey, (New York: Bantam, 1959),
p. 70; cf. Sigmund Freud, An Outline of Psychoanalysis tr. by James Strachey (New York: Norton,
1949), p. 20.

[7]Whitehead, PR, p. 427, cf. Whitehead, RM, p. 115.

[8]Whitehead, AI, p. 257.

[9]This point will be discussed in Chapter VII on
Evil.

[10]Ibid., p. 265, cf. PR, p. 359.

[11]Ibid., p. 264.

[12]Cobb, Natural Theology, p. 152.

[13]Cf. Ibid., p. 154.

[14]Whitehead, RM, p. 159.

[15]The concept and word is that of Cobb, Theology
and Pastoral Care, op. cit., pp. 46ff.

[16]Charles Hartshorne, Man's Vision of God (Chicago:
Willet, Clark, 1941), p. 244.

[17]Whitehead, RM, p. 99.

[18]Cf. Whitehead, _AI_, ch. XIX.

[19]Cf. Paul Tillich, _The Courage To Be_ (New Haven: Yale, 1952), p. 51.

[20]Bernard M. Loomer, "Notes on Beauty as a Design for Life," (unpublished paper).

[21]T. S. Eliot, "The Love Song of J. Alfred Prufrock," _The Complete Poems and Plays_ (New York: Harcourt, Brace, 1930).

[22]Erik H. Erikson, _Childhood and Society_, op. cit., p. 231; cf. Erik H. Erikson, _Identity and the Life Cycle_, Psychological Issues, Monograph 1, (New York: International University, 1959), p. 97.

[23]Cf. Daniel J. Levinson, _The Seasons of a Man's Life_, (New York: Knopf, 1979), ch. 14.

[24]Cf. Ernst Becker, _The Denial of Death_ (New York: Free Press, 1973), pp. 96, 97. Cf. Morton A. Lieberman, "New Insights into Crises of Aging," _The University of Chicago Magazine_ (July/August, 1973), p. 14.

[25]The book by Gail Sheeby, _Passages_ (New York: Bantam, 1977), deals in a popular style with these and other crises of the adult years.

[26]Erikson, _Identity_, p. 97.

[27]Jung, _Modern Man_, pp. 225-226.

[28]Abraham Maslow, _Motivation and Personality_ (New York: Harper, 1954), esp. chs. 5-8.

[29]_Ibid._, p. 136.

[30]_Ibid._, pp. 128, 132, 134.

[31] Ibid., p. 127. In his last book published post-humously, Maslow writes of these needs as being "biologically necessary" to "avoid illness" and to "achieve full humanness." Abraham H. Maslow, The Farther Reaches of Human Nature (New York: Viking, 1971), p. 316.

[32] Maslow, MP, p. 143.

[33] Ibid.

[34] Abraham H. Maslow, Religious Values, and Peak-Experiences (New York: Viking, 1964), p. XVII.

[35] William A. Christian, Interpretation, p. 302.

[36] Roberto Assagioli, The Act of Will (New York: Penguin, 1973). See also his Psychosynthesis.

[37] I am indebted to Prof. Cobb for sharing one evening his sense of the aims of God toward transcending any epoch.

[38] Danial Day Williams, The Minister and the Care of Souls (New York: Harper, 1961), p. 13.

[39] Ibid., pp. 26-29.

[40] Ibid., pp. 28, 29.

[41] Whitehead, RM, pp. 16, 47.

[42] Hartshorne, Man's Vision of God, p. 229.

It is more important that a proposition be inter-
esting than that it be true . . . [for its] primary function . . . is as a lure for feeling. . . .
                                Alfred North Whitehead

                    Chapter VI
     Pointers Toward the New: Lures for Feeling

     In the previous chapter I have urged that the
goal of all caring is to help one another create
instances of beauty which are instances of stretching toward intrinsic value. Such stretching is
occasioned by a richness of contrasts so deep and
wide that the experiencing person is constantly
being lured out of what was into what might be.
There is always some nudging of creative discon-
tent. At the center of this stretching is the
persistent aiming of the person, an aiming which
is never clear-cut and never statically targeted.
The aiming itself is in process, constantly modi-
fying itself as it feels contrasting lures which
beckon it.

     This chapter looks at some of these contrast-
ing lures which are calling us to adventure at
least into novelty and at best into moments of
novelty that are beautiful in their achievement.

     A grandmother shared with me a charming ex-
ample of a lure for feeling. She was caring for
her 2 1/2 year old granddaughter while the mother
was in the hospital having her second baby. The
granddaughter was obviously feeling the absence
of her mother and slight jealousy toward the one
taking her mother away. The grandmother cuddled
her in her arms in the rocking chair as she tried
to console her but with very marginal success.
Then she made what I consider a remarkable association: she told her the story of the Lost
Sheep. The little girl began to become quiet.
When the story was finished, she asked to have it
re-told again, and again, and again. Even after
the mother and the baby were home from the

hospital, and grandmother had gone home, she asked
her parents to tell her the story. Each time she
relaxed in the teller's arms. The grandmother
told me she knew her granddaughter had identified
with the Lost Sheep: sought out, found, cared
for. The story became the powerful lure toward
reassurance in her unsettled times around the
hospital experience.

A very rich Whiteheadian concept informs this
chapter, namely, the concept of propositions as
lures for feeling.[1] While I do not intend to get
into the intricacies of this concept, we do need
to understand what it is essentially getting at.

There are concrete actualities, the real
happenings in the world. Caesar did cross the
Rubicon. Jesus was a first century Jew. My
client this morning did cry. There are also pure
possibilities which are located in the eternal
nature of God. These are eternal potentials,
waiting to be grasped by an experiencing subject
putting itself together. Redness, pain, consciousness, hope are examples of these pure possibilities which tell no tales until they become in-
gressed in some actual occasion or better, in a
society of actual occasions, e.g., redness in a
Chrysler Imperial rose, or hope in a human soul.
But there is yet another kind of entity, propositions, which bring out of the vast realm of
potentiality a relevant grouping of possibilities
that beckon for actualization here and now.
Every person is aiming toward something new. But
the aiming is not toward undifferentiated potentiality. As Cobb points out, that would be demonic and destructive,[2] for such potentiality
would provide only a vague, general direction.
Aiming is guided by possibilities pried loose
from infinity and brought realizably close. What
pries them loose and brings them close is that
they are linked as predicates to a subject, that
is, to an actuality, whether simple or complex.
For example, a cancer patient writes (or speaks)
of his battle and of his victory. The words read

(or heard) by another cancer patient become a
lure for her. She is now the subject experiencing the possibility of hope in a very real and
challenging way. One cancer vanquished has the
meaning of hope for another. All about us are
possibilities which have become interwoven with
actuality. This hybrid formation becomes a lure
for feeling for the rising new occasion. Then
the new occasion's aiming or pointing or reaching
is guided toward, or by, that cluster of possibilities.

Whitehead calls attention to Hamlet's speech,
"To be, or not to be . . . ."[3] The speech is made
up of words, of course; but they are not words
forming sentences for the sake of being judged as
true or false. Their meaning is to be a lure for
feeling. They are thirty-five lines designed to
lure a theater audience toward aesthetic delight.
Whitehead also cites the illustration of a Christian meditating on a Gospel saying.[4] What that
believer is doing is to elicit the value of that
saying as an element in feeling. The Parable of
the Prodigal Son, couched in words, is a storied
proposition luring the reader to some attitude,
some act, some response that will be a new experience for him or her. The reader's aiming will
receive some direction from the possibilities
brought close to home by the primary functioning
of the story.

Life abounds in such lures for feeling as we
have been describing. Art-objects are images
whose primary function is to express concrete possibilities which might guide the aiming toward
novel realization. A natural setting, such as the
Glow-Worm Grotto in the Waitoma Caves in New Zea-
land, with myriad specks of light suspended above
illuminating the jutting rock and the calm water
below, might suggest a feeling to a tourist that
could issue in the ineffability of an Aha! experience. The turbulent waters of the gorge below might suggest to one looking over the bridge
rail the "What if" of suicide. But they might

also prompt that beholder to alter his carefully calculated vacation plans to include encampment beside those waters.

The primary meaning of any lure--statement, image, symbol, scene, etc.,--is to call forth feelings in an experiencing subject. The subject's own aiming is partially an imaginative response toward, and realization of, the possibilities which furnish the lure. These responses, which build upon God's aim given initially to the subject, help to guide one's way toward moments of new richness, even moments that are potentially transforming of life itself.

Some Important Lures for Pastoral Caring

In what follows I am suggesting four modes which can significantly serve as lures for feeling and which are appropriate to the ministry of caring. These modes are not exhaustive, of course, but they illustrate the value of pointing in the communicative context.

1. The first mode is the person of the carer. To this we shall relate Mead's notion of the Significant Other. This would also seem to be the context for a brief discussion of Transference which helps to constitute the Other as significant.

The carer herself provides lures for feeling by what she has actualized in her lifetime. Out of her subjective struggling she has defined who she is at any given moment of time. What she is, she is for the other, in our case, the client. What she is is a new objective fact in the world of the other to be experienced by the other. Through the process of becoming she achieves momentarily a complex unity of selfhood. That is her self-definition for this instant. In her selfhood she becomes a lure for feeling which the client will entertain as a feeling, perhaps of

124

wistfulness or strength or hope, or disappointment.
The carer may point to the possibility of quiet
strength. Quiet strength is always a possibility.
But in her it has become realized and is available
as an inspiration to the client. Perhaps the
client has always wished for a quiet strength
which he owned, but that seemed so impossible for
him. Now the carer is being experienced by way of
her quiet strength. "It is possible . . . perhaps
even for me," might be the prompting felt by the
client. What was abstract now becomes much more
real as a possibility thanks to the carer's mode
of being. In the concreteness of the carer's own
person, she points by way of what she is to an
alternative that might lure the client toward what
he may yet become. Her meaning for him, then, is
that she is the catalyst for his feeling toward a
possibility that is now real for him.

In Eugene O'Neill's Long Day's Journey into
Night there is a classic example of propositional
lure and a propositional feeling. It is that
pathos-filled scene after midnight when the two
brothers, Jamie, the older, and Edmund, are drunk.
His tongue loosened, Jamie inquires about his
mother:

"Where's the hophead? Gone to sleep?" Edmund strikes him a blow off the cheekbone in a
burst of rage. Then apologizes: "I'm sorry I
hit you. . . ." Jamie responds huskily: "It's
all right. Glad you did. My dirty tongue. Like
to cut it out. I suppose it's because I feel so
damned sunk. Because this time Mama had me fooled.
I really believe she had it licked. She thinks I
always believe the worst, but this time I believed
the best. I suppose I can't forgive her--yet. It
meant so much. I'd begun to hope, if she'd beaten
the game, I could, too."5 (Underlining mine).

In this example the older son, wanting so
badly for mother to be cured that he might have
new hope for himself, believed she was cured. The
mother provided the appearance for the belief but

125

not the reality. She had become a lure for Hope. His anger was his response to a lure that had only appearance but not reality. She was not what she seemed. The feeling of Hope, stirred by the lure of mother's seeming achievement, was dashed. The contrasting feelings issued in a subjective form of despondency. What might have been! Jamie felt the pull of Hope, made real by the alleged achievement of his mother. Despair was the form of anger when Hope was dashed.

Fundamentally, I see the carer as a pointer to a new alternative, hopefully not a deceptive pointer. The person as pointer is profounder than any word that person utters. For the person is the incarnation of meaning to which his words at best are symbols once removed from the reality. Carl Rogers has articulated this in these words: "If one wishes to give . . . real meaning he should put his hand over his mouth and point."[6] I am suggesting that every person is pointing out of his or her reality toward a new possibility for another. This would seem to apply with obvious significance to any therapist; but to a pastoral carer, because of her office and her professional identity, it may apply awesomely. If she rejects this burden, whether for theological or psychological reasons, the client may nevertheless invest her with it out of his expectations of who and what clergy are.

The dangers involved in a pastoral carer being such a significant other are immense and the temptations no less so. It would be easy for both pastor and client to look upon the carer as an example, especially a moral example, given the traditional Christian emphasis upon morality as of the essence of piety. It should be clear from the previous chapter that this would not be true to process thought nor, to my mind, to the best in Christian thought. Emerson has pithily made the point: "You know and I know that one of you is enough." It would also be an easy move for either carer or client to think of the person as an

example in terms of medieval piety or spirituality. I picture this in a series of emanations:
Jesus in the image of God; the pastor as a superior follower in the image of Jesus; and the
second-class Christian lay person following the
pastor who is following Jesus who is following
God. But the Imitatio Christi model of spirituality even in its most sophisticated form as in
Thomas a Kempis, The Imitation of Christ, seems
inappropriate theologically and unsound ontologically for it misses the uniqueness of each
concretion: Jesus' as well as ours. This model
so easily develops into a Jesus cult, makes his
vocation ours, and overlooks and overrides our
own unique locations in our world in our time.
Professor Edward Farley has analyzed this model
with his usual acuity.[7]

In the process conceptuality we are employing the carer is neither example nor model to
follow. Rather, she points beyond herself but by
way of herself to new possibilities which the
client will feel and to which he must respond.
The pastor is not a stained-glass saint to be
emulated but a fellow-traveler who is in the process of a peculiar formation called "disciple."
Her aiming is hopefully fixed on God as exemplified in the "classical instance" called Jesus
Christ. Her own formation is shaped in the struggle of her own becoming. Without doubt this
places a burden on the carer to struggle to be
shaped by the richness of her religio-theological
tradition, including those devotional exercises
and experiences which will aid her to be more
alert to God's Presence and so to make her aiming
more congruent with God's Aiming.

The paradigm of the pastoral carer which has
been so meaningful to me is Johann von Staupitz
who got Luther settled in a chair of theology in
the Wittenberg University. But Staupitz was more
than the settler of Luther's professional vocation. Roland H. Bainton traces how Luther came
to a new view of Christ and a new view of God,

127

and in that order. In the quiet of his study in the Augustinian monastery at Wittenberg, Luther came to see that Christ is not only the judge "sitting on the rainbow" but the Christ so identi- fied with humanity that he becomes "the derelict upon the cross." This view of Christ opens up a different vision of God for Luther: not only the hated God of wrath but also the all-merciful God of love. Luther came to see that this God is benevolently bent on the human's salvation.[8]

Behind this discovery is the person, Staupitz. Erik Erikson traces the influence in his <u>Young Man Luther</u>. Young Martin had suffered a very strenu- ous discipline in his childhood home. Arthur C. McGiffert in his <u>Martin Luther</u> helps document that discipline by quoting Luther: "Where such fear enters a man in childhood, it can hardly be rooted out again as long as he lives. As he once trem- bled at every word of his father and mother, to the end of his life he is afraid of a rustling leaf."[9] Continues McGiffert: ". . . driven by the harsh discipline of his early life to see God only in the aspect of a stern judge, Luther had hitherto been altogether blind to it [the comfort that God was merciful]. Gradually, under Stau- pitz's tutelage, his eyes were opened, and a new gospel dawned upon his gaze."[10]

Erikson provides the psychological bridge from the hated God, after the image of his feared- hated-loved father, Hans, to a new vision of God as benevolent, merciful, and loving. Staupitz became a new father to Luther as Luther acknowl- edged. Luther called him "father in the evan- gelium." Erikson finds in Staupitz the father- figure who struck the "long lost note of infant trust," giving "retroactive sanction to the effi- cacy of maternal trust. . . ."[11] There is no doubt, as Erikson points out, that Luther's feel- ings for Staupitz were ambivalent. But what is crucial for the paradigm is that Staupitz in his person was the bridge to a new view of Christ and then of God. Staupitz by his fatherly being and concern as well as his words seems to have provided the new possibility for a vision of God. As Erikson says: ". . . Luther always and ever referred to him [Staupitz] as the 'father' of these two ideas: that faith comes first; and that we can face God's son and look at him as a man."[12] Staupitz, as pastoral carer to the young Martin, was the lure pointing to a softer image of father or parent, and so to a relieved perspective on God. Martin followed the pointing far beyond Staupitz, but the pointing was crucial to a new vision. In this sense the pastor's being is a lure toward new possibilities.

Of course, everyone provides lures for feeling. Yet, there are what George Herbert Mead has called Significant Others. These include parents, teachers, neighbors, etc., and for some, pastors. When through empathy a carer locates herself in the "perceptual world" of the other, an experience so foreign to most human encounters, the client almost inevitably raises the carer to the status of Significant Other. When the client transfers feelings out of the unconscious, feelings, for example, that are a part of childhood conformal patterns, transferring them to the person of the carer, such transference tends to endow the carer with a projected aura of significance. The carer is projected as mother, father, lover, sibling, best friend, enemy, etc. Gathered in the transference are the feeling-tones appropriate to needs, desires, aims of other times; they color the carer with the tonality from "vaguer presences in the past."[13] This coloration focuses hopes, both reasonable and unreasonable, and fears, trust and mistrust, love and hate so that the carer is rarely seen for what she really is. Pastors, along with medical doctors, are especially vulnerable to such miscasting. Small wonder that disappointments on the part of clients are so common and anger so near at hand.

Transference, the phenomenon identified by Freud as essential to therapy and further explicated

by psychoanalytic thinkers,[14] can be given ontological status in process thought. Transference
is the projection of feelings, out of the past of
childhood on to a contemporary, e.g., a pastoral
carer. Every client visits the present with
freighted meaning out of his past. He may trans-
fer to the carer seated before him the love he
always wanted and never felt he had. Out of his
past he imposes meaning, probably extremely in-
accurate, on the carer.[15] Thus, the carer is
perceived by the client in terms of needs and
wishes arising out of the client's history. The
projected perception clothes the carer with the
client's set of feelings and so skews reality.
The projections on the part of the client create
much mischief since the resulting expectations
are so unrealistic. On the other hand, such projections help to underscore the important role of
the carer. A pastoral carer is bequeathed the
role of Significant Other and so is bequeathed
the power to be effective; that is, to become a
lure for feelings that points beyond herself to
possibilities scarcely dreamed of by the client.
The client is cautiously but wantingly open to
the carer the reality of whose life might point
to new beginnings. The client might feel the lure
of that life and aim toward possibilities that not
even that life has dreamed of.

Part of the task of the carer is to help the
client to understand and correct his transference.
The role of the pastoral carer is to accept the
meanings imputed to her, to lift them up for the
client to see, that is, to analyze, and gradually
to help the client to understand that he is skewing much of the present by making inappropriate
references to it out of the past. For example,
if he is conformally involved in oedipal feelings
toward his mother and if he has made of the pastoral carer a substitute mother-lover, he has projected on to her feelings appropriate to other
times but inappropriate now. If he can work on
his present projected perceptions of the carer,
perhaps he can go back in memory and uncover the

earlier feeling-tones with which he has been coloring the present. The carer thus helps the client to go back and forth between present symbol (carer) and past meaning (childhood conformal feelings).

Supporting this way of handling the transference phenomenon is the role of the carer as a Significant Other. She is laden with emotionality projected by the client. Imperceptibly, however, her role changes as she continues to lift the transference into the light of day. In the beginning he prehends her as mother and perhaps as oedipal lover, with all the unsatiated needs fueling his erroneous perception. Gradually he comes to have differing propositional feelings as together he and she lift up what he has been doing and how he has been skewing the present. Hopefully he can then follow more realistically in the direction of her pointing. He now more accurately perceives her as she is. Now he is learning to deal with every present more realistically. Her pointing now gives him permission and encouragement to aim toward a freed future and to follow his new aiming to create that strength of beauty in his own being that God's steadfast aiming has been envisioning for him. The carer as Significant Other and so a significant lure, may be the Socratic mid-wife in the providence of God to help the client toward new birth.[16] God employs such potentially powerful human lures, especially those of an I-Thou richness, to re-direct the aiming of the client so that he might escape from bondage into a more authentic unity of selfhood. In a carer-client relationship we can suppose that God entertains the carer's pointing and the client's appetition for the new goal suggested by the pointing. Thus God can make the transference material serve the divine aim.[17] God, enmeshed in the social nature of reality, relates client and carer that a richer synthesis of patterned contrasts might result in a new strength of beauty for the client, and by way of Transformation, for the carer.

131

2. A second mode by which propositional lures take place is the Gesture, and especially the gesture of significant others. The brilliant work of George Herbert Mead analyzes the importance of gestures. First, let us turn to the bodily gesture, with special attention to the face. Gesture is a social act for it elicits response.[18] In the "conversation of gestures," an individual responds to a facial gesture, a frown, let us say, which may be an unconscious communication, responding with fear. The one frowning, in turn, will respond to any bodily indication of fear, e.g., tensing up or moving back in the chair. Sociality is taking place and therefore the gesture is significant.[19] Non-verbal gestures serve as propositional lures to which we respond fearfully, happily, anxiously, coquettishly, etc. While such gestures are powerful for us all, they are especially so for the young and those already burdened by anxiety, doubt, perplexity, etc. Our gestures are deeply characteristic of us. Our body language is expressive of who we really are. Therefore, the carer needs to be sensitive to the responses of the client in order to understand the meaning of the social act which has taken place in response to gestures. It is incumbent on the carer to try to ascertain what she might have initiated. Mead has shown how significant gestures, especially those of significant others, are creative of the me to which the I reacts.[20] The me is a social "me," that is, the attitude of others constitute the "me"; or as I would prefer in process terms, the I constitutes the "me" out of a multitude of prehensions of community attitudes toward me. The "me" is the object of each concrescence, the unity I've achieved. The non-verbal gesture is a powerful factor forming that "me." The repetitive frowning of a parent helps to lure the "I" into a frown-ful feeling about "me," so that "I" might develop a residual feeling of rejection. The carer's cloudy visage can re-enforce that residual feeling, or an approving look point toward a new alternative. Bodily gestures contribute to the process of creativity as the concrescing subject feels the lure of those gestures.

Language, vocalized or written, is the most accustomed mode of suggesting propositions. George Herbert Mead argues: "The vocal gesture . . . has an importance which no other gesture has."[21] One cannot see his own facial gestures except in a mirror, but we hear ourselves speak and we not only hear the words but the tone as well if we are alert. This is important for both carer and client. When the client speaks, especially to an accepting carer, those words will arouse in him certain tendencies toward feelings, attitudes, actions. Thus his own uttered sentence becomes a lure. When the carer speaks, especially in well aimed words that may become compelling, they often lure into a follow-up of silence which the sensitive carer will encourage by her own silence. The significance of silence lies in part in the propositional feeling grasping the lure resident in the linguistic gesture. This is one reason why interpretations should be carefully timed, tentatively and briefly offered, and sparingly used. We can ground Mead's psychological insight on an ontological basis: the propositional role. Nothing in the caring situation replaces the vocalized propositional structure. The statement may be in the form of a question asked to provoke the client to reflect more deeply or to reach into the near future to grasp a new option. It may be in the form of a _tentative_ interpretation, viz: "Does it seem to you that you feel anger toward people in authority?" Or it may be to give permission; viz: "I could imagine that you felt that very angrily." But most of the therapeutic conversation encourages the client to articulate his feelings, to get them out through language to look at them. Thus he objectifies his feelings and the very objectification might become a lure for new feeling as he muses within himself: "Hmm, I said it. I said I was angry and she [carer] didn't jump down my throat. Maybe I don't need to feel so afraid." Most often it is the vocalization of the client, though sometimes the articulated thought of the carer, but in both cases the proposition sets before the client a lure if ever so slight toward a novel prehension.

133

To illustrate the power of the right word at the right time let us return to Staupitz and the young Martin Luther and see that relationship through the eyes of Erikson. We recall that Staupitz had become for Martin a father-figure, the benevolent, loving, gently confronting father Martin had not known. Erikson writes of Staupitz as being the "right man . . . in the right moment to support the total counterswing and the radical reversals inherent in Martin's budding thoughts. . . . Staupitz evoked enough trust so that Martin was able to experiment with ideas like those he was soon to find deep in himself. This is the therapeutic leverage: the therapist knows how to say that particular right thing which, given favorable circumstances and the condition of the patient's needy openness, strikes a deep note--in Martin's case, undoubtedly, the long lost note of infant trust. . . ."[22] It was in the context of the deep relationship built up between Staupitz and Martin that Martin heard numerous statements from Staupitz that served as lures pulling him toward new possibilities. A memorable one which Luther later talked about around the dinner table was Staupitz's admonition: "One must keep one's eyes fixed on that man who is called Christ."[23] Erikson's comment: ". . . [Staupitz] happened to say it at the right time and in the right place, perhaps under that pear tree in whose shade he gave Martin his first feeling in a long, long time of a benevolent paternal presence. This remark meant to Martin that he should stop doubting and start looking, use his senses and his judgment, grasp Christ as a male person like himself, and identify with the man in God's son instead of being terrorized by a name, an image, a halo."[24] This is an instance of a propositional lure at such a ripe time, what Tillich called the kairotic moment, that it contributed to the birthing of a new age. An appropriate vocal gesture helped to lure a struggling human being into a novel prehension of such importance that it has been a major effect in all subsequent western history.

134

3. Dreams, both sleep-dreams and awake-
dreams, or images, are propositional feelings.
This means that dreams do tell us much about our
aiming, for dreams are part of the content of our
aims. Freud may have overstated the case in his
identification of dreams with our secret wishes
which get by the censor; but there are dreams
which express hidden wishes which are hidden aims.
But dreams may also be warnings of danger, re-
vealers of conflict, indicators of compensation
as when we dream idealistically of one we under-
value, etc., as Jung has taught us. A client of
mine dreamed of dancing in a circle of people
with arms interlocked. She was joyous in her
dream, which revealed to her, her need of, her wish
for, her aiming toward, a support community.
Dreams, when utilized therapeutically, help to
objectify what aims are going on within the concrescence. Furthermore, when the carer helps the
client to tease out of dreams or images his
feeling-tones and perhaps meanings, she inevitably
provides by her pressing questions and statements
lures to attract the client toward new reaches of
insight. Then new syntheses are possible along
the route of one's becoming. Freud's understanding of dreams as the "royal road to the unconscious," a position fully accepted by Jung, though
his understanding of the unconscious was so different, might encourage the carer to travel that
road providing she follows the fellow-traveler,
the client. The concrescence is so plastic, God's
aiming so massive, propositional lures so powerful,
the subjective aim so educable that the client can
be trusted to lead the way through the imagery of
his weaving. The carer's role is to be a prompter
in the wings so that the richness locked up in the
image can literally speak itself out into the open.
As revelations come they in turn become propositions inciting further manifestations. Because
the carer is not in the precise stream of the
client, though her stream and his intersect, pastoral carers ought not to venture to interpret
dreams. But their interpretation is not needed.
The client can be trusted, with some prompting,

135

to explore his imagery-feelings. As he explores
those feelings new subjective forms can begin to
supplant old ones. A processive new birth is taking place.

For example: a young male client imagines a
horse grazing in a pastoral setting; trees on the
edges of the pasture are alive with singing birds;
the "feel" of the scene is one of contentment; and
yet on the edge, just out of sight, a large cat
is ready to pounce at the back of the neck of the
horse. This image, devoid of intricate detail,
begins to evidence itself in anxious twists as the
words describe it. The carer helps the young man
to stay with the image, to probe the imagery to
feel what the imagery is saying to him. Finally,
the young man with the trace of a smile and a sag-
ging posture, suggests its meaning: "The story
of my life: everything seemingly good but always
the threat, not quite in the picture, never overtly
attacking, but always the threat. . . ." Then he
drew the identification with his father, an identification Freud would have termed superego, and he
felt anger toward the internalized, threatening
father. The client worked on his feelings, full
of contrasts as the imagery was full of contrasts,
canalizing them and widening them. The carer's
task was to be a guide,[25] that is, to assist the
process of teasing out sub-images and thicker
feeling-tones which, when expressed, became lures
for further feeling, lures that were appetitive
toward release and toward a revised ordering of
inner harmonies.

4. Art, both as created by the client and as
offered to the client, is also a propositional
mode. I have in mind painting, sculpturing, music,
poetry, psycho-drama (including role-playing), and
the several possibilities open to children's play.
Art in itself and in its technical usage is a
powerful propositional lure and fits so readily
the ultimate valuational concern of Whitehead,
aesthetics.

An illustration of a powerful art-form for
caring is poetry and the novel, for as Wellek and
Warren conclude in their Theory of Literature, a
poem is "only a potential cause of experiences."26
The same would hold true for the novel. These two
art-forms, when judiciously utilized, can lure the
moving self to take up into itself sullen despair
or cold loneliness and transform these forms into
forms that bear a different coloration and a different stature. Emily Dickinson's poems are her
own redemptive aiming toward such creativity and
they can afford gradations of redemptive meaning
for her readers. Every carer should have a list
of great moments in literature which she can share
with the client, whether as "homework" between
counseling sessions or within the session itself,
or to be left with the client when the pastor concludes her visit. The Psalms, carefully selected,
in some cases with just a few lines pinpointed,
are powerful lures in their own right, but also
because of expectations projected on to them.
Some Psalms I have found valuable include 8:3-9;
16:1, 2, 5-11; 42; 51:1-17; 103; 139:1-18, 23-24.
Other Scriptures are also valuable, of course, such
as Rom. 8:31-39, and each pastor will have her
favorites which have prompted her. Timing and
relevance are the two basic criteria in suggesting
such readings. Significant poetry and novels have
possibilities for lure as well. T. S. Eliot's
"The Love Song of J. Alfred Prufrock," requiring
a sophisticated client, or his "The Cocktail
Party," are potentially powerful for the client
stuck in the Mid-Life doldroms. W. H. Auden's
"For the Time Being" (A Christmas Oratorio) is
useful, especially in a group setting, during the
Christmas seson with its pain of loneliness,
grief, and seasonal weariness. Robert Frost's
nature poems have the quieting, centering effect
so salutary to people whose inner motors are rac-
ing in neutral. Plays, such as those of Eugene
O'Neill, and novels by such master readers of the
human situation as James Baldwin, Albert Camus,
and Saul Bellow are powerful orienters to reality
and help to lift a person into a larger world.

A carer's list will be somewhat idiosyncratic.
Providing the literature is worthy of shaping a
person's intellectual character, the possibility
is large that what has found a response in the
carer will likely find one in the client, for
through the caring relationship something of a
common world is created.

Worship, especially corporate worship which
I regard as a potential art-form, is packed with
imagery that can lure. In fact, when worship is
reduced to rationality it loses its life, for its
esse is to draw the worshipper wholistically into
the presence of the Divine. Within that presence
new power can be gained to face chronic emotional
distress and stressful situations. Worship, so
seen, is preventive therapy as well as supportive
therapy. But much worship fails to be a lure for
feelings for a number of reasons: it is often
too singly cognitive in focus, too unimaginative,
too repetitive or conformal; it may lack transcendence which lures with the sense of awe, or
immanence, which lures with the sense of presence,
or sensuality, which lures with the sense of
warmth; it may lull into drowsiness by dullness
and/or incapacity on the part of the leaders; and
it may be denuded of expectation, which may be the
final vulgarity. I have assigned as homework for
some clients attendance at corporate worship
within carefully selected situations. The results
have been faithful to the theory of propositions
set forth by Whitehead. In my judgment pastors
could do an important service to their people by
reassessing worship within the guidelines of propositional theory.

Whitehead has written, "A proposition is . . .
a supposition about things."[27] As a supposition
its suggestiveness opens upon the future. The
future for so many clients has blinds pulled down
over it. Whatever can bring real possibilities
nearer home can help to raise the blinds and let
the future in.

138

NOTES

[1] For those interested in pursuing this concept the following will be helpful: PR, Part III, Ch. 4; Dean, Coming To, op. cit., Ch. 3; Christian, Whitehead's Metaphysics, pp. 315ff; William A. Beardslee, A House for Hope (Philadelphia: Westminster, 1972), Ch. VIII; John B. Cobb, Jr., Christ in a Pluralistic Age (Philadelphia: Westminster, 1975), Ch. 3; Lewis S. Ford, The Lure of God (Philadelphia: Fortress, 1978), pp. 65, 66.

[2] Christ, p. 74.

[3] PR, p. 281.

[4] Ibid.

[5] Eugene O'Neill, Long Day's Journey into Night. (New Haven: Yale, 1956), pp. 161-62.

[6] Carl R. Rogers, Client-Centered Therapy, p. ix.

[7] Edward Farley, Requiem for a Lost Piety (Philadelphia: Westminster, 1966) Ch. 2.

[8] Cf. Roland H. Bainton, Here I Stand (New York: Abingdon, 1959), pp. 54-67.

[9] Arthur C. McGiffert, Martin Luther (New York: Century, 1910), p. 8.

[10] Ibid., p. 31.

[11] Erik H. Erikson, Young Man Luther (New York: Norton, 1958), p. 168.

[12] Ibid., p. 169.

[13] PR, p. 271.

[14] See Sigmund Freud, Introductory Lectures on Psychoanalysis (New York: Norton, 1977), tr. James Strachey, Ch. XXVII; Clara Thompson (ed.), An Outline of Psychoanalysis (New York: Modern Library 1955), Chs. 28-32; C. G. Jung, Collected Works (London: Routledge, Kegan Paul, 1964), IV, Ch. 8 and C. G. Jung, Collected Works (London: Routledge, Kegan Paul, 1954) Part II, 3; Karl A. Menninger & Philip S. Holzman, Theory of Psychoanalytic Technique, (second ed.) (New York: Basic Books, 1973), Ch. IV.

[15] The background is Whitehead's suggestive concept of Symbolic Reference. See Alfred North Whitehead, Symbolism: Its Meaning and Effect (New York: Capricorn, 1959), pp. 8, 18 and passim; Also PR, Ch. VIII.

[16] Cf. William D. Dean, Coming To (Philadelphia: Westminster, 1972), pp. 112ff.

[17] Cf. Cobb, Natural Theology, pp. 156-57.

[18] George H. Mead, Mind, Self & Society (Chicago: University of Chicago, 1934), p. 80.

[19] Ibid., p. 81.

[20] Ibid., pp. 173-78.

[21] Ibid., p. 65.

[22] Erikson, Luther, pp. 167-68.

[23] Theodore G. Lappert (tr. & ed.) Table Talk Luther's Works (Philadelphia: Fortress, 1967), Vol. 54, no. 526, Cf. Erikson, Luther, p. 168.

[24] Luther, p. 168.

[25] The concept of Guide is that of Martha Compton, An Historical Survey of Mental Imagery Techniques in Psychotherapy and Description of the

Dialogic Method, rev. ed. (Montreal: Canadian
Institute of Psychosynthesis, 1977), p. 29.
This is an exceedingly helpful manual on the
use of Imagery. Also see Assagioli, Psychosynthesis, op. cit., Part II.

[26]As quoted by Donald W. Sherburne, A Whiteheadian Aesthetic (Hamden: Anchon, 1970),
p. 99.

[27]Whitehead, Al., p. 244.

Mankind carries the burden of guilt and the anxiety of dying in a humanity misshapen and bewildered by its own creations.

Daniel Day Williams
<u>The Spirit and the Forms of Love</u>

Chapter VII

Doing It Evilly: Fateful Decisions

Pastoral care, especially in its more limited expression as pastoral counseling, has been side-stepping the issue of evil for a long time. Even in its more traditional expressions, for example, around a terminal illness or a grief-situation, pastoral care has too often been tongue-tied or forked-tongue when confronted with evil. In either case pastoral care fails to deal with what Jung calls the shadow-side of human experience. It fails the basic human need for meaning when it does not lift up the experience of evil into the light of interpretation. It trivializes the richness of salvation when it circumvents the evil from which we are saved.

The reasons why pastoral care has skirted the problem of evil are several and important. For one thing, the form of pastoral care known as pastoral counseling has taken its direction from several psychologies as we noted at the beginning of Chapter III. That direction has led pastoral counseling away from strong theological concerns about God[1] and about evil. The various psychologies have notions about evil but evil in terms of mental or emotional disordering. For example, for Freud evil would be those imprisoning fixations around which the repressed Self rotates, thus impeding, distorting, and finally preventing the Self from a nice balance of appropriate instinctual gratifications and rational endeavor.[2] For Jung evil consists of the shadow-side of the Self, which is the "dark half of the personality,"[3] the irrational, negative side, when the Shadow is not taken up into the individuating Self. For

143

Maslow, evil is the failure of the instinctoid hierarchical needs to be satiated so that the apex-need, self-actualization, can take place. Gestalt psychology would equate evil with being locked out of the present, i.e., blaming the past or wishing for the future, locked into a static position, and with self-contempt because the self does not seem to be intrinsically valuable. Finally, Assagioli, who has so much in common with Maslow, would go beyond self-actualization to self-realization, which is the "experience and awareness of the syn-thesizing spiritual Center."[4] Then evil would be that which prohibits realization of one's true Self, i.e., domination by "subpersonalities" and failure to use the will creatively.[5]

None of these psychologies views evil in any metaphysical or theological way. This should not be surprising for they are horizontal or humanistic psychologies for which the ultimate good is the Self variously interpreted. Therefore, that which contradicts or defrauds the Self is evil. From the viewpoint of Christian theology, ostensibly a primary datum for pastoral care, all of these un-derstandings of evil, while suggestive and prag-matically helpful, are inadequate. Yet since these psychologies have largely shaped pastoral counseling, their views of evil have almost to-tally informed that discipline. Pastoral coun-seling, so informed, has thus been truncated by its very patterning. Its perspective on evil has been watered down vitiating its own history and theology. Karl Menninger has put the problem forthrightly: "Disease and treatment have been the watchwords of the day and little is said about selfishness or guilt or the 'morality gap.' And certainly no one talks about sin!"[6] Menninger intentionally points his finger directly at the clergy.[7]

No pastoral counselor worthy of his salt is going to lay guilt trips on his client and he will be wary about drawing causal connections between sin and sickness. Fortunately, Job's "friends" are not in modern day pastoral counseling settings. That need not mean, however, and should not mean, that evil plays no role in pastoral counseling. We shall return to this later.

Pastoral caring which is generic to pastoral counseling, and which has been much less informed by psychological data, has also the strange modern practice of ignoring sin and evil or misusing it. It misuses it when it surrenders too easily to the tendency to draw causal connections, when it apes the "friends" of Job, when, in the fancied service of evangelism or new birth/conversion tactics, it feels a compulsion to make the foil of evil so powerful that grace will appear more amazing. But probably pastoral care more often ignores evil, or talks around it, as though embarrassed by it or not knowing what to do with it. In this case the fundamental problem seems to lie not so much with the problem of evil as with the problem of God vis-a-vis evil.

Pastoral caring situations are constantly faced with the problem of evil. For example, a scaffolding collapses in St. Marys, West Virginia, hurtling 51 men to their deaths 160 feet below. A grief stricken woman interviewed on national television said, "I guess it was supposed to happen." Her statement might be taken as referring to the event as fated, whether by the Furies or a demonic and diabolical Force, or as predestined by God. How does the pastor deal caringly with that woman whose small theology includes an all-powerful God who is ultimately responsible for every event and who is also perfect in goodness, the consequence of which is that whatever happens must be accepted because it happens according to God's inscrutable will. She would have enormous difficulty in expressing her anger or even acknowledging it. She would tend to suppress and finally repress her grief. She could scarcely find a ministration of merciful comfort from a Presence who had just destroyed her world. Yet she would have to live with that God and she would undoubtedly

145

compartmentalize her religious affections by abstracting God from the daily commerce and repressing her negative feelings and questions. Her life would then be the more impoverished because she would have no way to take up the ambiguities of human existence into her theology and finally into her individuating self. In all likelihood at least a low-grade depressive emotional tone would pervade her being and color blue her relevant and long-term future. Much pastoral care, embracing that woman's theology, would be of little help in guiding her toward a different interpretation. So pastoral caring, even when it is not pastoral counseling, has a tendency to sidestep the problem of evil, preferring the pious dodge of leaving it enshrouded in "mystery," which is often a religious form of obfuscation.

At this point we need to draw some distinctions among the forms of evil. There is natural or physical evil which involves suffering, e.g., earthquakes that kill, cancers, floods that ravage. There is moral evil or sin. Whether this type of evil be interpreted as the misuse of rational freedom or as a willful intention, it is the evil humans cause whether to themselves, e.g., overindulgence, to others, e.g., scaffolds that fall hurtling 51 men to their deaths, to the rest of creation, e.g., uncontrolled strip-mining. A further distinction is that between intrinsic evil and instrumental evil. The former, termed by David Griffin "genuine evil," is "anything, all things considered, without which the universe would have been better."[8] I should think rape would be intrinsic evil. Instrumental evil, on the other hand, points to the actual effects of an act, say, a well-intentioned act, as when a mother, through ignorance, over-protects her child. She may become instrumental in her son's excessive dependency.

Our concern in this chapter is to lift up certain aspects of evil with which pastoral caring is most engaged. Since pastoral caring is our foremost concern, we will need to view evil from some ultimate perspective, that is ontologically and theologically, to see it for what it is as nuclear to the human condition (and not simply as descriptive of mental or emotional illness). Consequently, we shall be primarily concerned with that form of evil called sin, and with instrumental evil, whether from good intentions or bad.

Human evil is identified as sin because of its standing <u>before God</u> or in the <u>presence of God</u>. Walter Grundmann argues that "every individual sin committed by and against men acquires its significance before God and has before Him the character of guilt."[9] Paul Ricoeur says bluntly, "The category that dominates the notion of sin is the category of 'before' God."[10] If sin receives its definition "before God," then pastoral care requires that it articulate its notion of sin or moral evil and its notion of God so that the latter informs the former. Pastoral caring in its more customary practice must come to grips not only with evil and the variegated roles it plays in life's crises as well as normal living; it must also look again at the final Referent against which sin postures itself. And pastoral counseling, to be true to its theological ancestry, must develop a language about evil that points to a reality beyond the merely humanistic, one that draws the differentiation between mental disorder and human evil. The history of pastoral care, including real guilt, sin, confession, penance, absolution, requires that differentiation even though significant relations between the two exist.[11]

In the next section we shall examine a process conceptuality of evil that appears to fit the phases of concrescence and the secular vision of God we have described and that can be utilized with integrity by pastoral caring generally or pastoral counseling particularly.

Statement of the Problem in Process Terms

Good and evil are dialectically related. As
we have already seen in Chapter V the highest good
for Whitehead is Beauty. The goodness of Beauty
is that an actual occasion enjoys in its actualizing of itself the richest variation of contrasts
possible, which is the breadth of Beauty; the most
intense feelings canalized into depth, which is
the profundity of Beauty; and these contrasting
and intensive feelings integrated into a harmony
of subjective form. Peace is the culminating
benedictory feeling, the glow of the beauty experienced. Intrinsic goodness, conceived in its
highest form as Beauty, is not mere moral goodness,
though it includes morality (where relevant); nor
is it mere true statements, though it includes
truth; nor is it mere sensory experience, though
it may include the sensual. Intrinsic goodness is
Beauty achieved in the harmonized self out of multiple contrasts intensely felt.

Evil is to be seen over against this understanding of the good. David R. Griffin has provided a rich analysis of evil.[12] Following
Whitehead, Griffin sets two dimensions of evil
over against two dimensions of good. Good is intrinsic good when it is characterized by beauty
which fulfills the aesthetic criteria of harmony
and intensity. Evil is intrinsic evil when it
opposes harmony and/or intensity. Against harmony
evil is discord or disharmony; against intensity
it is triviality.[13] Evil as discord is the feeling of mutual destructiveness, the clashing of
experience. Schizophrenia might well be interpreted as a way of coping with the threats of disharmony. Depression would illustrate the subjective form of inner clashing and disharmony.
Compulsions, especially those of an obsessive nature, would be illustrations of triviality for
within trivial limits there is narrow harmony.
Griffin sees discord or disharmony as evil in an
"absolute or noncomparative sense" while triviality
is "evil only by comparison,"[14] that is, with what

148

could have been. But both must be overcome if the highest good, i.e., beauty, is to be achieved.[15] Evil so conceptualized must be seen in the concrescence itself. Within the droplet of experiencing the subject "chooses" disharmony or triviality and so minimizes any achievement of what was possible for it. Right here in the process of putting it all together each person "chooses," or "decides," or "does," evilly in actualizing less than the optimal possibility; or, in terms of God, misses the mark toward which the divine vision was luring him or her. For the moment I do not have in view the effects on oneself or on others of doing it evilly. Rather, I have in view the immediacy of the moment in which this person is failing his or her own best possibility! That is the genuine or intrinsic evil Griffin is pinpointing. This evil occurs when discord triumphs and/or triviality prostitutes the possibility. The metaphysical description of how an occasion becomes is at the same time the description of how genuine evil becomes actual.[16] The theological input is that the occasion has for that "moment" missed actualizing the beauty God envisaged for it. The sensitive pastor knows intuitively in his or her own life the failure of the aesthetic vision, and empathically knows the discordant, trivialized experiencing that is the agony of failure which has prompted the client's cry for help. In the next section we explore more fully what this understanding of evil means for pastoral caring.

Evil, however, is not limited to the experiencing moment. Much evil is inflicted upon us. Or to put it in process terms, every moment of actualized evil becomes a new datum for a new occasion to cope with. If I fail my best possibility by trivializing it with churlish anger, that realized anger is there for the next "moment" of me to cope with, as it is there for others around me to cope with. Cases of rape and incest, wife-beating and child abuse, are not only morally evil within the abuser himself as he fails optimal possibility; they are also morally evil in their

149

effect in the lives of those abused. Every event
is a cause within subsequent events; that is,
every event makes a difference to its successors.
One fundamental difference is the infliction of
suffering, pain, degradation upon successor events
through abuse, e.g., what the rapist inflicts upon
the woman raped. There are those who argue that
rape, evil in itself, might in the long run produce some kind of good, i.e., be the provocation
for the raped woman's turning to a vocation that
concentrates on helping other rape victims. That
might happen. But if it does, it does not minimize the evil effect of the rapist. Now we are
talking about a different set of occasions; viz.,
the rape victim, through intense suffering, creating a thing of beauty: a vocation of service.
These are different occasions: the woman redeem-
ing the evil perpetuated in no way transmutes what
was evil into potential good. It remains what it
was! Her creation is what she does with it. The
genuine evil of the abuser becomes instrumental
evil for the woman. Her dealing with it construc-
tively, even redemptively, does not make it less
evil. As Whitehead writes, ". . . beyond itself
it is evil in its character of a destructive agent
among things greater than itself."[17] What I am
insisting on is that there is real human evil, both
in subjective experiencing when it is rife with
discord and/or triviality, and in its effect as it
is inflicted upon its successors. A further clari-
fication is needed regarding instrumental evil.
It may be the effect of a good intention as well
as a bad intention. The evil intention to rape,
when carried out, bears instrumental evil in its
effect. But the good intention of a mother to try
to anticipate her young child's needs may become
instrumental evil when she pre-empts his need to
signal by prematurely providing for him. She thus
deprives him of a key element in his individuating
process, namely, to communicate his wants and needs.
His mother's pre-emption makes it more difficult
for him to separate from the symbiotic relationship
with the mother.[18] He might resign the struggle
and become complacent with dependency conformal
feelings.

150

So far we have looked at evil primarily ontologically, that is, within the process perspective
which illumines the inner struggling of the concrescence and the effect of the outcome of that
struggle on successor occasions. Still within
that perspective, but from a theological reference, we need to focus on God since it is "before
God" that sin receives its sharpest definition.
Since in process thought God aims the creation
toward divinely conceived goals for each moment,
sin is the reflection of any "divinely given ideal
aim."[19] Since sin is the intention not to maxi-
mize intrinsic good, it is the refusal of God's
lure toward the creation of Beauty. Sin, then, is
obstructive of the divine Working.

I have found Henry Nelson Wieman helpful in
describing how good comes about and what thwarts
it. He has two classifications of good: created
good and creative good,[20] and two classifications
of evil, destructive and obstructive.[21] Created
good is achieved value, and is always the result,
in part, of the working of creative Good. Wieman
identifies creative good with creative event, which
is an ongoing process toward the emergence of
value,[22] and the creative event with God,[23] who is
engaged in the transformation of the world. Evil
is destructive when it destroys created good in
opposition to God, the creative Good. However,
not all destruction of created good is evil. God
intends for created goods to be destroyed so that
novelty can be born. Otherwise, there would be
no zest in life. There is a "perpetual perishing." Destructive evil, therefore, is always relative. On the other hand, obstructive evil is
absolute evil, that is, evil that is evil every-
where and under all circumstances, unqualified,
ultimate, and confined.[24] It is absolute because
it opposes God who is at work producing value.
An illustration of both destructive and obstructive evil would be when a person, an intrinsic
good, is regarded and treated as a mere thing.
That person would suffer destructive evil, e.g.,
abused wife or battered child, and God would at

151

the same time be obstructively opposed. The heart
of Wieman's concern with obstructive evil is reflected in these words: "Man is beaten and destroyed if he gives first place to any other good
save what creates all good . . . ."[25] Wieman's
emphasis is on that kind of evil which is in opposition to, or obstruction of, the divine Working.

The contributions by Griffin and Wieman are
exceedingly helpful. There is genuine evil, the
possibility of which is ever-present and the experience of which is ubiquitous among the higher
forms of life, especially human. The experience
is located where all experience is actualized:
in the concrescing subject. Evil derives, as
Charles Hartshorne argues, from creaturely freedom.[26] It is the actual occasion which actualizes
disharmony and triviality. This evil is seen as
sin when it is set over against the Working of
God, obstructing that Working by refusing or skewing the divine Aim. This is the greatest evil
because it opposes that Working which provides
order and the zest for Beauty. Evil then is the
fundamental opposition to a cosmic Vision, an
opposition which disharmonizes or trivializes the
whole of creation, a creation groaning and travailing for its redemption. Lured on by God but
despoiled by its own aim the creation at any one
moment forms itself into the agonies of misused
freedom with now and then a taste of the Promised
Land with its milk and honey.

The pastoral carer sees these forms of agony.
To cope with the agony, penultimate goals, laudatory as far as they go, are not enough for pastoral
care. Whatever may be enough for other forms of
caring, the pastoral concern must understand evil
both as actualized in the concrescence and as a
tendentious force opposing the grace-aims of God.
The "tendentious force" would be the pile-up of
concrescence upon concrescence of disharmony and
trivialization. Such a repetition of evil concrescences would account for the perduring, tena-
cious, sedimentary character of evil which

traditional theology has labeled original sin but
without the locked-in-iron connotation given to it.
We can take evil with utmost seriousness without
surrendering our ability to do something about it.
With process understanding of evil pastoral care
would be struggling with the terrible reality that
made Paul groan under this "body of sin," that led
Luther to characterize it as "bondage," that
forced Kierkegaard to describe sin as a "sickness
unto death," and prompted generation after generation of theologians to speak of the human being as
guilty of hubris, and still deal with the concrescences redemptively.

Process theology locates sin both as actualized content, i.e., disharmony and triviality,
and as downright opposition that so often misses
the mark toward which God's constant aiming gently
and faithfully lures us. Pastoral care has to
answer Menninger's question, "Whatever became of
sin?" For its job is not yet done when the symptoms of psychological stress have been eased.
That could mask a deeper malady. As Tillich has
shown, health is multi-dimensional.[27] Failing to
help the client to full health, including wrestling
with the two dimensions of evil, leads to the phenomenon of what Tillich has called "unhealthy
health," which "comes about if healing under one
dimension is successful but does not take into
consideration the other dimensions in which health
is lacking or even imperilled by the particular
healing."[28]

Pastoral Care and Intrinsic and
Instrumental Evil

Pastoral care must struggle with evil as it
is actualized in persons, for we do actualize
ourselves evilly; and such actualization does constitute fateful decisions for ourselves and others,
for the subhuman creation, and for God. Process
thought has opened up the problem of evil in a new

way. Now we must try to assess what difference
the contribution from Process Thought can make to
pastoral care.

We begin by looking at the problem that evil
poses for pastoral care in two cases, one a family,
and the other, a re-visiting of the client we met
in Chapter II. What I shall venture to claim is
that while the data of pastoral caring cases will
differ, every pastoral caring situation involves
sinful actualizations which become destructive for
the concrescing subject and for others.

First, I propose that we look at a family of
five: father (Arthur), mother (Donna), Peter (16),
Diane (14), and Greg (12). The familial relationships can be visualized by dotted lines suggesting
strained relationships and solid lines, relationships tending to be more positive.

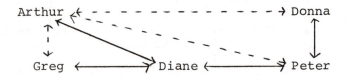

Arthur, an engineer, is exceedingly intelli-
gent, fancies himself as thoroughly rational, and
is anal-compulsive. He is a camping enthusiast.
He wants desperately to be liked. At work he en-
dures the normal frustrations and works out ra-
tionally crisis situations but he brings home his
frustrations, for home is a safer place to let
them out. At home he is overbearing, his compulsive nature dominating the relationships. He sets
the family agendas, running a taut ship whether it
is a pleasure outing or home maintenance.

Donna, housewife, is somewhat passive. She
has a very poor self-image, derived from a pile-
up of poor conformal feelings from childhood. Her
low-self-esteem is reinforced in her marriage. She
is somewhat mystical about life escaping into an

idyllic world now and then; is not very ordered in the daily journeying; is a bit scattered about her aims both for today and tomorrow.

The relationship between Arthur and Donna, although somewhat affectionate, is extremely frustrating for Arthur and destructive for Donna (hence the dotted line). It is tendentious for him to blame, and for her to feel she should be blamed.

Peter, the oldest, has been unduly the recipient of his mother's attention. To the father this has meant an alliance to which he was not really privy (therefore, the dotted line). The father's strenuous efforts to shape the son in his own ordered, rational image have been met by resistance by both mother and Peter. Warfare has ensued.

Greg, the youngest, has fared better thanks to his brother's bearing the brunt of the parental tug-of-war. But he has not escaped. The father's compulsive shaping has alienated him, too. The mother's overprotection has not created, however, a second alliance, but it has tended to be a counter-weight to the father's sterner, compulsively demanding ways. Nevertheless, the father sees a second mother-son alliance (dotted line).

Diane is the most fortunately situated child with no dominating alliance with either parent, (hence the solid line). She mediates somewhat between the brothers but more so between the father and her brothers. In some ways she is a bit above the battle.

Perhaps we have enough rough lines to indicate the destructive discord within this family which in my experience with families is not a-typical. The husband and wife want to make a go of their marriage and they both long for harmony in the family. Individually Arthur and Donna are attractive people who want to be affectionate and who long for peace. But destruction reigns among four of the five and Diane feels it as it swerls about her. What is amazing are the trivia which trigger the destructive tendencies, thwart the potential eros in the home, and blight the yearning for peace. The sons resist simple chores out of resentment; Donna "forgets" to shop for camping supplies for the weekend; Arthur's compulsive mind surveys what's not been done and, overloaded with frustrations from work, levels the family for another weekend of warfare.

With this family mix, destruction is inevitable. Evil in the form of destruction becomes the dominant subjective form of the family. But even worse, there is obstructive evil. God's individual aiming toward each of the members correlates, we must assume, with a composite aiming for the five transmuted into a family. However, the family is so obstructive of God's working that God's aiming is constantly thwarted. Each individual member seems to be expressing centrifugal tendencies, obviously to escape the pain; and at the same time all, but Diane, a stiff-arming resistance toward the other members. Therefore, any hope for Beauty and Peace in the family has no basis. Evil in the forms of obstruction and destruction permeate the family structure and together they find No Exit. Hopelessness is what has driven the family to seek help. In process terms the bottom-line of this family is that singly and together they have a patterned response of putting all things together evilly. Their decisions infect each other and their life together so that their future is fated.

Now I propose that we re-visit the client of Chapter II, whom we shall identify as R.D. I am going to begin with a categorical statement that R.D. actualized himself in part evilly. I need to remind ourselves of the analysis of evil within which this statement is made. R.D. is not "totally depraved" but he is suffering a "sickness unto death." He is not evil in the picayune

156

sense of moralisms and legalisms nor is he
drenched with debauchery. Neither is he a bad
fellow as society might stigmatize him. He suf-
fers from an enduring route of occasions which are
characterized by an evil series of subjective
forms. In the profound and tragic sense his life
is marred by disharmonies and trivia which are
both destructive and obstructive. He is a fellow-
traveler for whom evil became a dominant recurring
subjective form. This was his bondage.

We may recall briefly his history as he perceived it. His father was hard, demanding, sometimes brutal. His mother preferred his sister
and did not intervene as an ally against the father. He ran away from home in early adolescence
vowing not to return until he was a millionaire.
Upon leaving home he was befriended by a golf pro,
his first real adult friend. His first two mar-
riages ended in divorce. By his mid-thirties he
had fulfilled his vow and made his first million.
A foreman younger than himself became his "best
friend"; his third wife was devoted and accepting;
his wife's pastor was the third positive male in
his life. His early experience with "sawdust
trail" religion in which he could "Almost smell
the singeing flames of hell," and his identification of both parents with that religious persuasion, were the realities out of which he became
antithetical to the church. We need not fill in
the details of these abstract descriptions, nor
can we in any sense that will do justice to him
as a being made up of myriad concrescing moments.
But we have enough description to see R.D. as
essentially unhappy despite appearances of having
it made. Yet "unhappiness" is too mild a word.
The repeating subjective form at the center of his
being was disharmony and discordance.

Let us trace the routing of his prehensive
life.

There was his past, physically prehended as
all pasts are; a past conformally felt, actual

157

occasion upon actual occasion, so that there was
massive repetition. There was a future of new
possibilities, conceptually prehended as all
possibilities are. By association the past suggested some possibilities, perhaps his vow to
prove that he could be something after all; and
God aimed him toward possibilities by which his
life might be filled with harmony and meaning. So
God became a propositional lure at the unconscious
level while at the conscious level God was anathema
to R.D. There were other significant lures for
feelings: the golf pro providing R.D. with an
alternative image of what it means to be an adult
male; two wives confirming the weak mother; one
wife offering an adult love almost too good to
believe; a foreman, younger than himself but
evidently a surrogate father; a sister hated for
her favored position; preachers and evangelists
in whose images God was a tormenting fiend to be
repressed and denied that even minimal existence
might go on.

In each concrescing experience R.D. felt the
competing of past and possibility, the contradiction of lures, the contrast of feelings which re-
fused integrative attempts. Even years away I can
feel the torment of discord, the clash of disharmonies, and the banality of resulting trivia. The
vision of a constant working of Good to give him a
hope for what might be was my vision not his. His
own aim seemed at best to be deflected by residual
forms of anger, fear, unworth, hostility, anxiety,
depression, which compulsively dominated the routing of his life. Surely God's Aiming got stuck
again and again in this traffic jam. If "destruction as a dominant fact in . . . experience is the
correct definition of evil,"[29] then R.D. was suffering a sedimentation of evil. Yet, as Whitehead
has observed, discordance need not be wholly evil.
"Progress is founded upon the experiences of discordant feelings."[30] Through the clashes of intensities there can be stimulation toward higher
realization. "Thus the contribution to Beauty
which can be supplied by Discord--in itself destructive and evil--is the positive feeling of a

quick shift of aim from the tameness of outworn perfection to some other ideal with its freshness still upon it."[31] So R.D.'s life was in part a struggle against the sedimentation, and so there were experiences of Beauty. But when discord is the recurring clash of incompatibilities destruction becomes the dominant fact. Destruction was the dominant theme both as R.D. sensed his life and as that life affected others.

When discord is destructive, that is, when there is so much inner clash that a constructive realization is not possible, then evil is recorded. It issues in a sense of tornness, schizoid feelings, boredom, ennui, trivia, loss of direction, sense of stuckness, with attendant feelings of rejection, despair, depression, self-pity, hostility, futility, and the like. Perhaps the best descriptive word is Triviality. Among all the factors in the data of a person's life, there is no central coordination. No one feeling emerges as reinforcing another. There are too many incompatibilities without a coordinating core. Narrowness or canalization needed for depth and intensity is not possible.[32]

R.D. knew internal clash as destructive turmoil. The patterned subjective form that dominated the flow of feeling was hostility, mostly turned inward upon himself. Against this evil he had to bring some harmony if he was to survive as a psycho-physical organism. He tried to eliminate this evil by pushing it into the background, by suppression and habitually by repression, while propelling into the foreground a determination to "show them."[33] By whatever gifts of the gods come imaginative feelings, in his case to set up a novel determination to "make a million dollars," R.D. made that determination his controlling subjective aim. When he left home at fourteen what sounded like an idle boast was the deepest intention of his life. To that intention he paid such full attention that quite early he actualized that aim. But along the way discord seemed to

159

make of his life a frenetic adolescent wandering; while trivia for the most part constituted the tasteless menu of his later years. Even a million dollars, maybe especially a million dollars, is a triviality in some contexts! As a goal it was a creative intensity for R.D.; as a realization a triviality.

Now the question is: How does the notion of evil, worked through in process terms, contribute to pastoral care? What difference does it make? I am suggesting that it makes two considerable differences.

The first difference is the location of moral evil or sin: within the self-causing subject as it puts itself together. There is always the effective power of the past; but the present shapes its aims and so determines what it will do with the past. There is always God with the divine aim; but the present has the ontological capacity not to conform to the divine purpose.[34] We have seen in this chapter how process thought locates intrinsic evil in the concrescence of an actual occasion and instrumental evil in the effect that occasion has in its successors. It is precisely with the actual occasion, or those nexüs of actual occasions which Whitehead would call a person, that pastoral caring is concerned. Thus, evil is part of the struggle by which the subjective aim achieves its unity. If that unity is a discordant or trivial unity, lacking aesthetic Beauty, which is the union of Harmony and Intensity, evil domi- nates. Pastoral caring, working with this dis- cordant and/or trivial concrescence, can know the malevolence, and the pain of that malevolence, with which it is working. In pinpointing the malady by naming it, pastoral care can know the seriousness of that with which it is dealing. It will not simplistically interpret the ensuing struggle as a rift with codes of laws or behaviors, or even with the moral wisdom of a culture, al- though the struggle may include all of these. So it will not be concerned to help the other merely

160

to adapt, though adaptation may be a result along
the way. In fact, adaptation may continue or re-
inforce the discord or the trivia. Nor will pastoral caring rub the other's nose in his or her
subjective forms of evil by castigating or piling
on further guilt.

Pastoral caring will be concerned with the
struggle out of discord and trivia into intensity
and harmony. Through imaginative feeling the
carer will empathize with the flow going on in the
person of the client where change takes place.
Pastoral caring, already sobered by its historic
emphasis on evil, will not take lightly what is
going on in the other. But clarified by a fresh
interpretation of evil which locates it within
the processive formation of an actual occasion
where it can be dealt with, pastoral caring can
be much more specific both about what it is dealing with and how to go about the healing, saving
task. The pastoral carer will be aware that she
is a very significant person accepting without
condoning, so that the trust level within the
other can be built up; an authority figure giving
permission for the client to try without continuing to be frozen by the fear of a failure; a religious figure from whom is incurred neither blame
or guilt but a religious figure who confronts out
of a faithful love; a friend who can take transference which is a faulty reference to herself out
of the client's past, without counter-transferring,
lift the transference up into the light of consciousness, and thereby diffuse the pent-up feelings derived from a previous time. This much of
the approach to the evil in concrescence is uti-
lizing insights taught us by our humanistic
friends, but hopefully employing such insights toward a somewhat different sense of reality as that
sense is informed by the character of evil.

Since the carer also experiences evil within
her own becoming and is therefore involved in
struggles similar to her client, she has need to be
self-confronting and to be continually transformed.
Self-confronting, a part of self-transformation,

is most difficult alone. Seemingly only a few rare fellow-travelers possess the insight and muster the courage to take an unrelenting look within. Most of us require an alter ego to stand with us but also over against us and with the courage of agape-friendship say, "Thou art the person," as Nathan said to David.[35] The model I have in mind is that of the Spiritual Director in the tradition of the Roman Catholic Church.[36] Customarily this is a priest, but consistent with the doctrine of the Priesthood of all Believers, it could as well be a sensitive lay person.[37] The carer at propitious moments needs also to be a client. In that role she can explore the two evils of discord and trivia, can re-assess methodically her destructive aims, whether targeted on the self or others, and learn painfully the difference between destroying created goods that ought to give way and created goods that are intrinsically good and ought not be violated.

The second difference the process notion of evil makes is <u>how</u> it requires the role of God as Savior. Theology has always placed the salvific work of God over against the fact of evil however conceived. But a process notion of evil, placed within the context of a process view of God, puts God's work as Savior quite differently from the way traditional theology puts it. Wieman saw, as does Griffin, that the major evil is evil as opposition to, or obstruction of, the divine Working. Translated into Whiteheadian language this form of evil arrays itself against the divine Aim in each concrescence. The subjective aim of the concrescing occasion prehends the divine aim by opposing or obstructing it. Lured by other aims it might target a lesser good and so miss that unity which was most appropriate for it. It might defiantly, proudly, lustfully array itself against the aiming of God. In either case there is the tragedy of what might have been.

Over against opposing evil is the role of God as Savior. God is not only the initiator of a

definite outcome for each concrescence which is
the creative effect of God upon the world. God
also prehends the world, enjoying the world at
every instant in its determinate unity. Each
concrescing occasion, say, in its one-tenth of a
second duration, is experienced by God. God's
love is not unilateral, affecting the world but
unaffected by the world. God's love is bilateral.
The world is immanent in God.[38] The novelty of
each actual occasion is enjoyed by God in the full,
rich immediacy of God's experience. This means
that God is both changing and changeless: changeless in the envisagement of potentiality and in
the steadfastness of the divine subjective aim;[39]
changing because of the effect of the world on
the divine experience. God does not have to reach
back in memory to enjoy what the creation has experienced. The creation is prehended by God in
its fulness and it remains God's everlastingly,
the intense immediacy of divine experience.[40]
Evil is experienced by God in the fulness of its
fury, whether as destructive discord, triviality,
or opposition to the divine aim. The final unity
of each actual occasion, be it banality, hubris,
lust for one's own target, refusal to seek the
good of the relevant future, or whatever other
opposing form of evil, is woven into the divine
experience. God is the "ideal companion who
transmutes what has been lost into a living fact
within his own nature."[41] This means that every
puff of human existence, every actual occasion
making up the nexüs of human selfhood, including
the subjective form most demonically opposed to
God, is caught up into the everlasting experience
of God. That, by the way, is a model for acceptance infinitely superior to any psychological
acceptance. That is acceptance _as_ _is_, as Tillich
preached.[42]

What God does with evil is to flood back into
the subsequent actual occasion through the divine
aim God's vision of what now may be, taking the
evil fully into consideration. God handles evil
in the only way evil can finally be overcome:

acceptance into the divine Love where it is overcome by good, the steadfast goodness of God; and
so transmuted, it is offered back to the world in
the form of a new Aim of God toward a new aesthetic unity of Beauty. As Whitehead says:

> The kingdom of heaven is not the isola-
> tion of good from evil. It is the over-
> coming of evil by good. This transmuta-
> tion of evil into good enters into the
> actual world by reason of the inclusion
> of the nature of God, which includes the
> ideal vision of each actual evil so met
> with a novel consequent as to issue in
> the restoration of goodness.[43]

Salvation is renewal. What God brings to
each new occasion, out of the divine experience
of its predecessor, both its good and its evil,
is a fresh Aim by which the world can renew itself if it will. Grace is prevenient, the birthing grace of a new possibility. This is the persuasive power of God toward a new direction. God
is Savior: in tenderness embracing the full
actuality of the world, in wisdom using what in
the world is "mere wreckage," and in patience
leading the world toward adventure and harmony by
the divine "vision of truth, beauty, and goodness."[44] Salvation is congruence of human subjective aims with the fresh, relevant initial Aim of
God. God is about the business of trying to pull
wandering, stuck, opposing human aims into line
with the divine Vision so that a new episode of
Beauty might qualify the concrescing world.

With the role of God as Savior we have completed the secular vision of God begun in Chapter III. Whitehead has summarized the vision in
this fourfold way: first, there is God envisaging
all potentiality; second, arising out of this envisagement there is the origination of actualities;
third, the completed actualities pass into the
experience of God everlastingly without loss;
fourth, in tenderness, wisdom, and patience God

refashions what has been received into the divine experience and floods back into the world a redemptive vision for what might yet be. Whitehead uses poetic expression to point to the re-creative, redemptive working of God. ". . . the kingdom of heaven is with us today . . . . [It] is the love of God for the World. It is the particular providence for particular occasions. What is done in the world is transformed into a reality in heaven, and the reality in heaven passes back into the world . . . . In this sense, God is the great companion--the fellow-sufferer who understands."[45]

If the requirement of the client is such that it would be coercive or manipulative to introduce God as Savior, the pastoral carer can still assume the Working we have now finished describing. God is redemptively at work whether or not we acknowledge this to be the case. It will be shown in the next chapter how this salvific work of God will be more effective if consciousness of that Working has been raised. But even if there is no faith consciousness on the part of the client, the divine Ally can be counted on by the pastoral carer to be intent on saving the process. The words in the preceding sentence, that God is intent on saving the process, need emphasis. We are not saved by the process nor can we simply trust the process. As Professor Griffin has reminded me, clearly with all sorts of people the process has failed to a great degree. With our proclivity for doing it evilly, and with the process constituted by all the embodiments of creative (and destructive) power, any trust in process would have to be misplaced and blind. There is no built-in meliorism here. Yet there is an element in the process that is fully trustworthy: God. To believe in God means to trust this trustworthy divine element in the process. God is in tremendous struggle for any success within our environment saturated with so much opposition and so much destructive intent. The risk of God is with our capacity not to conform to the divine purpose. Yet God as Savior is intent on making of each a fresh creation,[46] by empathically receiving from the world, purifying what is received, and re-constituting the world with a new vision as fresh as the next puff of experience can stand. This is the Working with which the pastor can identify in his or her caring effort to come to grips with evil in its several forms.

NOTES

[1] Supra, Ch. 3.

[2] Freud was once asked what a normal person should
be able to do well. He replied, "To love and
to work." That reply is consistent with his
grounding of psychology in instinct and with his
desire to see the ego autonomous. The quotation
is from Erikson, Childhood and Society, op. cit.,
p. 229.

[3] Jung, The Archetypes and the Collective Unconscious, op. cit., p. 246.

[4] Roberto Assagioli, Psychosynthesis, p. 37.

[5] Cf. Assagioli, Will, pp. 70-75.

[6] Karl Menninger, Whatever Became of Sin (NY:
Hawthorn, 1973), p. 228.

[7] Ibid., pp. 223ff.

[8] David Ray Griffin, God, Power, and Evil (Philadelphia: Westminster, 1976), p. 22.

[9] Walter Grundmann, "Sin in the New Testament,"
tr. from Gerhard Kittel's Theologisches Worter-
buch zum Neuen Testament by Geoffrey W.
Bromiley, in Theological Dictionary of the New
Testament (Grand Rapids: Eerdmans, 1964), I. 311.

[10] Paul Ricoeur, The Symbolism of Evil, tr. by
Emerson Buchanan (Boston: Beacon, 1969), p. 50.

[11] Cf. John T. McNeill, A History of the Cure of
Souls (NY; Harpers, 1951), Ch. XV passim;
Seward Hiltner, Preface to Pastoral Theology
(NY: Abingdon, 1955), pp. 94-98; Seward Hiltner,
Theological Dynamics (NY: Abingdon, 1972),
Ch. 4; Albert C. Outler, Psychotherapy and the
Christian Message (NY: Harper, 1954), pp. 130ff,

233ff. Also, a brilliant paper by Edward Farley, "Psychopathology and Human Evil," unpub. Schaff lectures, Pittsburgh Theological Seminary, Spring, 1975.

[12] David Ray Griffin, God, Power, and Evil: A Process Theodicy, esp. ch. 18.

[13] Ibid., p. 282.

[14] Ibid., p. 284.

[15] Ibid., p. 285.

[16] Cf. ibid., p. 24.

[17] RM., p. 95.

[18] Cf. Margaret S. Mahler and Manuel Furer, "Certain Aspects of the Separation--Individuation Phase," The Psychoanalytic Quarterly (vol. 32, 1963), pp. 3 and 4.

[19] Griffin, God, Power, and Evil, p. 292.

[20] Henry Nelson Wieman, The Source of Human Good (Chicago: University Press, 1946), ch. III.

[21] Ibid., p. 86.

[22] Ibid., p. 56.

[23] Ibid., pp. 264, 275, 305ff.

[24] Ibid., pp. 90-92.

[25] Ibid., p. 158.

[26] Charles Hartshorne, "A New Look at the Problem of Evil," in Current Philosophical Issues: Essays in Honor of Curt John Ducasse, ed. by F. C. Dommeyer (Springfield, IL: Thomas, 1966), pp. 207-208. Cf. Griffin, op. cit., pp. 292ff.

[27] Paul Tillich, "The Meaning of Health," Religion and Medicine, ed. by David Belgum (Ames, IA: Iowa State, 1967), pp. 6-11.

[28] Ibid., p. 11.

[29] Whitehead, Adventures, p. 259.

[30] Ibid., pp. 259-260.

[31] Ibid., p. 257.

[32] Cf. PR, pp. 170-172.

[33] Such ego strength as R.D. marshalled persuades me that Hartmann and other ego psychologists are correct in affirming that ego has partly at least an independent origin, that it has autonomous functions, and that it has a conflict--free sphere. Cf. Heinz Hartmann, Ego Psychology and the Problem of Adaptation (NY: International University, 1964).

[34] Cf. Griffin, God, Power, and Evil, pp. 24, 278ff.

[35] II Sam. 12:7.

[36] For a splendid contemporary illustration see Henri J. M. Nouwen, The Genesee Diary: Report from a Trappist Monastery (NY: Doubleday, 1976).

[37] From his writings I detect that Dr. Paul Tournier fulfills something of this role.

[38] PR, p. 528.

[39] PR, p. 523. Cf. Christian, Whitehead's Metaphysis, op. cit., p. 300.

[40] PR, p. 524.

[41] RM, pp. 154-55.

[42] Paul Tillich, _The Shaking of the Foundations_ (NY: Scribners, 1948), Ch. 19.

[43] _RM_, p. 155.

[44] _PR_, p. 525, 26.

[45] _Ibid._, p. 532.

[46] II. Cor. 5:17.

Only a socially constituted, all-retaining memory
can give all of life a long-run meaning, and only
a socially constituted deity can have such a memory.
Charles Hartshorne, Reality as Social Process

Chapter VIII

The Role of God: A Religious Vision

In this chapter as in Chapter III, I am again
following the strong lead of Whitehead who goes
beyond the secularity of God's role to a religious
vision which I find commanding both in its force on
me as a person and in its potential power for
pastoral caring. What Whitehead said about the
religious vision bordered on poetry, especially
in Part V of Process and Reality and in Adventures
of Ideas. I shall attempt to delineate the
religious vision to see what it might hold for us,
hoping as I do so, not to evaporate the power of
the vision itself which perhaps is best preserved
in Whitehead's own artistic form.

In Adventures of Ideas, Whitehead makes a
striking move from his secular vision of God to a
religious vision. For the secular vision, he
leaned on Plato whose final conviction was "that
the divine element in the world is to be conceived
as a persuasive agency and not as a coercive
agency."[1] Whitehead accomplished with this
insight what Plato failed to do: he built it
systematically into his metaphysics. It is by the
divine persuasion that "ideals are effective in
the world and forms of order evolve."[2] This is
the vision we embraced in Chapter III.

What Plato "divined in theory," Whitehead
saw Christianity making concrete in what for it
"is the supreme moment in religious history."[3]
For the concreteness of the religious vision,
Whitehead appealed to the life of Christ "as a
revelation of the nature of God and of his agency
in the world."[4] While much traditional Christology

171

would agree with these words, it then goes on to
see God's presence in Jesus as sui generis, an
isolated specimen. Process Christology, on the
other hand, looks to Jesus as the supreme exempli-
fication of how God relates to us: "the poet of
the world, with tender patience leading it by his
vision of truth, beauty, and goodness."[5] It is
important to quote Whitehead with some fullness
here:

> The record is fragmentary, inconsistent,
> and uncertain. . . .But there can be no
> doubt as to what elements in the record
> have evoked a response from all that is
> best in human nature. The Mother, the
> Child, and the bare manager: the lowly
> man, homeless and self-forgetful, with
> his message of peace, love and sympathy:
> the suffering agony, the tender words
> as life ebbed, the final despair: and
> the whole with the authority of supreme
> victory.

Then Whithead concludes:

> I need not elaborate. Can there be
> any doubt that the power of Christianity
> lies in its revelation in act, of that
> which Plato divined in theory?[6]

Whitehead gives credit to the early Christian
theologians for rejecting Plato's notion of mere
imitation, though Platonists they were, in favor
of a doctrine of actual divine immanence, both in
the world and in Christ. But he scolds them for
not building that discovery into a general metaphysics. Because their God was exempted from
metaphysical categories and because they got stuck
on unqualified divine omnipotence, they could not
make full use of their doctrine of divine
immanence.[7] Whitehead has pinpointed the doctrine
of divine immanence in what Pittenger calls the
"classical instance"[8] of religious faith, at least
for Christianity, the Christ-event.

172

It is my purpose to suggest the relationship
between God and Jesus as revelatory both of God's
persuasive Agency and of the impact upon God of
the divine immanence. Then it will be time to see
what all this might say to pastoral care.

I

Jesus cannot be lifted out of the metaphysical
framework within which we are working. At any
"point" in Jesus' history there are the full, rich
data of causal efficacy. The Old Testament
recounts some of those data, relevant to Jesus as
to any other first century Jew, though the relevance would be graded in keeping with the uniqueness of each self. The early Gospel geneological
and birth narratives likewise recount some of those
data and come to us highly interpreted. But the
point is that Jesus conformally related to the
data of causal efficacy and so the past became
immanent within him. But along with the data
physically prehended, Jesus was confronted with
divine aims for his fullest, richest becoming.
God was persuasively bringing to Jesus God's
vision, yes, intention, for Jesus at each instant
of his becoming. Thus, God was "luring" Jesus
along lines of the richest fulfillment for Jesus
the person and beyond Jesus to a future envisaged
by God as fulfilling of the world. I am insisting
that God had a unique aim for Jesus' future, as
God does for each future, but an aim that was to
be potentially creative for all the futures of the
world. ("Potentially creative" here means redemptively new in the sense of a "new creation.")
Here I am in complete agreement with Cobb when he
regards it as arbitrary to deny to God "freedom to
differentiate his relations to particular occasions." On the contrary, he concludes, ". . .we
may suppose that God may well take the initiative
in presenting himself to human occasions with
peculiar force and specific efficacy prior to and
quite independently of their self-preparation or
desire for this occurrence."[9]

173

I interpret the relationship of God to Jesus
in terms of a "gift"; that is, that God in full
divine freedom chose to give to Jesus an intention
for his becoming that would establish his personhood, his career, and his ministry, with "peculiar
force and specific efficacy" for the purpose of
redemptive effectiveness in the world. It may not
be too much to symbolize this as "virgin birth,"
accentuating a remarkable uniqueness to the Christ-
event, though, tragically, the powerful metaphor
is debased by the trivialization of literalism.
Perhaps it is too carnal to have been otherwise.
The powerful relationship between God and Jesus
can be expressed in several ways. Two will
suffice: The Fourth Gospel says: "The Word
became flesh." This would be the Communicative
Event[10] par excellence, the divine Word shaping
the creation out of multiplicity into unity.
Christologically it would be the Word tenderly
persuading Jesus the person through all of that
marvelous history toward a vocation of redemption
of a creation "groaning and travailing," longing
for renewal. It is the Communicative Event as
"creative transformation," to borrow from Cobb,[11]
which aligns itself with Jesus to make concrete
in the world the process by which God renews
life. It is God, communicating the divine Aim
for more and more Beauty in the occasions of
history, whose tender persuasive love united with
Jesus to effect a "fresh creation" for the world.
Jesus can be seen as the "luminous moment" of the
"Persuasive agency of God,"[12] for Jesus internalized this self-communication of the Divine.

Jesus, himself, the intended recipient of the
gift both from others and from God, had ontologically to put it all together. In his own being
it had to become actual. Jesus in marvelously
rich sensitivity to the divine purpose, in the
exquisiteness of his self-consciousness, and in
courageous commitment to be loyal "in spite of
consequences," prehended positively the divine
persuasion, made it his own subjective aim, and
worked out the consequences of a life of devotion

174

to God, in the form of servanthood, consonant with the divine behest. The word which may get at the heart of the God-Jesus relationship is congruence. Jesus in his subjective aim was congruent with the Aiming of God for his life and the renewal of the world. Precisely here I find at least part of the meaning of "deity" in the traditional effort to define the uniqueness of Jesus. While we are incongruent most of the time with the Initial Aims of God, Jesus was congruent. The miracle of his life was that in the midst of popularity and isolation, hostile enemies and turn-coat friends, threat, suffering and death, he was obedient to the divine Aiming. His obedience was the congruence of his aiming to that of God who was calling him forward. Jesus was fully persuaded.

In a very suggestive section, Cobb argues that the religious experience is such that at least for some there is experience interpreted with reference to the presence of God. His position is that God is apprehended as one among the many data which crowd upon us and clamor for attention. Consciousness of the God element is usually low or nil, lost among the multiplicity. But some sensitively interpret that element, e.g., God, as a constant presence and find their "interpreted experience dimly qualified by that experience." (underlining mine). Furthermore, there are "intense experiences of the numinous, and ecstatic experiences of union and communion."[13] While a person's disbelief does not nullify God's initial aim toward value for that person, it does affect that person's own aiming. For disbelief colors our aims as does belief. Furthermore, disbelief may put a hindrance upon what God can do, as belief may help to keep one open so that God's aiming can take advantage of that openness. One's past beliefs are among the most important things determining those possibilities toward which God can seek to lure us.[14] Perhaps it was that a vigorous belief structure on the part of Jesus, inclusive of "intense experiences of the numinous," helped

175

keep Jesus sensitive so his subjective aim was
congruent with God'a aiming. Jesus' intense awareness of God throughout his life, including the
climactic agony of the last hours, would allow God's
aiming to have its way to an extraordinary degree.
The numinous and ecstatic experiences would most
naturally be prehended as communion or even union
without necessitating a notion of deity for Jesus
that would violate metaphysical structures.   In
fact, how might the community of believers better
note the unique relationship of God to Jesus than
by the notion of deity ascribed to Jesus?   In the
Jesus-event God was so wonderously and totally
apprehended by Jesus that Trinitarian formulas
came to express best that particular Incarnation.
But the dogma can be dangerous when it is miscon-
strued; viz. God in the fullness of divine subjectivity and Jesus in the richness of his own
subjectivity are made equivalent. That constitutes
a confusion of entities.

     We have been looking at the God-Jesus relation-
ship.   In summary, it would appear that God chose
Jesus for special ministry and persuasively
communicated the divine Vision; Jesus made that
Vision his; and the outcome was a total Servanthood
in which Jesus was wonderfully faithful to the
unique calling laid upon him.   That calling was to
be redemptively effective in the life of successive
generations by way of his obedience even unto
death.   Those successive generations have so
prehended the mighty acts of God in this Jesus as
to constitute themselves the Body of which Jesus is
the Head.   Staying close to Jesus, so conceived,
who was uniquely close to God, has proved to be the
central standpoint of the Church.   God continues
to "lure" the church into servant positions after
the manner of Jesus.   The church's corruption is
the failure of that vision and, therefore, its
falling away from Christ.   Its glory is to be
girded with a Towel and with Basin in hand to wash
the feet of the world.   The church's model is
Jesus whose own servanthood is the transparency of

the servanthood of God. God's servanthood is the
way God expresses love for the world.

II

In pointing to God as revealed in the Christ-
event as Servant of the world, we have been tracing
God's constant Activity, illuminated in Jesus, to
shape the world. But God's love is revealed as
well, and perhaps more poignantly, in how the
Divine prehends the world. God does shape the
world, but the world also shapes God. This, too,
is revealed in Jesus. Charles Hartshorne offers
the "simple suggestion that Jesus appears to be the
supreme symbol furnished to us by history of the
notion of a God genuinely and literally 'sympathetic'
(incomparably more literally than any man ever is),
receiving into his own experience the sufferings
as well as the joys of the world."[15] The
Consequent Nature of God about which Whitehead
writes so lyrically in Part V of Process and
Reality, and which we looked at briefly toward the
close of the last chapter, interprets God's love
to be bi-lateral and not unilateral. God prehends
the world and has a full and exquisite immediacy
of enjoyment of the world so prehended. The
divine immanence is so sensitive, the divine love
so "sympathetic," that God not only receives from
the world but treasures the experiences everlastingly. Whitehead employs the imagery of "a
tender care that nothing be lost."[16] Quite
clearly Whitehead has in mind Jesus as the
"supreme symbol" of the love of God patiently
persuading the world, eagerly enjoying the world,
and tenderly saving the world. [17]

Whitehead summarized his formulations about
God and the world by way of six antitheses. Two
of these are appropriate here:

> It is as true to say that the World
> is immanent in God, as that God is
> immanent in the World.

It is as true to say the God creates
the World, as that the world creates
God.[18]

Since the World is real, that is, has the power to
make a difference, it has the power to make a
difference to God. The world contributes novelty
and richness to the divine experience. God's
experience grows literally by "buds or drops of
perception"[19] as God, one actual entity, ingresses
every other actual entity in the full splendor or
poverty of its final self-creation. Because God
does not require excluding prehensions, the whole
of every actual occasion is included into God's
subjective enjoyment. Further, such enjoyment is
preserved everlastingly by God.[20] So the world is
the instrument of novelty for God as God is the
instrument of novelty for the world.[21]

Put in terms that can command awe, the
existence of each person means that God is different
in some respects from what God would be had that
person not existed. God would not cease to be God
if that person, say Carolyn, did not exist, but
because Carolyn does exist, she is immanent in
God and creative of God as God is immanent within
her and creative of her. God's enjoyment, in the
full technical sense of that Whiteheadean concept,
is different because of that divine Entity's prehension of Carolyn from what it would have been in
a world without Carolyn. If Carolyn can stand for
the client, this metaphysical insight begets powerful religious reverberations. The utter significance and very sacredness of the person who makes
a difference within the being of God usually gives
to the person who is not overwhelmed by it a sense
of worth and destiny that is redemptive beyond my
ability to express. It is akin to Maslow's peak-
experience, a Wow! or an Aha! experience that enables
a person to stand on tiptoe, perhaps for the first
time in his or her life.

The ontological fact that God prehends our
sufferings and joys, adding thereby to the growing

178

experience of God, makes life meaningful. When a
person hurts, God hurts. When a person achieves
a momentary satisfaction on the finer side of
life, God's own joy is finely intensified.
Hosea's intuition that God felt deeply the childhood of Israel and responded by leading them with
the "cords of compassion, with the bands of love,"
and that God wrestled against giving up Ephraim,
prompted Hosea's putting into the mouth of the
Divine these words: "My heart recoils within me,
my compassion grows warm and tender." This is the
intuition that the divine love prehends sympathet-
ically as well as gives persuasively.[22] And the
words of Jesus that even the hairs on our heads
are numbered and that we are more valuable than
many sparrows are not mere hyperbole but an
authentic insight into the center of the divine
experience. Charles Hartshorne has put the
significance of attributing to God real change as
the divine love takes into itself our contributions
in these rather beautiful words:

> What is the significance of this
> attribution? The significance is
> clear and immense. It means that
> what happens makes a difference to
> God, that he has a future, and that
> we help to determine each new stage
> of the divine life as it becomes
> real or present. For by his
> sympathetic omniscience, our free
> acts are participated in by God,
> for weal or woe according to the
> quality of living which we present
> to him in these acts. Hence, we can
> feel that every moment of our lives
> contributes a unique quality to the
> divine experience, and the finer the
> quality the richer the life of God,
> so far as derived from us. Thus,
> we find at last an answer to the old
> question, what does it all matter,
> since time swallows up each precious
> joy in the great emptiness of the

past. The past, we can not feel, is
not empty, but is the inconceivably
beautiful and sublime record of all
experience in the divine memory. And
we have made a little of that imper-
ishable beauty, and perhaps also have
tinged it imperishably with tragedy.[23]

The Christian doctrine of the cross is raised
to metaphysical status by the above attribution.
Far from being immune to suffering, God is vulnerable to the evil and pain of our human condition
with which pastoral care struggles. Guilt and
grief, for example, two persistent problems for
pastoral care, are caught up into the divine
experience, held significantly and everlastingly
there, and out of that experience God labors to
persuade us into new directions informed by the
suffering but creatively advancing on it toward a
finer wholeness. This vision of God's prehending
and persuasive love became wonderfully incarnate
in a gentle Galilean.

III

We must now investigate what effect the
religious vision we have been discussing might have
on pastoral care. I submit that the theme of
servanthood is implicit in God's relation with the
world and is lifted up in Jesus whose life
actually mirrors the Subjective Aim of God which is
love. I believe, therefore, that Servanthood is a
proper conceptual locus for pastoral care. There
is no intended denigration of other helping
professions when I urge that the uniqueness of
pastoral care is its servant motif. While
Christian pastoral care has many indebtednesses,
its own decisive subjective aim is to be in the
servant-tradition. It is beholden to Jesus as
Jesus was beholden to God; or put more carefully
and precisely, it is beholden to God after the
manner of Jesus. That servant-tradition neither
began nor stopped with Jesus. It was there in

180

Deutero-Isaiah in the painful servant songs from
Isaiah 42-53 and again in 61 with which Luke was
Jesus identifying in Jesus' sermon in Nazareth
(Luke 4). And it continues in the tradition of
Jesus with poignant reminders along the way such
as Francis of Assisi, Albert Schweitzer, and Martin
Luther King.

If servanthood fulfills the Galilean Vision,
to borrow from Whitehead, and were to become the
key concept of pastoral care, several significant
results should follow.

1. Pastoral care would become incarnational
   in nature. The notion of servanthood we
   have been examining is not merely descriptive but prescriptive. Part of the meaning of the uniqueness of Jesus is that he
   revealed something of God. His revelation
   was not new but it was decisively clarifying. God has a ministry to the world:
   to create and re-create the world. Neither
   by power nor by might, but by persuasive
   spirit, does God make all things new.
   Pastoral care is in this tradition: never
   to absent itself from any situation but in
   every situation to seek the mind of God
   for the good possible in that moment.
   Jesus was accused of favoring harlots and
   tax collectors, of eating and drinking
   with sinners. He sought them out, as the
   texts clearly show. Pastoral care would
   seem not to be faithful to the Galilean
   Vision when it relies solely on knocks on
   the study door, scheduled appointments,
   therapeutic conversations with the right
   people in the right places. Nor does the
   pastoral carer have a leg to stand on when
   she complains about the sad lot she has to
   work with. The laboratory for pastoral care
   is the people in the parish: boorish, innovative, whining, courageous, ugly, beautiful,
   dull, brilliant, repetitive, and aloof. Perhaps

181

one experience of servanthood is to be an
It to the client; that is, to be willing
and able to be made into an object for
awhile, against which the client can project anger, frustration, bitterness. The
servant is used, as our prayers use God in
our distraught moments. Sooner or later
the carer must help the client to enough
self-esteem that he need no longer "dump"
on the It. When the relationship changes
from I-It to I-Thou, healing and salvation
are in the works. To do pastoral caring
is to be set down in the midst of a people
with whom God is patiently at work to help
them inch their way to "a mode of satisfaction deeper than joy or sorrow."[24]

This does not mean that the pastoral carer
gets himself confused with Jesus. He had
his mission; we have ours. We dare not don
Messiah-complexes. They do not fit because
they do not belong. They only rob us of
our proper responses and so of our
integrity. Yet. . .within the Servant-
tradition, it is not always easy to know
when we are being had. It is fairly
simple for a supervisor to tell us that
our Messiah-complex is showing, as though
he is saying something witty and profound,
but it is not so easy to determine if it
is only our psychological ego needs that
are pleading for strokes or if it is our
religio/theological commitment that
is impelling us to walk that second mile on
feet already dead tired. Probably more of
us fail the servant-tradition than fall
prey to the need to be a savior. A life
sensitive to God, whose servants we are,
will usually feel the impress: draw
aside for a time and rest. . .and take
stock.

2. When pastoral care is located in the
    servant-tradition, acceptance of the other

as _is_ is easier to come by. To be in the
society of Jesus is to be there as a
recipient of grace. To be a servant of
that grace and in its ministry is to have
a self-consciousness that is actually
incapable of lording it over another.
Neither to condone nor to condemn but to
accept is to be at the side of the other
in his or her route of concrescing, to
share his or her reality so that in the
commonness of that sharing a new reality
might be born for both. That new birth,
which is a term generally descriptive of
the passage of time over against a "perpetual perishing," seems not to be genuinely possible when there is not this
acceptance. Then the other becomes an It
deployed by our cleverness, impressed by
our superiority, frightened by our correct-
ness, awed by our knowledge, depressed by
our having made it, overwhelmed by our
sanity, and perhaps destroyed by the self-
image we communicate. Only when the two
meet in the community of I and Thou, which
is the community of acceptance as is, is
there that openness into which God's ideal
aim can find the fertile soil for producing
thirty fold or perchance one hundred fold.

3.   In the context of servanthood, transference
would seem to have the best chance for
effective working through. At the same
time transference may well be a severe test
of servanthood.

Transference requires of the carer the
willingness and capability to absorb the
transference of the other neither in a
masochistic way nor a stoic way. The
absorption is in the context of agape-love;
that is, a love that can be willed to stand
firmly with the other in spite of consequences. It is also an informed agape-
love: informed by the causal efficacy out

183

of which the transference emerges and so
is intuitional rather than analytic;[25]
informed by such a degree of self-
knowledge on the part of the carer that
counter-transference does not take place;
informed by good theory out of the social
sciences; and informed theologically.
So it is a tough and responsible love as
Erich Fromm calls for in The Art of Loving
or Daniel Day Williams in The Spirit and
the Forms of Love. The model for such
servant-love is Jesus the Christ in which
event God's love is mirrored. The
crucifixion is the moment when the world's
brutal and pent-up hostile transference
was visited upon Jesus who absorbed the
worst the world could do without responding in kind. There is no indication of
masochism or stoicism in the Gospel
accounts of that death. Rather, Jesus'
servanthood is lived through in a persuasive loving of his enemies. There was
no counter-transferring. Instead there
was raw pain, raw hurt, raw isolation,
raw anguish. If we see in Jesus a
"luminous moment" of God's eternal ministry,
we have a model of servanthood in the
transference/counter-transference
phenomena. In fact, Good Friday and
Easter are the ultimate symbols of how to
deal with transference: absorption of
the projected evil out of causal efficacy,
and a benediction, a final good word, that
forgiveness in the full dimension of that
experience is assured. Transference had
done its worst; the worst had been
absorbed; the final Word is an absolution
with outstretched hands over a suffering
world: You are absolutely clean, a fresh
creation; accept God's acceptance of you
and start to live toward the more
abundant life.

4. To be a servant requires the transformation
    of the self. It is not natural to be a

184

servant. It is natural to lord it over
others; to have others below us in the
pecking order, i.e., males over females,
parents over children, whites over blacks,
blacks over Puerto Ricans, nation over
nation, the "we-group" over the outsiders,
etc. It is unnatural to gird oneself
willingly with a towel and with basin in
hand to wash dirty feet. This is why
servant acts are prehended by so many
either as incredible or as a sure sign of
pathology. But servanthood is indigenous
to the religious intuition. Luther put it
so unforgetably: "A Christian man is the
most free lord of all, and subject to
none; a Christian man is the most dutiful
servant of all, and subject to everyone."[26] Servanthood may be the ultimate
subjective form of the religious person:
out of one's solitariness to develop
consciously, cost weighted as it is, the
"project" of being a servant. This would
tie together Whitehead's characterization
of religion as what an individual does
with his solitariness, which refers to
the concrescence, with Whitehead's
emphasis upon the revelation in the life
of Christ of the divine agency as
persuasion in tenderness, patience, and
wisdom.[27] Servanthood was the dominant
subjective-form of Jesus. It would seem
to me to be the requisite dominant
subjective-form of the pastoral carer.

When I speak of servanthood as being the
"dominant subjective-form," I must make
clear what I am excluding. I am excluding
Mr. Milk-Toast, a doormat supineness, a
whimpering dependency, a masochistic
enjoyment, a martyr-complex, a stoic
inevitability, a cringing faith, a
routinized religious misunderstanding, and
a reaction-formation defending an angry
ego. I am intending servanthood out of

185

strength, a whole-hearted response to the givers and gifts of life, a thoroughgoing life-project as commitment to the gracious persuasive Agency luring us by an Ideal of a new Humanity the first fruits of which are engraced in the faithful servant.

This requires transformation of the carer-self not as a single once-and-for-all act but as a lifelong process of ingressing ideals by which the divine Persuasion is seeking to renew the world.

Transformation is a social phenomenon. It is social through and through. This denies any Kierkegaardian abstraction which locates the self primarily on a vertical plane with God, as it denies the social evolutionist abstraction which locates the self solely on a horizontal plane, a fond theory of some liberal theologians in the twenties and thirties. It insists that transformation occurs in the social milieu in which everything inter-penetrates everything else. The doctrine of social immanence in process thought is that each "stand-point" is a togetherness of the world. When my world includes the client, RD, my world will be changed by RD. To be a cause in process thought is to "make a difference." Whitehead agreed with Plato's dictum: ". . .the definition of being is simply power."[28] What has real existence has the power to make a difference. Translating this into pastoral care terms, the client either has power and hence will make a difference to the carer or the client is non-existent. The servant stance insists that the client has power, that the carer must be open to the transforming risks of that power, and that the carer will never be the same again. This is the risk of love.

To support that risk, some regularly sustained practice of the spiritual life would seem to be required. There is an emerging insight that spiritual formation, or as I prefer, faith forma-tion, be correlated with pastoral care.[29] This insight once more attempts to locate pastoral care

in its own rich history; it serves to remind ourselves, especially in pastoral counseling, that our
traditions have also to offer, along with insights
from the various psychologies, their own unique
caring tools such as spiritual readings, meditation,
and prayer; it urges us to rebuild the spiritual
bases of human life as preventive therapy for the
handling of life crises; and it calls us to
revitalize the faith of the pastoral carer for
her heavy work in ministry. It is with this fourth
purpose that I am primarily concerned now.

Pastoral caring loads can quickly drain a
pastor if she does not drink deeply from the
artesian wells of God's plentitude. Or to change
the imagery but still maintain the oral event, if
her becoming is not continuously fed as she feeds
others, her own organism will become depleted. If
pastoral care is to be housed in servanthood, an
unnatural role for all of us, it requires worship
which fulfills two major functions.

The first function is to relate us to God.
Private and corporate worship do not have as
laudatory goals paying metaphysical compliments to
God. Nevertheless, as Wieman correctly argues,
worship has everything to do with God, for in worship we find the way to participate in the divine
Working.[30] Worship helps to sensitize us to the
Divine; that is, it assists us to pay attention to
God that we might be more open to the divine
directivity. Paying attention to God, which is a
way to put the meaning of obedient hearing of the
Greek verb ὑπακούω, is necessary for a variety of
reasons, not the least of which is to discriminate
the datum, God, out of the multiplicity of data
that come through causal efficacy. Since God
comes to us primarily below the level of consciousness, worship can attune the trajectory of the self
in its movement from unconsciousness to consciousness[31] so that our aiming might be more on target
with the aiming of God. Worship helps to tell us
where to look. As Cobb says, ". . .those who
affirm the presence of God may so form their sub-

187

jective aims that God's causal efficacy for them may be maximized."[32] Worship can open us to this possibility.

The second function worship fulfills is to give perspective. It provides the vision by which life in its many facets may be viewed sub specie aeternitatis. It was a colleague of Whitehead's at Harvard, William Ernest Hocking, who developed the principle of alternation between worship on one hand and life in its several aspects on the other. We live and work among the parts of life: i.e., work, play, eating, talking, friendships. But this tends to divide us up around partial objects and so we become splintered. Hocking held that worship is that pursuit which alone brings wholeness. To regain wholeness from time to time, we need to worship and from that experience of wholeness move on to our partial tasks, alternating back and forth between worship and life's demands.[33] Hocking was especially concerned with the alternation between worship and work. He thought work might thus be saved since work provides its own arrest.[34] My experience is that pastoral care, intensive and problematic as it is, is a work especially providing its own arrest. It is especially demanding for the pastoral carer who must not only listen intensively to the client but listen as well for the "soundless voice" of God. Worship "puts behind its back. . .all partial loves"[35] as it focuses upon God who is the unifying Fact of our lives. Not to participate in this principle of alternation is to become diffused and finally worn out. Perhaps herein is a reason why women and men give up the ministry or complain bitterly about what a drain their people are. Infused with a lively sense of God's Presence through spiritual readings, including Scripture, meditation, and prayer, and through corporate worship, the pastoral carer can move back to her full ministry better able to handle that strenuous vocation. Thus the ministry itself might be suffused with a Shekinah glory. This is on the order of the vision of Thomas Kelly, Quaker and student of Whitehead's, who called for us to live on two levels: the upper

188

and outer level of external affairs and the inner and profounder level of divine immediacy, with the fruitful interplay between.[36]

But there is also a role for attentiveness to God within the caring conversation itself. When we looked at the secular vision of God in Chapter III, we did not propose any religious activity within the relationship. However, the religious vision, when it is shared by both carer and client as is most often the case in pastoral care, opens up rich possibilities for the use of several means of grace, and especially prayer. Prayer when chastely used, that is, when it is artfully timed and carefully articulated, can focus the attention of the client on his problem in the context of God's prehension of his stress and of God's aiming for a new resolution. Prayer is a powerful reminder of a sympathetic Ally who actually envisages ways out not even anticipated by carer or client. Prayer can help to coalesce wavering human aims with the divine vision so that a measure of congruence is possible. Perhaps the essence of prayer is training in "attention"; that is, prayer focuses attention on God so that the client's appetitive nature is on alert for the divine leading. The prayer, usually by the carer, needs to be short, targeted but without directing God what to do, and so phrased that the prayer itself can be used by God as a propositional lure. Prayer may have a primary effect upon God, not to change the divine Subjective Aim, but to allow God to come back to the client more relevantly and more persuasively because God has experienced the prayer and because the client's consciousness of the divine Presence has been raised. So the pastor's prayer might form as Lewis Ford suggests, the "passions of God," that is, how God feels us in our needs, allowing to God the divine rationality to determine what new aim is appropriate to the felt needs.[37]

The pastoral carer, employing process categories, may be able to use the rich resources of the history of caring more freely, wisely, and fruitfully than in those formulations in which God orders and controls all things according to an inscrutable will, for whom the future is already actualized, and for whom there is no experience of novelty because there is no possibility of change within God. It is really the religious vision of a divine love so reciprocal that it cherishes every perishing and bestows zest on every becoming that gives importance to pastoral caring.

NOTES

[1] AI, p. 166.

[2] Ibid., p. 167.

[3] Ibid.

[4] Ibid.

[5] PR, p. 526.

[6] AI, p. 167.

[7] Ibid., pp. 167-169.

[8] Norman Pittenger, Christology Reconsidered (London: SCM, 1970), p. 133. Cf. pp. 88, 110.

[9] Cobb, Natural Theology, p. 237.

[10] Cf. William Temple, an early process thinker, Nature, Man and God (New York: Macmillan, 1949): "The Eternal God is such as to communicate Himself; co-eternal with His ultimate Being is His Word, which is His mind in self-expression." p. 445.

[11] See his Christ in a Pluralistic Age (Philadelphia: Westminster, 1975). See also Wieman, The Source of Human Good, op. cit., ch. 4.

[12] AI., p. 169.

[13] Ibid., p. 233.

[14] Cf. David Griffin, A Process Christology (Philadelphia: Westminster, 1973), chapters 9 and 10.

[15] Hartshorne, Reality as Social Process, p. 24.

[16] PR, p. 525; cf. p. 527.

[17] Cf. PR, p. 520 and AI, p. 167.

[18] PR, p. 528.

[19] PR, p. 105 where Whitehead quotes William James who employs these words to describe how reality grows.

[20] PR, p. 527.

[21] PR, p. 529.

[22] Hos. 11:1-9.

[23] Hartshorne, Reality as Social Process, p. 151. Cf. Reinhold Niebuhr: "By this freedom [power of mercy beyond judgment] He [God] involves Himself in the guilt and suffering of free men who have, in their freedom, come in conflict with the structural character of reality." Niebuhr points approvingly to Hartshorne's handling of this problem in his The Vision of God. See The Nature and Destiny of Man (New York: Scribner's, 1943), II, 71. Also cf. D. M. Baillie, God Was in Christ (New York: Scribner's, 1948), pp. 190ff.

[24] AI, p. 172.

[25] Supra, p. 12.

[26] Martin Luther, "The Freedom of the Christian Man," Luther's Works, ed. by Harold J. Grimm (Philadelphia: Muhlenberg, 1957), V 31, p. 344.

[27] Cf. RM, p. 47 and AI, p. 167.

[28] AI, pp. 119ff.

[29] Cf. the work of Adrian van Kaam and Susan Annette Muto, Center for the Study of Spirituality, Duquesne University; Morton Kelsey, Encounter With God (Minneapolis: Bethany, 1972); Henri J. M. Nouwen, The Wounded Healer (New York:

Doubleday, 1972); the work of the New Wineskins
Center, Columbus, Ohio, and especially the
creative work of Barry Woodbridge, in Meditative
Prayer; and Jack Biersdorf's work as Director
of the Institute for Advanced Pastoral Studies,
Bloomfield Hills, Michigan.

[30] Henry Nelson Wieman, Methods of Private Religious
Living (New York: Macmillan, 1929), pp. 28-30.

[31] Cf. Jung, Supra, ch. IV.

[32] Cobb, Natural Theology, p. 233.

[33] William Ernest Hocking, The Meaning of God in Human
Experience, (New Haven: Yale, 1952), ch. XXVIII,
passim.

[34] Ibid., p. 418.

[35] Ibid., p. 421.

[36] Thomas R. Kelly, A Testament of Devotion (New
York: Harper, 1941). For some helpful readings
in process thought on such topics as prayer,
Eucharist, spirituality, commitment see Cargas
and Lee, Religious Experience and Process
Theology, op. cit.

[37] Lewis S. Ford, "Our Prayers as God's Passions,"
Religious Experience and Process Theology, op.
cit., ch. 26.

For the spiritual "I" need not remain itself, but can, instead, always transcend itself. Thus, spiritual existence is radically self-transcending existence.

John B. Cobb, Jr.
The Structure of Christian Existence

Chapter IX

Recovery of the Soul: Toward Creative Transformation

With the resurgence of biblical theology in this century, the traditional Christian notion of the Soul which had been based upon a Platonic understanding of the soul as an immortal essence encapsulated within the body had to be abandoned.[1] While biblical theology re-interpreted "soul" with a decidedly Hebraic cast, the re-interpretation has not caught on in any significant way in the life of the church. One need only preach a sermon on the resurrection of the body, and in doing so deny the immortality of the soul, to prehend the wrath of many in a congregation and to validate the depth of conformity to the unbiblical notion that there is an eternal spark within us. Whether pastors are wearied by resistance and ire on the part of congregants, or whether they are embarrassed by soul-language in our technological times, or whether the concept is simply no longer meaningful, many have tended to drop "soul" from their vocabulary; and in so doing have given up a great deal of significant imagery and perhaps a point of contact for the rich dimension labeled spirituality. I am not meaning to suggest that the loss is solely due to the surrender of a word though words have the power of signification. I am suggesting that the very concept of soul has been lost or at least eviscerated.

Most of the psychologies which have informed pastoral caring, and especially pastoral counseling, have aided the evisceration. Jung, Frankl,

Maslow, and Assagioli are major psychologists who have tried to recapture soul-imagery and conceptuality; but largely the secularity of the informing psychologies is evidenced by their eschewal of such imagery. Maslow is especially critical of his scientific colleagues, as he is of "dichotomized religion" and "liberal religionists," for "leaving out too much that is precious to human beings," namely the spiritual, or sacred, or transcendent, viz., those values that cluster around the Soul.[2]

With the loss of the traditional meaning of soul, even in pastoral care there has been some reduction of the human being to a psycho-somatic organism for whom the psychological side has primary reference to mental and emotional states of being. With our cultural surrender of transcendence and our capitulation to a positivism of technology, scientism, and secular humanism, pastoral caring has perhaps compromised away too much of its spiritual identity and vitality.

The thrust of this chapter is to recover what can be recovered with integrity. It is salutary that a philosopher of the stature of Whitehead is not timid about using soul-language carefully defined; but more importantly, he embraces value-laden experience as of the essence of life. We shall begin with Whitehead. Then we shall proceed to an interpretation of soul within Hebraic thought and note the close correlations between that interpretation and Whitehead's. Finally, we shall suggest what difference a rediscovery of soul can mean to pastoral care.

I

Soul Within Process Thought

In beginning his treatment of the human soul in A Christian Natural Theology Cobb insists that if we are to understand Whitehead's doctrine of

196

the human being, we must begin by grasping his thought on the soul.[3] We begin by disassociating Whitehead's understanding of soul from that of Plato although he is appreciative of Plato's emphasis. In Whitehead there is no immortal essence called soul, imprisoned in the human body, to which things happen as in Plato.[4] Rather, the soul fits the categories of process thought, although it is unique to higher life since it seems to require an appropriate nervous system and cortex for its functioning at least in our present bodily experience. The soul is not foreign to animal and human nature, that is, it is not a supra-natural entity.

The soul as understood by Whitehead can be described as the synthesis of the accumulated life experience to date within the human organism. (While animals have souls, as Hebrew thought also taught, we shall concentrate on the human soul.) The soul is self-constructed out of the prehensions of all those data which are transcendent to it. Its closest neighbor is the brain where Whitehead locates the soul.[5] The soul is a society of occasions whose occasions prehend the occasions which compose the brain. In turn the occasions that make up the brain prehend the rest of the body along the many pathways by which one part or another feeds the brain. For example, the occasions of the brain prehend the occasions of the eyes feeling sensations of light. In its turn the body prehends through its myriad occasions the external world. For example, the occasions of the feet feel the occasions that make up the pavement. This is an ever widening environmental circle of the soul beginning with the adjacent brain and expanding to include the widest stretches of the external world. As Whitehead notes, ". . . nature in general and the body in particular provide the stuff for the personal endurance of the soul."[6] Whitehead continues, "Let us ask what is the function of the external world for the structure of experience which constitutes the soul. This world, thus experienced, is the basic fact within those

197

experiences. All the emotions, and purposes, and
enjoyments, proper to the individual experience
of the soul are nothing other than the soul's re-
actions to this experienced world which lies at
the base of the soul's existence."[7] So Whitehead
can conclude, "The soul is nothing else than the
succession of my occasions of experience, extending from birth to the present moment."[8]

In our experiencing ourselves we experience
most directly our soul, which is a society of
actual occasions. We experience our soul in the
immediacy of its self-enjoyment: the thrilling
to a golden sunset across an infinity of ocean,
the excitement of a world series game, the depression over the discovery of a battered child, the
captivation of a new idea, the ecstatic feeling
in the momentary awareness of the goodness of God,
the fear and anger over the Three Mile Island
nuclear nightmare, the oceanic feeling of an
orgasm. But I also am aware, often vaguely, of
myself in memory and in anticipation. These are
current experiences of previous occasions of my
soul, memories I am re-presenting and re-living;
and current experiences of wishes and dreams reaching out toward the future, anticipations being
enjoyed in prospect.

Much of the soul's awareness is preconscious
in the Freudian sense; that is, available to consciousness but not in immediate conscious awareness. What I am mostly aware of is my soul as it
looks back in memory, as it dreams or anticipates
future possibilities, and as it is the primary
locus for the present struggle of multiple prehending, aiming and re-aiming, and realizing. Up
to now I have occasionally used person or self in
the customary way of denoting the total organism.
Those terms, person or self, require the notion
of soul because that is the society that is the
synthesizing center of personal ordered existence.

The soul is a high-grade society. The body is permeated by low-grade occasions so far as mentality is concerned; the soul is composed of high-grade occasions.[9] That is, mentality in the soul rises to high levels of conceptual functioning including consciousness, intellection, imagination, and integration.

The soul is the presiding society of the organism. Located in the brain it gives order, perspective, and duration to the flow of the myriad occasions in the course of the route of personal development. In the hierarchy of occasions and societies that make up me, I have some direct intuition of a presiding monarch, informed by the total environment of the world, my body, and God. This presiding monarch, which is my soul, is effecting some kind of order among the feelings responding to the environment. A human life is a hierarchy of societies from low-grade experiencing centers like the big toe to the pinnacle of personhood, the soul. A vegetable is more like a democracy with no culminating, dominating society, e.g., soul. Human life is more like a monarchy in which the soul is that high-grade society of dominant or presiding occasions within the environing brain.[10] It is the constantly moving, changing intersection of the traffic that informs it and which it to some extent directs. From the body it inherits; and subsequent occasions feel that inheritance modified by the soul's vision.[11] Thus, as Cobb points out, the soul as the "center of experience in its continuity through time," plays a decisive role in the "functioning of the organism as a whole."[12]

A primary function of the soul is memory, which Cobb argues persuasively to be my personal sense of identity.[13] Whitehead through his doctrine of hybrid prehensions explains the possibility of memory.[14] We inherit from our immediate past as when I laughingly respond to a joke just told me. We ingress a new possibility as when I am lured by a child's forthright question. The

199

former is a physical feeling, meaning that it is derived from the contiguous past. The latter is a mental feeling, meaning that it is derived from the future so pregnant with possibility. But our souls can roam over the entire past without a con- tiguous past event. I can remember my father, dead thirty years, by re-presenting him in present experience. I know that in essential ways there is a continuity of myself now remembering with my- self then directly experiencing his gentle arthri- tic hand on my arm. That is a soul-function. Memory is a hybrid experience of the soul: feel- ing the novel features of long-ago (or recent) ex- periences, themselves once puffs of experiencing vitality, and now data to be re-presented in the present moment--what we call remembering. Without any adjacent occasion mediating our memories, our souls can roam over the past to recover mental images which fill us with delight or sadness'or anxiety. These are the memory traces, abstracted from, or lifted out of, the rich feelings of which they once were a part. Since these memory traces constitute a large part of the agenda, much of it painful as in grief situations, with which pastoral care must deal, the remembering soul, the organ par excellence of memory, is always before the carer.

The soul is also appetitive. Whitehead urged that ". . . the primary meaning of 'life' is the origination of . . . novelty--novelty of appeti- tion."[15] The soul is teleological; it has an ap- petite for the future, the tense of creativity. While the soul prehends its past, it simultaneously prehends the future, that is, God's aim (as well as the aims of others) for that concrete instant. The soul is challenged by a new possibility. Since the soul is a society of high-grade mental occasions as well as physical feelings, it theoretically is the society in the organism most alive to the novel possibilities God is persuading upon it. The soul, by nature appetitive, is the agency above all others in the human being by which the past is renewed and surpassed. It is the primary agent of change in the human organism.

The human soul develops its aims most often, I should think, in concert with bodily satisfactions. But it often develops aims unrelated to the body, and even possibly contrary to bodily satisfactions.[16] The history of mysticism is replete with illustrations of the soul's insistent urge toward spiritual peace at the expense of bodily pleasures. We may neglect food, or sex, or sleep to focus on the possibility of a "peak" experience, or to fulfill a social or moral duty, or to finish a book. There is no body/soul dualism even implied here. Rather, the appetitive dominance of the soul is underscored. In its forward reaching it may fulfill a hierarchy of needs beyond lesser bodily experiences. This pull of the soul would seem to be the base for great creativity. It may also create for the self times of tension, schizoid feelings, despair, and, contrary as it may seem, malaise of spirit as one wearies of the battle.

The nature of the soul is to aim with the far view as well as the near view in perspective. It hungers and thirsts for Adventure. It grows sad, shrivels and dies in the ennui of mere repetition. It is the experiencing center of vitality when it is a well soul; it is cast down when it is sick. And it is well when it is true to its nature: far-reaching in memory, abounding with vision, enjoying in its immediacy a unity of diversity and intensity. Thus the function of reason, as Whitehead has defined it, is one function of the soul: to live, to live better, to live best, that is, to promote the art of life.[17]

Before we move to specific applications to pastoral care, I propose what might seem an excursus: to look at a remarkable essay by Johs. Pedersen in his classic, Israel Its Life and Culture, I-II. The essay describes the Israelite sense of the soul. The reason for including a

201

brief summary of that 84-page essay on the soul
is to show affinities between Whitehead's understanding of soul and that of the Old Testament as
understood by one of its scholars. The obvious
benefit for pastoral care is to facilitate the recovery of its own biblical tradition about the
notion of soul. If there is the affinity I am
suggesting, that recovery lodged in an ontological
psychology should be all the richer.

II

Soul in Hebraic Thought

The soul is best characterized as an organism.[18] As such it possesses life, some souls
possessing great life, some less. In sorrow a
soul may shrink, losing its fulness or strength.[19]
The soul, nephesh, forms a unity with the body,
basar, and animates it. Yet the two terms are used
approvingly of the whole person from different
perspectives. But the soul is the preferred structure to express life and vitality whether of human
beings or beasts.[20] Indeed, the human being in
its total essence is a soul.[21]

This organism is volitional. As Pedersen
says, "The soul can never exist without volition,
because its certain character directs it along a
certain course."[22] It is the subject of appetite,
its appetition charged by emotion. "The nephesh
hungers and thirsts; is greedy; is satisfied;
feels joy, sorrow, love, hatred, hope, despair,
etc."[23] All these subjective forms derive from
its aim or thrust. In its volitional nature it
is often characterized as will and the Hebrew word
for heart, lev, is used to express both the desire
of the soul and the emotion implicit in the desire.[24]

In its essential volitional nature the soul
strives after totality and movement. The soul is
absorbed in its orientation "towards something to
which it is led or towards which it directs

itself." So the soul in its desiring "comprises everything that may add to the capacity of the soul, both the ideal values and the satisfaction of the claims of the body."[25] David has a king's desire, viz., to rule over Israel. That desire is total for David and leads to movement and action. Similarly the Israelite has a desire to "remember" Yahweh and his name. When the desire is sated the soul is complete, happy, restored.[26] If it is not filled it is anguished and "poured out." The soul then lacks strength.[27]

The soul must always be centered, and it centers itself around a point of gravity. This point of gravity is where the volition or desire takes form, and where the resulting fulfillment of the appetition is located. "Centering" is important to the Israelite because there is defined the essence of the life. The soul that is "lifted up to God," (Ps. 25:1; 85:4), "hopes in and glories in God" (Ps. 33:20; 130:5, 6) (Ps. 34:2; 35:9), and rests in God (Ps. 62:1, 5), becomes centered in God.

Spirit (ruah) is also part of soul when it is the human being's spirit. To have ruah is to be filled with spirit whether the spirit of wisdom and obedience or of harlotry and disobedience. Ruah is most consistently used, however, as a controlling notion. Some outside ruah other than the human person's own ruah is controlling, "as if controlling him and dominating him from the outside."[28] The Israelite's soul aspired to be controlled by the ruah of Yahweh, at least in Israel's finer moments. Its shame was to be controlled by the ruah of Baal or any other harlotry.

Consciousness, either of thought or of feeling, is not identified with the whole soul. "Consciousness plays a subordinate part in the psychological basic conception . . . what actually is in the soul may be there without our knowing it . . . ."[29] Under the surfaces of a person may be a stronger, that is, a potentially bursting,

203

soul to be called out by one with a penetrating vision, i.e., a prophet. So Samuel saw the latent forces in Saul.[30] Thus a soul, held under the control of consciousness, may be an impoverished soul because its great potential power is not unleashed. A soul, say, that of a prophet, senses it is owned or possessed when the ruah of God enters it. Compare Jeremiah: "My bowels, my bowels! I am pained at the walls of my heart; my heart thrills within me; I cannot hold my peace." (Jer 4:19). The soul has power to expand, burst its limits. It can be called forth and new depths and new elements make themselves known.[31]

While souls have their center, as we have noted, that center is not sharply defined as to space. Souls act on each other; they interpenetrate each other. The life of the soul "consists in constantly renewed combinations with other souls."[32] Through and through souls are social. There is mutual interchange, souls receiving from each other strength, sadness, joy, etc. When souls are united they gain a common will. So totalities are created. Israel is a unit when it is impressed with a common character running through the souls within it.[33] A soul is partly an entirety with itself and partly an entirety with others. Thus new unities and new centers are constantly being created.[34] Pedersen says, "That which is received into the soul must influence the character of the whole, just as, in its turn, it takes its character from the given stamp of totality."[35] In this context it is important to note that in Hebrew thought thinking is not abstractive. It is investigative with a practical bent: ". . . it consists in directing the soul towards something which it can receive into itself, and by which it can be determined."[36] The soul is responsible for the ideas it contains. Furthermore, it will act in accordance with those ideas because they harmonize with its essence and general character. "Therefore, it is of the greatest importance which ideas fill the soul."[37] The king going to war must fill his soul with victory

before the fight. If he does not win it is because he did not go to war as a soul of victory."[38] Action is part of the idea within the
soul. It is critical what the soul strives for,
since that determines what it is filled with,
which in turn determines its totality, its peace
(shalom), its satisfaction.[39]

     To summarize the salient points Pedersen has
made: The human soul is an organism whose predominate capacity is appetitive and volitional.
It is wholistic in its desiring, thinking, feeling, acting. It is dominated by spirit; and happy
or fulfilled is Israel when it desires and is possessed by the ruah of Yahweh. Consciousness is a
surface phenomenon not identical with its essence.
It is composed of the unities of other souls which
interpenetrate it and so it is social through and
through. In its totality it is marked or impressed with a common character. For Israel that
common character came from the wise soul seeking
the Lord with its entirety and being blessed.

     We are now able to assess the affinities be-
tween the Old Testament view of soul as characterized by Pedersen and that of Whitehead.

     Both view the soul as an organism: lively,
growing, decreasing, full of flux, but always a
unity whatever the state of affairs of the soul.
For both the organism is informed from without but
is responsible for how it puts together the world
which informs it. It is social through and through,
receiving from others and participating in others.
Both view the soul as appetitive: with desires,
yearnings, aims, ideals; in short, seeking adventure. Both see the soul as volitional: a corollary of the appetitive nature. In both consciousness is important but is only a small part of the
soul. Whitehead sees the soul as the dominant
society of the human being; with this Pedersen
would agree especially when the soul is truly itself, that is, when it is possessed by God. In
Hebraic thought to be possessed by the ruah of God

205

is to meet the soul's most basic need, which is to
be directed. Whitehead would agree that the soul
seeks direction and finds its need ideally met in
God as Lure. The ontological structure of the
soul, the dominant society directing the organism,
is met in its appetition by the incarnational activity of God.[40] I should think the soul as described by both Whitehead and Pedersen would be
the primary locus for responsible human existence,[41] because it is the primary meeting place
between the Divine and the human.

III

The Soul and Pastoral Care

If the soul is recovered, or to the extent
that it is, such a happening would invest pastoral
care with a uniqueness quite its own. I see four
aspects of this uniqueness, the first three to be
dealt with briefly and the fourth at some length.

1. The soul has capacity for novelty. Other
societies of occasions have capacity for novelty,
ranging from almost nil to considerable. But the
soul, located within the environment of the brain,
is that dominant society of major occasions whose
mental pole is wonderfully equipped for intellectual and imaginative feelings. It is pitched toward the entertainment of the richest possibilities
imaginable and beyond imagination. Even if the
soul itself is in bondage to conformation so that
it is succumbing to the "slow paralysis of surprise,"[42] with intensity flattening out, and even
if it is a cooperating victim of the trivial in
which life has lost its taste, the soul yet has
the capacity for novelty. Most if not all of pastoral caring cases feel the bondage and taste the
flatness of their lives, whether chronically or in
crisis. Their souls have become disquieted, down-
cast, desensitized by distraction, unable, even if
momentarily, to become zestful societies aiming
for new adventures. A case in point is a "normal"

206

grieving situation. By "normal" I mean one that does not continue past a year more or less into melancholia.[43] Three movements are involved in grieving and can be illustrated in the loss of a spouse. The widow had cathected, to borrow Freud's technical term, her husband; that is, she had invested herself in him, depositing herself in commitment to him. With his death she must decathect, slowly, painfully withdraw that cathexis lest she live in the illusion that he is not dead. Thus she gathers herself back into herself once more. After approximately a year, with its cycle of anniversaries and uniquely meaningful days including the anniversary of his death, she is ready to re-cathect the world with new commitments. Of course, some re-cathexis has been slowly taking place for months. In this situation of mourning where grief-work has been going on, the pastor may have confidence that the widow's soul has the normal capacity for renewal and transformation. Empathic support on the part of pastor and other friends will be helpful to introduce gently and patiently contrasting aims toward something new into the flow of concrescences in the life of her soul. But the pastor can count on a structure of soul-life in the hurting one with the capacity to grasp proffered aims and work toward novel satisfactions. We recall that the soul is volitional, appetitive, striving after movement toward wholeness. When its center has been disrupted or dislodged, its nature is to seek to be re-centered. This locates Carl Roger's insistence that every client has the capacity for his or her own righting.

Of profound importance in understanding the capacity of the soul is its effect upon the rest of the societies of the body. As the dominant society within and over the myriad societies that make up each of us, it can spread its virility throughout the human organism, infusing even the sick parts with its will and its appetition. I am thinking of cancer cases, my own included, in which a relatively healthy soul has given the

organism the courage to be and to do despite sometimes horrendous odds. A dear friend, Lois Jaffe,
had been in and out of leukemia remission for five
years. Relatively unafraid to die but with a zest
toward life, her soul carried that contagion of
spirit throughout the occasions and societies that
made up her body and especially her blood system.
A professor at the University of Pittsburgh, and
herself dying, she offered a course in death and
dying both to deal with her own feelings and to
be a catalyst to youth not too intimidated by
death to take the course. In Whitehead's language, in imagination she was roving in search of
novelty.[44] Whereas conformal feelings can fixate
us and block imagination, which is the peak of consciousness, she used imagination to deal with the
constant temptation to conform to moments of despair and ennui. Her sensitive and committed at-
tending physician, whose own healthy soul was a
continual lure for her, saw in her ensouled-
capacity the essence of her psychosomatic struggle. Current research seems to support the position that inner capacity of psychic health, which
I am locating primarily in the monarch which presides over the organism, is crucial to recovery
from cancer.[45] The soul, guided by "its ideal of
itself as individual satisfaction and as transcendent creator,"[46] has the capacity for that
novelty of aim which is necessary for organismic
healing.

2. The soul is the primary society of Hope.
We have referred to Hope several times in these
chapters, for it is necessary to the aesthetic
project of a human life; it is that possibility
perhaps beyond all possibilities to which propositions point; and it is the novel subjective form
in the process of salvation. Perhaps no psychological thinker has made so much of hope, although
rarely using the word, as has Victor Frankl.[47]
His thought, as is well known, was forged in the
infamous concentration camps of the Nazis where
he found meaning and its corollary, hope, crucial
to survival. I am suggesting that the soul is the
human locus of hope necessary to lesser as well as

greater survivals. Hopelessness is a predominate subjective form of most clients. The world appears bleak, empty, walled in. That was the concentration camp feeling for most, according to Frankl. It is the experience, whether temporary or of long duration, for many the pastor counsels with and cares about. So often they feel existence is not worth the struggle.

A client of mine, overpowered with feelings of rejection, derived first from parents and reinforced by a hammering and belittling husband, made a habit of hanging the world in black crepe. One evening she came to her appointment looking very glum. She announced that she had been promoted to be secretary to a company vice-president. Knowing I must not congratulate her I waited. "You know what they are trying to do," she finally struggled to say. "Put me in a position where I can't do the work so they can fire me." Her soul was sick. There was no health in her, and so no life, and so no hope. Until she could take a new aim on the future, she had not the luring power of hope. Without hope her soul, sick unto death, could only look back. But that was precisely the problem: to have hope she needed a hearty soul to look forward.

The responsibility of the counselor, by his presence and his words, was to introduce very gently slight, wan possibilities of hope that in the passage of time (a three-year duration) her own soul would prehend and would turn, if ever so slowly, toward hope. The capacity was there. That is the nature of souls. She had to let go compulsive patterns as she guardedly let her own capacity take hold. Several times as she left the counseling room she would subtly threaten, "I'll see you next week if I'm still alive." I interpreted that to be movement within her soul, partly because it came a year into the counseling relationship, and partly because of the voice tone and the facial gesture. I replied, "I trust the direction in which you are moving. I'll see you

209

next week." I could be comfortable because I trusted her soul's capacity toward the future and I sensed hope was being born in the turning soul. Hope did become prominent among her subjective aims. In Old Testament language her soul gradually became fat and she herself almost visibly leaned into the future.

Pastoral care of the aging, a vast field about which we have important gerontological studies but about which we have little first-rate correlated pastoral material, would seem to be an area of concern primed to test the thesis of this section. Hope is shut down or made difficult for many aging not only because of infirmity, poverty, and aloneness, but more importantly because of crass socio-cultural animosity, denial, indifference, and disaffirmation, surely in part as defenses against reminders of our finitude and our own aging processes. Ministry to the aging will find a strong lead in correlating the soul as described by Whitehead and Pedersen with genuine hope. Such hope is here and now an article of experience as well as an eschatological event yet to be fully realized. The theologians of Hope such as Moltmann, Pannenberg, Ritschl, and Alves, and the Marxist-humanist Ernst Block, provide significant theological material, but material which must be sensitively related to the structure of the soul with its natural capacity for hope and not to an abstract human nature whose appearance we sense but whose reality we are not in touch with. It will be the formidable task of pastoral theology to do the relating and the sooner the better.

3. The soul may be the vessel for intercessory prayer. A primary contribution of pastoral care is praying in behalf of another. Whether the one praying is at the bedside of the other or across the country is not fundamental to the proposal I am making. Rather, the suggestion depends upon the immanence of souls in each other and in God, and God's redemptive responsiveness. Only

sketchily do I make the proposal here. Cobb
writes, "The soul in each momentary occasion prehends not only its environing brain but also its
own past occasions of experience and the experiences of other souls. The prehensions are not
mediated by the body."[48] These are hybrid prehensions of the mental poles of other souls and these
prehensions constitute our memory system. Souls
are the loci of immanence of each person in the
other. Cobb accounts for the "extreme vagueness
with which other souls are prehended directly in
this life" as being due to bodily interventions.[49]
But Pedersen's understanding of the social nature
of souls, Whitehead's insight into the social nature of all reality, and our own vague experiences
argue for the immanence of soul within soul.

There is also theological argumentation. God
prehends the souls of all, grasping each momentary
soul-experience into the divine nature. The immanence of human souls within the experience of
God must mean that in that immanence each is part
of the other as they are together in the immediacy of God's experience. As part of the everlasting nature of God we are not isolated from each
other but socially intertwined. It is out of this
profound organismic setting in God's experience
that God comes back to each soul with the particular aim most appropriate to that soul. God weaves
the multitudinous experiences of the world into a
Harmony within the divine Nature and offers out of
that Harmony a new lure for the next moment in the
world.

Translated into intercessory prayer, this
would mean that my mother, 2,500 miles away,
stroke-ridden with only fragments of durations of
awareness, is prehended by God. I, praying a simple prayer that she might be at peace, am prehended by God. Isolating those two prehensions
within the total experience of God, there my mother
and I meet. God brings those two prehensions into
Harmony within the vast divine redemptive work.
In turn, God floods back upon my Mother an aim--

211

for Peace?--appropriate to her condition as well as upon me appropriate to my needs (anxiety over her state of illness?). God does not need to be reminded to care for my Mother nor how to care for her. God's graciousness is to experience us as we actually are; and then to use those experiences in luring us into transforming moments. Perhaps God uses intercessory prayers to enrich our love for one another and to provide a way for our bearing responsibility for one another whether close by or far away. Each intercessory prayer is an actuality which God must (ontologically) and does take into account in persuading the world from moment to moment. Perhaps such prayer opens up for God the opportunity to persuade by a radical new possibility. Perhaps the divine patience and humility are God's waiting upon such actualities as intercessory prayer to let them be a creative part of the divine aiming. Might this be a way in which the Spirit intercedes with our spirit, as Paul suggests, and by which we become laborers with God? Even if God could do it all, which experience and process ontology deny, our sensitivities, far from reaching new levels of Beauty, would stultify and be degraded, the nadir of evil.

The process understanding of Soul when coupled with process insight into the relation of God with the world allows the three Souls--my mother's, mine, and God who is the Soul of the world[50]--to be mutually prehended. Perhaps language or perhaps sheer intercesssory feeling can reach from one soul to the other through the gracious Agency of God as mediator, and so have an effect, that is, make a difference, in each. God offers the divine life as meeting-place, uses the emotion of intercession to relate appropriately to the world, and lends out the divine Soul to lift our human souls into new reaches of existence.

4. The soul is the center of spirituality. Immediately I must clarify what I do not mean by center of spirituality. It should be clear by this time that Whitehead does not see the soul as

212

some kind of supernatural pre-existent element as in Plato's conceptuality but as a natural human element.[51] Thus spirituality does not mean a dualism which elevates soul and deprecates body. The spirituality envisioned is not that of Medieval piety, which is dualistic, although it may be enriched by the formidable models derived from the desert Fathers and monastic life. It rejects the medieval Imitatio Christi model as inauthentic and unbiblical when it would copy his life and apply his stigmata, demanding rather that each fulfill her or his vocation as Jesus fulfilled his.[52] It rejects a piety of laws, rules, and regulations as not appropriate to free people in Christ, although it can usefully employ the suggestion in Psalm 119: 24 as translated in Today's English Version: "Your instructions give me pleasure; they are my advisers." It also rejects as abstractions a check-list of Christian virtues, although they may be as helpful as they are dangerous as guides.[53] Reinhold Niebuhr reminded us how easily virtues become vices.

There are movements in psychology which point to the kind of spirituality envisioned. Carl Jung represents one such thrust. Critical of Freud's theories based upon biological drives, Jung wants to press to the "deeper spiritual needs of the patient." By these needs he means fundamentally the need for meaning, asserting that it is "only the meaningful that sets us free." He continues: "The patient is looking for something that will take possession of him and give meaning and form to the confusion of his neurotic mind."[54] Spirituality, for Jung, occurs when the conscious life has obtained "meaning and promise" through the painful individuation of the Self out of the collective and personal unconscious.[55] Jung is correctly searching for meaning. My criticism is that he finds it on a trajectory out of the past.

Frankl, too, would relate spirituality to meaning which he derives from ideals and values for which one is willing to die. These ideals and

values are not resident in the human being but
are over against her confronting her. Thus, he
criticizes the archetypes of Jung as merely self-
expressions of humanity. Frankl is frank to use
the term spiritual (as did Jung) to stand for the
aspiration to meaning which is the basic need of
each. That need is indeed more than an aspiration; it is a basic "will to meaning," a why to
live for.[56] The essence of existence, according
to Frankl, is responsibleness; that is, the responsibleness of each to decide "for what, to
what or to whom he understands himself to be responsible."[57] What one chooses, one will live for.
That is the essence of being spiritual. Frankl
underscores the existential decision and the pri-
macy of aim which are nuclear to the concrescence
described by Whitehead. But he does not show
where values are lodged or how values arise and
this deficiency is crucial when compared to process thought.

Maslow, like Jung, is critical of Freud for
his reductionism, especially as he reduces values
to biological drives. He argues that psychoanalysis does not supply us with a psychology of
the "spiritual life, of what the human being
should grow toward, of what he can become. . . ."[58]
Maslow talks of of our "higher nature," our "spiritual values," which he no more wants to base on
a traditional supernatural explanation than does
Whitehead.[59] Our higher nature is Being-nature
which in Motivation and Personality is the self-
actualizing need-fulfillment to which he attached
a number of values. He later refined the value-
descriptions involved in B-living in his Religions,
Values, and Peak-Experiences detailing 14 complex
B-values.[60] He repeats these with elaboration in
The Farther Reaches of Human Nature, Ch. 9. These
B-values are intrinsic values, constitutionally-
based, instinctoid.[61] Yet not all people realize
these B-values. This has led Maslow to recognize
"peakers" and "non-peakers," two types of person-
alities. The former are more open to mystical experience, to incursions of the unexpected, to

"transcendent" experiences by which he means "natural, human peak-experiences."[62] Non-peakers are inclined to the strictly rational, to institutional life such as the church, to legalisms; in short; they are those who "concretize the religious symbols and metaphors. . . ."[63] Maslow was a prophet in behalf of helping all people to grow toward the Being values which he felt he had empirically uncovered in his research. His list not so strangely resembles middle-class virtues of the Western world since his subjects were mostly college students. He thought these were indigenous to each self and would be achieved if the needs of the self could be progressively satiated and the person released to actualize himself. Any list might make one nervous, reminding one of old trait-theories. But a list would especially raise the eyebrow of a process thinker since the realm of eternal objects is an infinity of possibility hardly reducible to a two-page listing. Furthermore, values do not arise on a trajectory out of causal efficacy, where instinctoid material would be located, but out of the future as God offers them for human aiming. Nevertheless, Maslow points to a spirituality that is beyond adherence to the actual, urging an intrinsic and constant connection with the ideal. So he quotes Dewey approvingly: ". . . endeavor for the better is moved by faith in what is possible, not by adherence to the actual."[64]

Assagioli identifies his thinking with both Jung and Frankl but especially with Maslow. But he moves beyond Maslow's self-actualization to self-realization which is gained from the Higher Unconscious, the source of our higher intuitions and inspirations. Assagioli insists that the highest realization of the self is by way of synthesizing those values such as the ethical, aesthetic, heroic, religious, and altruistic which can generally be termed spiritual and which are the contents of the superconscious.[65] These contents are the "strong 'call from above,'" and are the "pull of the Self. . . ."[66] Whitehead would locate this "call from above" and the "pull of the Self" in

the persuasive agency of God, or in the divine
Directivity, as Cobb has named it. Such a location fulfills the ontological principle that everything has to be somewhere, that is, in an actual
entity. Assagioli's Superconscious sounds like an
abstraction needing to be housed. Whitehead provides the housing.

Jung, Frankl, Maslow, and Assagioli are struggling for a break-through in psychology that will
embrace the realm of values. Because of this emphasis they, especially Maslow, are third-force
psychologists informing the growth potential movement. They can be enriched, however, by the ontological vision of process thought which carefully
locates values within its metaphysical system.
Their intuitions toward spiritual values would
thus be secured beyond instinctoid needs, innate
trajectories, free-floating values, and an abstract superconsciousness.

The spirituality I envisage is a new existence
(the biblical "fresh-creation" of Paul) constantly
transcending itself as its appetitive reach grasps
the lures of God. While God lures each occasion,
it is the soul which is the natural point of contact for God's richest luring. It is the soul
which is equipped to respond in imaginative feelings to make concrete Maslow's inspired vision of
each self reaching for the "farther reaches of
human nature." But it is God, essential to process but peripheral to even third-force psychology,
who makes the basic difference. The soul has the
capacity for spiritual existence, but whether or
not it is spiritual depends on what ruah controls
its vitality, as Pedersen has shown. When God's
aiming, fresh each instant, possesses the attention and direction of the soul, then no list of
values as ends to be realized can do justice to the
small and large miracles of novelty possible to the
soul. In fact, lists might make the vision myopic.
That would be another false piety, for God's vision would have to conform to our list. The spirituality envisioned refers to the "radically self-
transcending character of human existence that

216

emerged in the Christian community," as Cobb has put it.[67] Yet no Christian community can contain it for every community also needs to be self-transcending. God's lures are always relevant, but they beckon toward what Simone Weil has called "a new saintliness, itself . . . without precedent."[68] The "new saintliness" of which she spoke so eloquently is to be "bound to the creation in its totality,"[69] and that is possible only when one is possessed by a willed love to God that out of that Attachment no single lesser attachment will tyrannize us. Spiritual existence is self-transcending existence that lives from the initiative of God,[70] and is therefore open to radical existence fronting on a future pregnant with surprises. It is not particularly heroic existence. It is trusting existence. Simone Weil has put it simply: "For as to the spiritual direction of my soul, I think that God himself has taken it in hand from the start and still looks after it."[71] It is an existence that "exercises its new freedom in love," as Cobb reports.[72] "Such love is the possibility of openness to the other as another. . . ." But such love itself is possible by the "gift of an undeserved love."[73]

I conclude this chapter by paraphrasing Whitehead: The soul lives by its incarnation of God in itself.[74] If its adventuring can meet the directivity of God, a process of radical self-transformation can go on making all things new (Rev. 21:5). In the flow of concrescences the new person emerges. In turn that new person offers herself or himself as a love-offering to the world. This is the soul's vocation: to answer the summons of God to individual self-transcendence; and the occasioning Beauty offers to the world a new datum pointing toward its own transcendence. Whitehead has written, "The power of God is the worship He inspires."[75] The soul's perishing to the old self and rising to the new is its adventure of spirit: the ultimate worship and the ultimate testimony.

One implication of this radical spirituality is preventive pastoral care. It might be the most significant pastoral caring that a pastor does when she helps to point a soul toward yet unrealized possibility: a) through her life, created out of the world's (and God's) offerings, and offered back to others (including God); and b) through her sermons, teaching, administering, professional and personal caring. Quickened by the summoning of God, the soul, while not protected from life's stresses and crises, would have the sense of direction and the discovery of meaning Frankl found to be the sine qua non of life in its most naked moments. The vocation of the pastor to care for her flock so that their souls may become congruent with the Soul of God is a vocation potential of producing health as well as salvation. And, incidentally but importantly, it might take the boredom out of so many ministers' lives.

NOTES

[1] See Plato, _Phaedo_. But it must be remembered that Plato was trying to say something terribly important when he talked about the soul.

[2] Abraham H. Maslow, _Religions, Values, and Peak-Experiences_ (NY: Viking, 1970), Chs. II-VI.

[3] Cobb, _Natural Theology_, p. 47. Cobb's treatment of the Soul is the richest and clearest expression in process thought. See Ch. II.

[4] Cf. Plato's dialogue, _Phaedo_.

[5] Alfred North Whitehead, _Modes of Thought_ (NY: Capicorn, 1938), p. 166.

[6] _Ibid._, p. 222.

[7] _Ibid._, p. 223f.

[8] _Ibid._, p. 224.

[9] Cf. _A.I._, p. 208.

[10] Cf. _PR_, p. 166 and Cobb, _Natural Theology_, p. 49.

[11] _PR_, p. 166.

[12] _Natural Theology_, p. 48.

[13] _Ibid._, pp. 71-79.

[14] For a technical discussion see _PR_, p. 163, 469; also, Cobb, _NT_, pp. 50-54.

[15] _PR_, p. 156.

[16] Cf. Cobb, _Existence_, p. 39.

[17] Whitehead, _The Function of Reason_, pp. 4, 8.

[18] Johannes Pedersen, _Israel, Its Life and Culture_ (London: Oxford, 1926), I-II, pp. 145, 151.

[19] Cf. _The Interpreter's Dictionary of the Bible_, "Soul," _in loc._, pp. 428f.

[20] Cf. Henry Snyder Gehman (ed.), _The Westminster Dictionary of the Bible_ (Philadelphia: Westminster, 1970), p. 901.

[21] Pedersen, _Israel_, p. 99.

[22] _Ibid._, p. 103. Bultmann writes that Paul's understanding of Soul is along these lines of an intentional vitality directed toward an end. By soul Paul means the tendency of one's will, the vitality of oneself as a "striving, willing, purposing self." Rudolf Bultmann, _Theology of the New Testament_ (NY: Scribner's, 1951), tr. by Kendrick Grobel, I, pp. 204-205.

[23] _Ibid._

[24] Cf. _ibid._, p. 108.

[25] _Ibid._, p. 126.

[26] _Ibid._, p. 148.

[27] _Ibid._, p. 149.

[28] Cf. Norman H. Snaith, _The Distinctive Idea of the Old Testament_ (London: Epworth, 1944), p. 149.

[29] Pedersen, _ibid_, p. 132.

[30] _Ibid._, p. 156f.

[31] _Ibid._, p. 162.

[32] _Ibid._, p. 165.

[33] _Ibid._

[34] Ibid., p. 166.

[35] Ibid., p. 106.

[36] Ibid., p. 109.

[37] Ibid., p. 141.

[38] Ibid., cf. p. 143.

[39] Ibid., cf. p. 108.

[40] Cobb's naming God's aiming as Directivity correlates precisely with the soul's appetite for
direction. Cf. Theology and Pastoral Care,
pp. 46ff.

[41] Cf. Brunner's analysis of "responsible existence"
which is existence "before God." Emil Brunner,
Revelation and Reason, tr. by Olive Wyon (Philadelphia: Westminster, 1946), pp. 52-57.

[42] AI, p. 286.

[43] See Sigmund Freud, "Mourning and Melancholia,"
Collected Papers (London: Hogarth, 1957), IV,
Ch. VIII.

[44] AI, p. 245.

[45] Cf. O. Carl Simonton, Stephanie Matthews-Simonton,
and James Creighton, Getting Well Again (NY:
Martin, 1978).

[46] PR, p. 130.

[47] Cf. Victor E. Frankl, The Doctor and the Soul
(NY: Knopf, 1968); and Victor E. Frankl, Man's
Search for Meaning (NY: Washington Square, 1963),
a revised ed. of From Death-Camp to Existen-
tialism.

[48] Natural Theology, p. 66. Cf. AI, p. 208.

[49] Ibid., p. 67.

[50] Cf. Charles Harshorne, "Whitehead's Idea of God," The Philosophy of Alfred North Whitehead, ed. by Paul Arthur Schilpp (NY: Tudor, 1951), p. 550. Also, Man's Vision, op. cit., p. 200.

[51] Cf. Cobb, Natural Theology, p. 48.

[52] Cf. Jung, Modern Man, op. cit., p. 236.

[53] See Edward Farley, Requiem, op. cit., for elaboration of some of these rejections.

[54] Jung, Modern Man, p. 225.

[55] Cf. ibid., p. 233.

[56] Man's Search for Meaning, pp. 155-164.

[57] Ibid., p. 173.

[58] Maslow, Peak-Experiences, p. 7.

[59] Ibid., pp. 36f.

[60] Ibid., pp. 91ff.

[61] The Farther Reaches of Human Nature, pp. 315f.

[62] Peak-Experiences, pp. 19, 20.

[63] Ibid., p. 25.

[64] Peak-Experiences, p. 15.

[65] Psychosynthesis, pp. 17; 36ff.

[66] Ibid., p. 54.

[67] John B. Cobb, Jr., The Structure of Christian Existence, p. 119.

[68] Simone Weil, _Waiting for God_ (NY: Capricorn, 1959), p. 99.

[69] _Ibid._, p. 98.

[70] Cf. _Christian Existence_, Ch. X.

[71] Weil, _op. cit._, p. 73.

[72] _Christian Existence_, p. 123.

[73] _Ibid._, pp. 134, 36.

[74] _RM_, p. 156.

[75] Alfred North Whitehead, _Science and the Modern World_, (NY: Mentor, 1925), p. 192.

Ultimately, it is the community that cures.
Philip Rieff, <u>The Triumph of the Therapeutic</u>

Chapter X
Church: A Society of Caring

The focus of caring in the preceding chapters
has been on the professional, e.g., pastor or
pastoral carer. This is partly because traditionally the pastor has been seen as the sole pastoral
carer. Furthermore, focusing on the professional
in the caring role enabled us to keep concepts and
applications more focused. With process thought's
atomistic analysis of actual occasions any individual self is already an enduring society of
occasions and therefore incredibly complex. To go
beyond the individual would be to deal with a yet
larger collective and perhaps obscure the genius of
process thought.

Nevertheless, in this concluding chapter we
must look at the church, or better the churches, as
loci of pastoral caring. We shall still remain
with individuals as the focus of pastoral caring
and so the analyses and applications in which the
pastor has been the focus will apply with equal
force to the so-called laity. I say "so-called"
because actually the people of God are all laity
including the pastor.[1] The purpose of this chapter
is to see the society of God's people as a society
of caring within process categories for the sake
of their participation in the common ministry of
caring. Furthermore, their involvement is the only
way in which the tremendous load of pastoral caring
can be borne. A friend of mine who is a psychiatrist in private practice and on a medical school
faculty once told me that if psychiatrists had a
community behind them as clergy persons have
behind them, they would long ago have found out how
to use such a community. Whether they could make
good on that statement I do not know. But almost
without exception clergy have not learned how to
use the community as a significant resource for

225

caring. Yet there are exceptions which highlight
the great value of equipping the rest of the people
of God or at least some of them to do pastoral
caring.[2]

In this final chapter we shall look at the
church in process terms and suggest a model for
equipping the rest of the laity, or rather a
remnant, for pastoral caring.

I

The Church in Process Thought

We must remember that the primary or basic
unit according to process thought is the actual
occasion. Each actual occasion bonds with other
actual occasions to form nexüs or societies, e.g.,
a molecule. These societies bond with other
societies to form ever larger societies such as a
person which is a society of societies of societies,
at the base of which are the actual occasions.

But quite obviously there are larger societies
which are collectives of persons. Such a social
network is the church. The social structure of the
church must be seen as a collective of myriad
societies which in turn are the interrelatedness of
a vast multiplicity of actual occasions. In this
chapter we are seeing the church, then, as a society
of societies of societies; in short, social through
and through. Its sociality is its internal
relations in the basic unity of an actual occasion
and permeating ever increasing complexities of
unity which we visualize or customarily think of as
church. It is an organism, the member parts of
which: a) grasp conformally an incredibly massive,
rich, and varied tradition; b) reach out to ingress
a future of possibility known only to God in its
infinitude and yet immediate relevance; c) put
together in the throbbing immediacy of each moment
their world of past and future so that new instants
dawn upon the world; and d) themselves so created
become insistently available to fresh moments

arising in the restless flow of time. Hartshorne
has written of sociality: "To be social is to
weave one's own life out of strands taken from the
lives of others and to furnish one's own life as
a strand to be woven into their lives."[3] The
church is one social organism among many fulfilling
this description.

In describing the church, that is, a congregation of people, we are describing a society which
is permeated by a common form. What constitutes
any society, e.g., family, church, is that there is
a form which is common to all of its members.
These are its bench-marks which give it its
identity over against other societies. The church
has a very complex set of defining marks which have
continually defined and re-defined it through the
years. For example, Calvin designated the defining
marks of the church to be the Gospel rightly
preached and heard and the sacraments rightly
observed. Bernard Lee, a Roman Catholic process
thinker, sees the Jesus-event as the common form
defining the church. By this he means a "faith
in the importance of Jesus" and that importance
showing forth the revelation of God's love which is
radical redemptive love.[4] Stating it differently
but driving to the core of the Gospel with his
"marks of the church," Calvin would agree with Lee.
The Jesus-event is the common form defining each
member and so is constitutive of that society in
which those members, marked by that common element,
relate, and inhere in each other. The church is
the embodiment of the Jesus-event, each one making
the dominant form or forms of that Event hers or
his. Each shares with others his or her own
peculiar form of that event which is how each has
grasped that event; and so each is partly creative
of the others through the process of receiving
from, and passing on, the Jesus-event.[5] So the
church is the unique society remembering Jesus and
passing on its own formations of that memory.

Through causal efficacy, the mode of reception
from the past, the church in process makes new

227

responses to the Jesus-event and passes those responses on to be grasped by new individuals in the flow of time. In chapter VIII we suggested how Jesus prehended God. The history of the church is 2000 years of prehensive history, the church prehending the Jesus-event at the center of which was Jesus' faithful prehension of God's self-communication as Christ. As Jesus internalized God in a remarkable uniqueness, so the church, taking in the entire Jesus-event (heritage, life, teachings, suffering and death, and resurrection) internalizes in heightened consciousness what Jesus had prehended: God. In Jesus the church has always uniquely sensed that it was in touch with the reality of God. The defining characteristic of the church by which it is ordered is Jesus as the Christ. It has other defining forms, to be sure, for its roots are in the Old Testament, the New Testament which is the interpreted memory of Jesus, and its own traditions. It is a part of all that it has met coming out of an infinite past. But its crucial form, exemplified in each member as each is genetically related to all, is the very complex definition of Jesus whose primary defining form was God's communication of agape-love which Jesus made his own. So Jesus as Christ is the center of the church's life.

Causal efficacy, the route by which the past is present to the present, is the mode by which Jesus is really present in his church. It is in unity with him that the church has its basic definition. Cobb and Griffin, using Whiteheadian conceptuality, show how the "real presence of Jesus" is that event which "literally plays a constitutive role" in the history of the church. They have suggested field theory symbolism in which to locate this constitutive event.

> In the case of Jesus we have to do not only with an event of great intrinsic power but also with one that has produced the church which accepts as its task the amplification of the

field of force. Millions of persons
have made decisions to be constituted
by the event of Jesus in such a way
that its potential for constituting
others is increased. These decisions
have shaped sacraments, whose purpose
it is to re-present the events for en-
hanced efficacy in the lives of
believers. Thus the church is the
community that is consciously dedicated
to maintaining, extending, and
strengthening the field of force
generated by Jesus. To enter such a
community is to be engrafted into
that field of force and thus to experience the real presence of Jesus
constituting one's own existence.[7]

The tragedy of the church, that above all else
which might make it seem demonic, is that we, its
cellular structure, have not been definitely constituted by the "real presence of Jesus." Jesus is
the titular Head, but titles do not constitute much.
We resemble Jesus so faintly who imaged God so
decisively. Of what is this image? Charles
Hartshorne has argued that the "universe as a
going concern must be a monarchical society, if it
is a society at all."[8] God, he argues, is the
monarch of the world society.[9] But, for Hartshorne,
God is cosmic monarch not political monarch, "world
boss."[10] God is neither tyrannous nor coercive.
God is the Servant of the world. Indeed, Hartshorne
affirms that "God is the only genuine servant of
all, who grieves in all griefs whatever, who longs
for the fulfillment of all desires actually enter-
tained. . . .God is the monarch or king of all only
through being in a real sense the slave, nay, the
scourged slave, of all, infinitely more passive to
others, more readily 'wounded' even, than anyone
else can ever be."[11] This divine servant or slave
is the suffering God who has for "nearly twenty
centuries been symbolized by the cross. . ."[12]

Hartshorne has thus suggested the transition
from God the servant to Jesus the Servant of God.

The Lordship of Jesus is by way of his servanthood.
I am arguing that the decisive characteristic of
Jesus, if one can be singled out, is that he exemplifies in a remarkable way what God is fundamentally about: serving the world which is agape-
love incarnate. Now if Jesus as the Christ is
Head of the Church, the monarch in Hartshorne's
understanding of the term, the Church's defining
characteristic should become quite clear, viz.,
to follow its Head, who followed God, in the
servant tradition. The formula would be: Like
God--Like Jesus--Like People. But this formula
has had rough going in becoming translated into
the life of the church. If the Christ is the
creative activity of God, prehending all life and
constantly struggling to transform all life, and
if this Christ was grasped by Jesus and became
constitutive of Jesus, the Society of Jesus should
be shaped by that which fundamentally constituted
him. The Body of Christ, constituted by the real
presence of Jesus as Christ, should be a society
forever being transformed and forever transforming.
This is the Servant-role.

     The church, instead, so often resembles the
first Adam, to borrow a biblical figure. Destructive discord, majoring in trivia, staleness and
dull habit, closedness to change, suppression of
adventure, opposition to the Creative Good, backing
into the future, are process ways of expressing
what traditional theological language has called
sin. Whatever the language, the reality is
oppositional so much of the time to the real
presence of Jesus and the transformation that
presence seeks to actualize within us. Cobb and
Griffin say straight-forwardly: "Openness to
Christ as creative transformation is rightly feared
as a threat to the extant churches."[13]

     That fear correlates with the church's pre-
occupation with maintenance. The institutionaliza-
tion of our defining form has blunted the radical-
ity of the love which is the essence of that form.
We are not transcending ourselves by living totally

from the initiative of God which became incarnate
in the Jesus-event. This was the new Existence
into which the early church was born with obedient
love its defining characteristic. The tragedy is
that the churches, with some beautiful exceptions,
have succumbed to the vulgarity of maintenance.
There is an odor about church order; it is the odor
of decadence. Thus spiritual existence, which is
existence expressing itself in love, is denied for
it requires radical self-transcendence,[14] that is,
a perpetual aiming beyond itself to be congruent
with the divine aiming.

Freud has called religion restrictive.[15] While
his data are partly pathological and partly pre-
judicial, an honest appraisal from within the life
of a religious institution must plead guilty to
this charge even though there are other data supporting a different conclusion. If the ego
defenses of individuals are restrictive, and if
those individuals are grouped together in a local
congregation, the ego defenses of that group are
not going to be somehow freer. Defensive structures
are implicit in institutional life for institutions
tend to be self-protective and self-serving. They
are maintenance prone. If the church were only an
institution, promising no more, that might be less
noisome. Since the church is the redemptive fellow-
ship of God on earth, its ministry the ministry of
reconciliation, such defensiveness is intolerable.
The Ephesian picture of the church (Eph. 6:10-17),
loins girded with truth, feet shod with the gospel
of peace, sword of the Spirit in hand, which is a
picture of the quick and the nimble, confronts in
stark judgment the massive, self-protective church
to today, which one young friend described as a
"beached whale."

All of this means that the church is hardly the
"nurturing matrix" or the "communal ground"[16] out of
which we should expect spiritual existence or radical love to be born. Nor do I entertain much hope
that the churches will alter their existence in any
important ways. At least I do not see any basis for

231

such hope. For pastors, many of whom are also
maintenance prone, to expect their congregation
to be turned around very soon would seem to me to
be indulging in wishful thinking and to be inviting
new visitations of guilt upon themselves. Rather,
I see a new possibility for creating a leaven
within the lump by developing a Remnant community
of caring. In the next section I shall describe
the concept and in the Appendix detail a program
for training "lay" pastoral carers.

II

The Remnant Concept of Church

The model for the Remnant society[17] which I
have in mind is the culminating picture in the Old
Testament of Yahweh's servant. It is found in the
four servant-songs of Isaiah, 42-53. The first
servant-song, Isaiah 42:1-4, pictures the Servant
of Yahweh chosen for mission to the nations. But
in 42:19, 20 the Servant is seen as blind and deaf,
that is, disobedient. This would seem to be the
nation Israel and points back to the reasons for
the Exile. The second song, Isaiah 49:1-6, hears
the Servant soliloquizing about having "spent my
strength for nothing and vanity"; yet the Servant
knows he is forgiven and has been assigned a two-
fold mission: to Israel and to the nations. This
would seem to point to an Israel within Israel, a
part of the People with a redemptive mission to the
rest of Israel, as well as a renewed mission to the
nations. In the third song, Isaiah 50:4-9, the
Servant is again soliloquizing, determined to fulfill his mission which will entail suffering,
certain that Yahweh will vindicate him and his work.
It is obvious that the personification of Israel,
if that is what it is, is much sharper than in the
two preceding songs, so much so that an Individual
may be emerging. The fourth song, Isaiah 52:15-
53:12, is a much more detailed personification, or
if an individual has truly emerged, the profile is
very personal. In this song the mission is to be
fulfilled through suffering and death.

Throughout the four songs the identity of the
Servant is a most perplexing problem.[18] The most
satisfying solution seems to me to be a collective
interpretation with an emerging sharpness of detail
as to be either a highly personified Israel or an
individual Servant in the future which sums up the
nation in faithfully performing its mission. I see
an Israel of the whole, disobedient to its mission;
then a Remnant is selected from within the disobedient Israel, purged and mandated with the
double mission to redeem the rest of Israel and
the world; that Remnant becomes highly personified
as it becomes increasingly conscious of mission
through suffering and death.[19] The Remnant is the
witness to the righteousness of Yahweh whose saving
acts redeemed the Remnant and assigned anew its
mission to be the redemptive agent of God.[20] As
McKenzie concludes: "The mission of service will
never die and never fail in Israel; for Israel must
become the Servant, its corporate personality, if
it is to survive as the people of Yahweh."[21]

The model of the church as a caring community
is tremendously rich. First, there is God whose
monarchy is that of suffering servanthood,
receiving the grief, pain, evil from the world and
tenderly working to redeem the world. Second,
there is the entire Jesus-event whose Lordship is
identified by a servanthood both in his own
identity and the identification of the early
church (Isa. 61:1, 2; Lk. 4:16-19). Third, there
is the servant motif of Deutero-Isaiah which I
have identified under terms of Remnant. When this
rich servant tradition is focused on the local
congregation, it would seem to have very persuasive
power. The congregation, or a part of it, itself
disobedient, might be lured to embark on a faith-
journey to be obedient. The Remnant responds to a
call to be in the tradition of Servant.[22] The
servant enters into a compact to bear the cost of
servanthood. The title of servant, as McKenzie
notes, designates a peculiar relationship to
Yahweh. The servant is one who has a peculiar
commission from Yahweh; the title, servant, is not

a polite form of self-deprecation.[23] Servanthood
correlates with covenant. God covenants with a
people to become the People of God. They are
formed as the grace-gifts of God are made their own
in the creative responses of obedient love. The
cost of the covenant will include a determination
to aim toward self-transcending love, intensive
training for the ministry of caring, and the caring
itself.

Taking the Remnant concept seriously and concentrating our labors on the church within the
church does not need to mean a neglect of the other
members. Their needs are great and they as persons
must be respected and served as well as drawn into
serving roles. The Remnant will have part of its
mission to this larger group. They will fulfill
this ministry as they become newly effective in the
life of the congregation as well as by their caring
within the specific needs of the people. Working
more intentionally, but not exclusively, with this
Remnant pastors might find that they are working
with manageable proportions so that they can do
more in depth, inculcate more growth, hope for more
spontaneity and creativity, and locate a people
more likely to be a servant people. There will be
the risk of envy on the part of some of the rest
of the people. So careful interpretation must be
made and the risk courageously faced. There is also
the risk of spiritual pride and the dangers attendant upon a "we-group" mentality. Again the risk
must be faced; but holding the biblical model before
the Remnant will soften the risk as it focuses upon
the luring activity of God. If we are intimidated
by either risk we lose sight of what might be by
way of a self-transcending community of people, and
we succumb to the trivia and staleness that marks
congregational life. It is from that tragedy that
we hope to be delivered.

How might this Remnant be identified? There is
no simple answer to this question and any attempt
at one may in itself become a new restriction. But
suggestions can be made. A sensitive and alert

pastor knows most of the Remnant within his congregation. But there are guidelines for the
selecting process. The Remnant should not be
self-selective. That is an invitation to those
who may not be emotionally or religiously prepared
to care in ways that are appropriate to pastoral
caring theory and practice. The Remnant must not
be equated with members of boards or committees
for it belongs to no officialdom. Neither is the
Remnant to be measured by the criterion of activity
because activity in itself may be a major defense.
Nor is it to be identified with the so-called
healthy-minded. There may be neurosis in the
service of the ego and especially in the service
of the Gospel. (Though neither is mental nor
emotional illness a criterion for Remnant.)
Perhaps the underlying concern would be that
Remnant-people have a healthy sense of freedom and
in their freedom there be a content of loving
awareness and the promise of creative imagination.

While I believe that Maslow's distinctions
between "peakers" and "non-peakers," that is,
between those more open to peak-experiences and
those more maintenance and institutionally oriented,
are overdrawn,[24] nevertheless his two types are
very suggestive for the selection process.
Obviously, "peakers" might point to Remnant
possibilities. Likewise, Gordon Allport's distinctions between intrinsic and extrinsic people,
the former having internalized their religion and
made it nuclear to their life while the latter
see their religion basically in terms of utilitar-
ian values, are helpful in pointing to those most
likely to be Remnant types.[25]

The psychological model I have in mind is
Erikson's adult person who is capable of genuine
intimacy, generativity, and wisdom.[26] He is no
paragon but rather a very human fellow whose
humanity has not been so blocked by defensive
stratagems that he is profoundly inoperative. He
is at least open enough to be opened more! Finally,
the Remnant must be of the Spirit's choosing, and
this is not said to avoid a hard question. It is a

theological judgment: the church is God's and God is free. Because some prospective Remnant may appear unlikely to the eye that is culturally blinded and others improbable to criteria that are taken from a defensively impoverished society, the role of the Spirit is an empirical necessity. Some bound, some freer will become involved as Remnant. Some from the present nucleus of congregational life, some from the periphery, will find in the new direction what they have been longing for. And some may come from the outside altogether although they may have been secret "insiders" longing for a significant group with which to identify and a purpose worthy of commitment.

To train the Remnant would seem to be a high priority for pastors. It would be an intensification of their own aiming with the almost certain benefit of a new dimension of aesthetic beauty derived from the new Adventure. Furthermore, they would be helping to develop a laity of disciplined carers to help minister to the rest of the flock and to the world beyond. This would make concrete the ideal envisaged in the doctrine of the priesthood of all believers and in the correlative doctrine of servanthood whereby the people of God are the ministry of God. In the appendix I am proposing in broad outline a three year training program with suggested resources.

The Remnant concept would seem to be a viable approach toward the re-constituting of the church. I am bold enough to suggest it looks toward a somewhat different ecclesiology based on self-transcending agape-love within the rich tradition of Servanthood adumbrated in Isaiah and made concrete in Jesus. John Cobb's trenchant remarks deserve to be quoted in this context:

> To reconstitute the church as a
> community that evokes and strengthens
> spirit requires more than the effort
> to reinvigorate worship and Bible
> study. The full range of pastoral

236

care is called into play. It is
time that the church created more
contexts in which, without embarrassment or false piety, Christians
can discuss their deepest aspirations,
encourage one another in the purifi-
cation and strengthening of these
aspirations, and test their relative
success in being transformed in the
direction of their aspirations.[27]

The Remnant model for ministry would appear to
furnish such a context. It is biblically based. It
is faithful to the categoreal system of process
thought: a personal society, that is, an Individual,
participating in a yet larger society, the Remnant,
which in turn is within the matrix of the more
massive society, the church, whose Monarch is God
exemplified so concretely in the suffering servant
of the New Testament which was adumbrated in
Deutero-Isaiah.

Perhaps God in and through the Jesus-event can
yet lure the church to become that fresh creation
which stands on tiptoe to transcend itself in radical love. Lee has written, "The presence of God to
Jesus and to the world comes about when we allow the
defining characteristic of his love to define the
shape of our love."[28] To love after the manner of
God is the defining form of the Society of Jesus;
to be constituted by that form is to be in the
image of God. The climax of pastoral caring is the
ministry of the people of God who in response to a
beckoning grace live beyond themselves in radical
love. Such love is response to the call of God to
high Adventure the finest quality of which is
Beauty and the consummate enjoyment, the gift of
Peace.

NOTES

[1] Cf. Paul Tillich, The Protestant Era (Chicago: University Press, 1948), tr. by James Luther Adams, p. 175.

[2] For a careful review of the literature in the general mental health field and in the church toward the preparing of para-professionals see Joan Fenner Weber, "The Ministry of Presence," unpublished Master of Theology dissertation at Pittsburgh Theological Seminary, 1979, ch. 6.

[3] Hartshorne, Reality as Social Process, p. 136.

[4] Bernard Lee, The Becoming of the Church (New York: Paulist, 1974), p. 186. The word "importance" can seem weak unless it is filled with Whitehead's meaning which is the "final unity of purpose in the world," the "immanence of infinitude in the finite." Modes of Thought, op. cit. pp. 16, 28. Cf. Lee's defining form with that of Daniel Day Williams, The Spirit and the Forms of Love (New York: Harper, 1968), pp. 187-89.

[5] Ibid., pp. 175ff.

[6] Cf. Whitehead, Process and Reality, p. 51.

[7] John B. Cobb, Jr. and David Ray Griffin, Process Theology An Introductory Exposition (Philadelphia: Westminster, 1976), pp. 107-08.

[8] Hartshorne, Reality as Social Process, p. 39.

[9] Ibid., pp. 39f.

[10] Man's Vision, p. 203.

[11] Ibid., pp. 203-204.

[12] Reality as Social Process, p. 123. I consider it significant that a philosopher of the stature of Hartshorne, without the need for any special theological pleading, makes the point of God as Servant and the relationship between that servanthood and the cross.

[13] Cobb and Griffin, Introduction, p. 131.

[14] Cobb, Christian Existence, ch. 10, esp. pp. 119, 124, 125, 139.

[15] Sigmund Freud, Civilization and Its Discontents, tr. by James Strachey (New York: Norton, 1961), p. 31.

[16] On "nuturing Matrix" and "communal ground" see Meland, "The Self and Its Communal Ground," op. cit., pp. 363-369.

[17] Another model which is suggestive is the Society in Early Methodism. It was a part of a congregation gathered together "in order to receive the word of exhortation, and to watch over one another in love, that they might help each other to work out their salvation." Herbert Welch (arr.), Selections from the Writings of the Rev. John Wesley (New York: Eaton & Mains, 1901), p. 96, also 98, 99. I am indebted for this suggestion to Ervin K. Kerr in his unpublished doctoral dissertation, "The Appointive Itinerant System of the United Methodist Church," Pittsburgh Theological Seminar, 1979.

[18] For the full review of the literature see H. H. Rowley, The Servant of The Lord and Other Essays on the Old Testament (London: Lutherworth, 1952), pp. 3-57; for a more recent review see John L. McKenzie, Second Isaiah (Garden City: Doubleday, 1968), pp. XXXVIII-LV.

[19] I am indebted in forming this interpretatin to a cluster of authors who share important components

of this view. See H. Wheeler Robinson, The
Cross of the Servant (London: SCM, 1926), ch. 1;
H. Wheeler Robinson, Corporate Personality in
Ancient Israel (Philadelphia: Fortress, 1964),
esp. pp. 15-20; Rowley, op. cit., pp. 49-57;
McKenzie, op. cit., pp. LIII-LV.

[20] Cf. McKenzie, op. cit., p. LIV.

[21] Ibid., p. LV.

[22] When in the following pages I locate pastoral
caring in the servant-tradition, I am aware that
other areas ofthe church's life, such as ethics,
including its total global responsibility, could
as well be included under that motif. In fact,
I believe Liberation hopes have an appropriate
home within the sense of servanthood I am
suggesting. But since the focus of this book is
pastoral care, I am limiting the inclusion to
that aspect of the church's life.

[23] Ibid., p. XXXVIII.

[24] Cf. Maslow, Peak-Experiences, ch. 3.

[25] Cf. Gordon W. Allport and J. Michael Ross, "Per-
sonal Religious Orientation and Prejudice,"
Journal of Personality and Social Psychology (Vol.
5, November 4, 1967), pp. 432-443. Cf. Russell
O. Allen and Bernard Spilka, "Committed and
Consensual Religion: A Specification of Religion-
Prejudice Relationships," Journal for the
Scientific Study of Religion (Vol. VI, 1967),
pp. 191-206.

[26] Cf. Erik H. Erikson, Childhood and Society, pp.
229ff. Another valuable model would be Maslow's
self-actualizing person as presented previously
in these pages.

[27] Cobb, Theology and Pastoral Care, p. 19.

[28] Lee, The Becoming of the Church, p. 183.

Appendix

Program to Train a Remnant
in Pastoral Caring

In the following model I am being very
specific. Training pastors will modify the model
to suit their situations. I am suggesting three
years in order to introduce carefully the program
and to provide a period of training with sufficient duration to allow the data to become
causally efficacious throughout the organism of
each individual and the society of the Remnant.
New subjective forms take time to coalesce. The
duration is minimal for the re-directing of one's
aims so that one becomes intentional about his
being open to self-transcending love in the
Servant tradition.

Year One: Preparation

The Remnant will be part of a larger society.
That larger society, to whatever extent it can
participate, should be involved in the new program.
These four steps are proposed to prepare for the
Remnant and to raise the consciousness of the
entire Body.

1. A careful explanation to the governing
board of the church, patient and unhurried, so that
only persuasive power after the divine model is
used, with the goal of securing a commitment in
depth for the program.

2. Enlisting the congregation, or as many as
possible and especially the "shut-ins," to pray
intercessorily for the program.

3. An intentionality to raise the consciousness of the gathered people of God through worship,
including sermons, and in educational opportunities
to develop openness and incite as much of the congregation as possible toward novelty.

241

4. Recruiting the Remnant, a group of not more than twenty, anticipating some attrition. Others capable of objectivity should be consulted by the pastor in the selection process. But the pastor should issue the invitation on a personal basis in face to face encounter. Two or three conference periods may be required. This would underscore the importance of the program, get it clarified for the person being invited, and give time to develop a compact with each member of the Remnant. The compact is crucial for it should spell out as precisely as possible what is involved in the way of training, the amount of time required over the next two years, and what the call to a caring ministry within the servant-motif means.

Year Two: Basic Training

October-November: an eight-week study shaping a Theology of Pastoral Care. The pastor's own basic theology will come out and would need to be cor-related with the ministry of caring.[1] There is an abundance of theological resource; for example: if the Process model were to be employed, there would be the resources suggested throughout this book;[2] if a Barthian model were used, there is Eduard Thurneyesen, A Theology of Pastoral Care (Richmond: John Knox, 1962) and Thomas C. Oden, Kerygma and Counseling (Philadelphia: Westminster, 1966).

January-March: an eight-week study on Human Development. A number of outstanding resources have been suggested throughout these pages, but I would encourage the use of Erikson's eight stages of human development which are clear and form a progressive outline from early infancy through the aging process.[3] If the pastor felt it necessary to have help in the training program, this would be an area in which professionals in the mental health field, especially CPE-trained chaplains, could make an excellent contribution.

242

Post-Easter: an eight-week program around the principles of pastoral care.[4] As a part of this segment the pastor should take members of the Remnant, two by two, with him or her into typical pastoral caring situations. The pastor would need to be sensitive to those situations which should be excluded from on-the-job observations by teams of the Remnant. Such observation of the pastor at work enable the Remnant to get a sense for caring as well as insight into the practice of caring. These observations need to be part of the compact. Members should obligate themselves for three hours a month for two months.

Summer: a two-month program, three hours per month, in which members of the Remnant would undertake limited pastoral caring assignments, two by two. The assignments should be made by the pastor. The Remnant should meet for a couple of hours each of the two months for mutual sharing and supervision with the pastor.

Year Three: The Practice of Caring

October-November: a minimum of four bi-weekly sessions over case material with short verbatims. The Remnant would be involved by now in simple to intermediate caring situations, either singly or two by two, which would be the basis for the bi-weekly sessions. These sessions with the Remnant would be supervisory in nature but would provide the opportunity for the raising of theological, psychological, and caring questions. The pastor should also meet at least monthly with each member (or team) in a private supervisory session.

January-March: a continuation of the bi-weekly sessions based upon intermediate caring situations.

Post-Easter: a continuation of the bi-weekly sessions with the gradual introduction of more varied caring situations.

243

Another training program could now be offered to a new class of Remnant people with the trained Remnant participating in appropriate ways. There is almost an unlimited number of ways for the trained Remnant to be used. Brister,[5] Southard,[6] and Clinebell,[7] among others, are suggestive. If a couple of neighboring pastors or a group of pastors try to implement some such program as proposed, they can stimulate each other's imagination for the enrichment of Remnant ministry.

[1]Four helpful resources which lay back of any
particular theology are: Seward Hiltner, Preface
to Pastoral Theology, op. cit.; John T. McNeill,
A History of the Cure of Souls, op. cit.;
Albert C. Outler, Psychotherapy and the Christian
Message, op. cit.; David E. Roberts, Psychotherapy
and a Christian View of Man (New York: Scribner's)
1950).

[2]Two other sources should be added: Don S.
Browning, Atonement and Psychotherapy (Philadelphia: Westminster, 1966); James N. Lapsley,
Salvation and Health: The Interlocking Process
of Life (Philadelphia: Westminster, 1972).

[3]Cf. Erik H. Erikson, Childhood and Society, op.
cit., either old edition or revised edition;
Erik H. Erikson, Identity and the Life Cycle,
op. cit.

[4]For helpful material see C. W. Brister, Pastoral
Care in the Church (New York: Harper, 1964);
Howard J. Clinebell, Basic Types of Pastoral
Counseling (New York: Abingdon, 1966); Howard J.
Clinebell, Growth Counseling (Nashville:
Abingdon, 1979); Seward Hiltner, The Christian
Shepherd (New York: Abingdon, 1959); Milton
Mayeroff, On Caring (New York: Perennial, 1971).

[5]Brister, op. cit.

[6]Samuel Southard, Comprehensive Pastoral Care
(Valley Forge: Judson, 1975), is a very helpful
resource on enabling laity to share in pastoral
ministry.

[7]Clinebell, Basic Types, op. cit., ch. 16.

146, 148
Descartes, 3
Dewey, John, 215
Diagnosis, 9, 10, 11,
12, 14
Directivity, 59, 64,
105, 110, 187
Dreams, 135f.
Education (Adler), 92ff.
Ego-psychology, 45, 169
Eliot, T.S., 107, 137
Emerson, 47, 126
Empathy, 12, 13, 15,
59, 129, 161
Enjoyment, 77, 80, 82,
178, 198
Erikson, Erik H., ii,
11, 33, 36, 45, 109,
128f, 134, 235, 242
Evil, 39, 63, 79, ch.
VII, 230
Existential Analysis, 12
Experiencing moment, 4,
15; center (as sub-
jectivity), 3, 8, 9,
14, 15, 27, 76, 78, 80f,
83, 201; unity, 50
Family, 59ff; counseling,
61
Farley, Edward, 127
Final cause, 50, 93, 113
Fixation, 29f, 33ff, 36,
69, 208
Ford, Lewis, 189
Francis of Assisi, 181
Frankl, Victor, 78, 195,
208f, 213f, 215f, 218
Freud, 3, 9, 11, 12, 16,
23, 25, 33ff, 36, 45,
49, 69, 71, 75, 77,
84f, 87, 89, 92, 101,
104, 129, 135f, 143,
167, 198, 207, 213f,
231

Fromm, Erich, 95, 111, 184
Gestalt theory, 14, 15, 18
34, 55, 93, 144, 155
Gesture, 132ff.
Goals, 100, 108f, 112f,
114f, 131; and death,
101; operational, 115;
penultimate, 47, 115, 152;
ultimate, 47, 53, 108, 115
God, and aim, 26f, 37ff,
48ff, 55f, 58f, 61, 70f,
73f, 76, 82, 101, 104ff,
113ff, 131, 149ff, 153,
160, 163, 173ff, 206,
211f, 216ff, 234; as
Ally, 53f, 56, 58, 61,
189; and beauty, 106,
108; and consequent
nature, 177ff; as
Creator, 26, 41; and
evil, 147ff, 156, 162;
and family, 60f; image
of, 71, 106, 237; and
immanence, 172f, 177f,
211; a metaphysical
requirement, 47ff; miss-
ing from pastoral care,
45f; as Monarch, 229;
and persuasion, 38f, 62,
93, 164, 171ff, 179, 181,
186, 200, 212, 215; and
possibility, 72, 122,
158; and power, 39, 83,
145; and presence, 55ff,
62, 127, 138, 145, 147,
175, 189; as Savior,
162ff, 210f; a secular
concept, 51f, 53, 55,
57, 62, 64, 171; and
servanthood, 177, 229f,
233; and soul, 200, 211,
216ff; and value, 56,
104, 106
Good (creative and cre-

248

Plato, 33, 171f, 186, 195, 197, 213
Possibility, 71ff, 76f, 85, 91, 101, 114, 122ff. 130, 149, 158, 200, 206, 208, 212, 215, 218, 226
Prayer, 189; intercessory, 210
Prehension, 5, 14, 25, 30, 48, 76, 82, 85ff, 95, 97, 157, 177f, 197, 200, 209; Hybrid, 40, 199f, 211; Negative, 26, 40, 178
Projection, 130
Proposition, 122, 125, 131ff, 138, 158, 189, 208
Providence, 58
Psychosynthesis, 18, 74, 113
Racial memory, 34f, 76, 81, 200
Reality as social, 94f, 98
Reason, 91f, 201
Regression, 29f, 81
Rejection, 92, 209
Relativity, 76, 94; and sociality, 76, 94
Reversion, category of, 71f, 96
Ricoeur, Paul, 147
Rieff, Philip, 225
Rogers, Carl, 1, 12, 18f, 45, 57, 111, 126, 207
Sartre, Jean Paul, 51, 105
Satisfaction, 5, 100, 182
Saul, Leon J., 40
Schweitzer, Albert, 181
Self-actualization, 110, 112, 144, 214
Servant, 175, 176ff, 180ff, 184ff, 232ff.
Significant Other, 124, 126, 129ff.

Silence, 57f, 133
Soul, 2, 28, 41, 93, 100f, 108, 116, 122, ch. IX
Spiritual Director, 162
Spirituality and pastoral care, 186ff, 212ff.
Staupitz, Johann von, 127ff, 134
Subjective aim, 14, 26, 38, 40, 50f, 60, 70ff, 76, 80, 85, 103ff, 113, 121, 159f, 162, 164, 174ff, 188, 210
Subjective form, 14, 15, 25ff, 30ff, 34f, 39, 53, 77f, 81, 91, 136, 148, 156f, 159, 161, 163, 185, 202, 208f.
Superego, 35, 77, 136
Teaching parenthesis, 54
Teleogy, 71, 74f, 91f, 104, 200
Temple, William, 191
Tillich, 46, 134, 153, 163
Tournier, Paul, 169
Transactional Analysis, 45, 93
Transference, 89f, 112, 124, 129ff, 161, 183f.
Transformation, 84, 93ff, 114, 124, 131, 151, 161, 184, 186, 195, 207, 212, 217, 230
Trust, 115, 161
Truth, 99f, 148
Unconscious, 34, 76f, 103, 213
Value, 50, 56, 62, 103, 108, 114, 121, 151, 196, 213ff; and valuation, 42
Weil, Simone, 217
Whitehead, i, ii, iii, 2, 3, 7, 8, 11, 12, 14, 25, 26, 27, 31f, 34, 36, 39, 46ff, 49, 53, 55, 57, 69, 71, 76, 78, 87, 91, 92, 100, 102, 103f, 106, 111, 116, 123, 136, 138, 148, 150, 158, 160, 164, 171f, 177, 178, 181, 185, 186, 188, 196f, 199ff, 205f,

208, 210f, 212, 214ff,
217
Wieman, Henry Nelson,
46, 151f, 162, 187
Williams, Daniel Day,
12, 53, 115f, 143,
184
Worship, 138, 187f, 217

Gordon E. Jackson, Ph.D., The University of Chicago, is Professor of Pastoral Care at the Pittsburgh Theological Seminary and also an Adjunct Professor at the University of Pittsburgh. He has served as guest professor at the Facultad de Teologica, Campinas, Brasil, San Francisco Theological Seminary, and the School of Theology at Claremont. Professor Jackson is the author of You Are My People and numerous journal articles.